Integrated Value Management

D1617414

Integrated Value Management

Peter Gomez

HD
31
.G5895
1999
West

INTERNATIONAL THOMSON BUSINESS PRESS
I T P® **An International Thomson Publishing Company**

London • Bonn • Johannesburg • Madrid • Melbourne • Mexico City • New York • Paris
Singapore • Tokyo • Toronto • Albany, NY • Belmont, CA • Cincinnati, OH • Detroit, MI

Integrated Value Management

Copyright © 1999 Peter Gomez

I(T)P® A division of International Thomson Publishing Inc.
The ITP logo is a trademark under licence

British Library Cataloguing-in-Publication Data
A catalogue record for this book is available from the British Library

Library of Congress Catalog-in-Publication Data
A catalog record of this book is available from the Library of Congress

First published in Germany by ECON Executive Verlags GmbH, Dusseldorf, Vienna, New York and Moscow

This edition published 1999

Typeset by LaserScript, Mitcham, Surrey
Printed in the UK by TJ International, Padstow, Cornwall

ISBN 1–86152–240–1

International Thomson Business Press
Berkshire House
168–173 High Holborn
London WC1V 7AA
UK

http://www.itbp.com

Contents

CHAPTER THREE

The strategic methodology of integrated value management   71

CHAPTER FOUR

Integrated value management: back to basics or the rise of a new paradigm?   205

List of Tables

List of Figures

Preface

How to increase the value of a company is one of the greatest challenges to corporate leadership in the 1990s. An increasing number of executives will be judged on their achievement of this particular goal. In the 1970s and 1980s the fight for competitive advantage was central to strategic management. The benchmark of a good manager used to be success in the marketplace. But today the motto is: increase the value of your company by exploiting its internal and external potential. Of course market position will continue to play a crucial role in the future. However, the potential of areas such as procurement, information technology, finance, human resources, mergers and acquisitions, organizational structure, etc., will grow in importance. Strategies for creating new markets will be supplemented by diversification, disinvestment, restructuring and financial engineering.

Increased market share and greater profits will remain an important measure of success. Investors, however, will insist increasingly that market success is also reflected in the value of the company and that the attained and available cash flow is commensurate with a return that is appropriate to the risk. An increase in value should not benefit simply the investors but should benefit all stakeholders in a company: management, employees, clients, suppliers, and even includes the state and society in general. A company can be deemed successful only when all these stakeholders receive what is theirs by right.

Integrated value management is a comprehensive strategic approach that can combine all the various new requirements of corporate management. On the one hand, it is a new way of thinking, on the other it is a concerted deployment of differing strategic concepts. It is not actually a new paradigm – the popular name given to conceptual thinking which breaks radically with tradition – but neither is it a re-formulation of well-known strategical concepts into easily changed or improved forms. Integrated value management combined with its strategic methodology integrates a variety of old and new strategic approaches based on thinking in network patterns, and so marks out the path towards a significant increase in the value of a company.

Conventional business analysis is no longer sufficient to overcome the complexity of present-day corporate affairs. Its techniques pick out individual areas or functions of a company and then try to optimize them, using every option available. This divisive thought process is reflected in the division of a company into different departments: procurement, production, sales, finance and personnel, for example. It is equally visible in the division of university faculties into different business administration departments. Yet corporate practice shows that it is much more important to combine the different divisions and functions effectively than have one single area functioning smoothly. To put it another way, different divisions running smoothly do not necessarily ensure the smooth running of the company as a whole. That is precisely why a systemic approach is essential to the development of strategy. Integrated value management incorporates this approach by the methodology of thinking in network patterns. Network thinking means understanding the interdependence of various corporate activities and then developing an action plan based on the understanding of these patterns and their inherent dynamics.

This book starts with the vision of a corporation which has looked at systemic or network thinking seriously and made it into its guiding principle. For all corporate activities it tries to find a balance between economic success, environmental sustainability and social responsibility. This has meant that the competition-oriented approach, which until quite recently was considered so important, has lost out in favour of exploitation of the many and varied other potentials of the company. What's more, the interests of different stakeholders have been incorporated too but the base line is still that economic success steers healthy future development. Bearing all this in mind, the first part of the book looks at the important strategic concepts of the 1970s and 1980s. By discussing and illustrating the strengths and weaknesses of those tactics it will become clear why a comprehensive and integrated value management is now necessary.

In the second part of the book I will introduce the components of integrated value management. They are: the corporate concept, the strategic approach and the yardstick for success. The corporate concept is based on the idea of network thinking as well as on the new St Gallen Management Concept. Network thinking creates a methodical prototype that allows corporate activity and the various areas it affects to be understood. The St Gallen Management Concept provides a coordinated system for identifying and classifying managerial problems. These two approaches combine to form an excellent device for the practical implementation of systemic thinking, which I will illustrate later by taking the example of a 'multi-domestic' company.

By using integrated value management one can fundamentally differentiate between three different strategies which then have to be developed and implemented in mutual coordination. They are the business unit strategy, corporate strategy and owner strategy. I will show how each of these strategies can be developed and what are the most important tools for their implementation. Practical examples will play a key role in this and are used constantly throughout the book. I aim not only to show that the suggested procedures and tools have been successfully applied in real life but also to encourage readers to incorporate them into their own workplace – particularly in the case of the corporate and owner strategies, as they are only now gradually being put to practical use.

I also intend to show how the success of these strategies can be measured. It soon becomes clear that using profit as a yardstick is not sufficient and in future must be replaced by free cash flows attained by using the three strategies. A key point to the models in this book is how to identify these cash flows.

The heart of this book is to be found in its third part, which introduces the strategic methodology of integrated value management. It is presented as an eight-step plan. At each step strategic principles are developed and illustrated with a selection of practical examples and the reader is accompanied throughout the whole sequence by a strategic study DELTA. Step one consists of identifying the strategic areas, including defining the strategic business units, setting the boundaries of the company *vis-à-vis* its environment and identifying the owner's area of influence. In the second step a vision is developed and aims and objectives are defined. The interests of the stakeholders must be explicitly considered while developing the vision so that the groundwork can be laid for a balanced model and a comprehensive listing of objectives.

The next step analyses the business and its environment. The three strategies – business unit, corporate and owner – have to be analysed separately as each contains very different issues. Networks are the most important tool of this phase of information gathering and their application will be shown for each type of strategy. The results of this analysis are shown as 'strength-weakness/opportunity-threat' profiles (or SWOT profiles) and as possible value potentials of the company or owner respectively. In order to develop these strategies a step system is reserved for each strategy type. The development of the business strategy consists of fixing a plan of action with the help of a selection of tried and tested tools, followed by the creation of alternative strategies. The corporate strategy concept has three parts. To start with the company is mapped out as an independent unit. The desired integrated strategies build on the value potentials and the core skills of the company. Then restructuring possibilities such as disinvestment, reorganization or optimization of finance and tax are studied in depth. Finally, strategies for cooperation are examined where one has to differentiate by degree between alliances, acquisitions into similar areas and diversification. Foremost in the development of the owner strategies are those potentials which actually lie outside managerial responsibility. As the owner is interested not only in increasing the value of his company but also in optimizing the value and risk of his personal wealth, management has to play its role with a special sensitivity.

In the following part the business unit, corporate and owner strategies will be evaluated on their chances of success, taking into account quantitative as well as qualitative considerations. In terms of quality, the strengths and weaknesses of various options have to be compared. In terms of quantity, the value increase achieved through a particular strategy has to be set out in figures. This should lead to a promising choice of strategy combinations for success. As part of the last step of this system these are then implemented and anchored in the company. Implementing means taking concrete measures at an operational level. Anchoring means guaranteeing the long-term success of these strategies. Essential prerequisites include the development of an early warning system to detect any divergence as well as a specification for strategic control, to allow for adjustment to a changed premise of the strategy.

The fourth and final part of this book offers some ideas on how to place integrated value management into present-day strategic thinking. The answer to the question: 'Is it back to basics or the rise of a new paradigm?' actually lies somewhere between the two. Integrated value management develops conventional concepts and integrates them onto a higher plane by means of network thinking. At the same time it is constantly being seen in terms of practical experience.

Three objectives summarize the purpose of this book:

1   to provide an integrated framework based on network thinking in order to develop business unit, corporate and owner strategies;

2   to present the system of integrated value management which not only covers strategic development, but which also lays out a systemic approach to information gathering and points the way to competent strategic assessment;

3 to illustrate the proposed concepts and tools with practical examples. These will be in a form which is comprehensible and easy to apply and not simply the usual success stories.

The examples I have chosen are mainly European ones. I have done this deliberately to contrast with the US examples generally used and to illustrate independent development in Europe. The companies are mentioned by name if the information being discussed is already in the public domain. In a few cases I have had to generalize the actual context in order to protect confidentiality. However, every example is based on actual projects from the business world.

Finally, I would like to express my thanks. The individual modules of integrated value management are the result of long-term work I have undertaken with treasured colleagues from both the academic and the business world. Systemic corporate thinking was developed from numerous research and practical projects carried out with Hans Ulrich, Gilbert Probst and Knut Bleicher. An intensive and invaluable exchange of ideas with Cuno Pümpin and Günter Müller-Stewens laid the foundations for the prototype of the three strategies: business unit, corporate and owner. Bruno Weber's input into the module for using integrated value increase as a yardstick for success was decisive. This book would not have been possible without my various contacts in the business world. I am therefore indebted to all corporate leaders from whom I had the privilege to learn over the years. My assistants and students also deserve acknowledgement, for offering their constructive criticism. I thank Mrs Sabine Köhler for her diligent and competent administration of this book, and Georg von Krogh and Göran Roos for encouraging me to have this book translated into English. The harmonious family environment, where writing books is a joy, is thanks to my wife Monica and to my daughters Claudia and Isabelle.

Peter Gomez
St Gallen, Summer 1998

CHAPTER ONE

Strategic Management – past, present and future

'We want to ensure the prosperity of our company beyond the year 2000 by striking a balance between our economic, social and environmental responsibilities.' Thus Ciba-Geigy AG (known as CIBA) introduced their vision of systemic company management, which at the end of the 1980s kicked off a deep-rooted change in this leading chemical multinational. In 1996 the Swiss-based company with more than 85,000 employees succeeded in turning over 23 billion Swiss francs (sFr) with its broad range of chemical and biological products. In 1997 it merged with Sandoz A6 to become Novartis.

What was it that persuaded Dr Alex Krauer, the President, and Heini Lippuner, its Chief Executive, to set a new course for a company which had already been so successful in the 1970s and 1980s? The major disasters at chemical plants in Seveso, Bhopal and Schweizerhalle were not the only reason, although these had considerably undermined public faith. Rather, those in charge were acknowledging a far-reaching transformation in the values of society. These were reflected in a feeling of disquiet about modern technology and a growing scepticism towards continuing technical and economic advance. At the same time the 'anything is possible' belief of the 1970s and 1980s was disintegrating and in its place came consideration of one's own limits and potential. The result was a movement away from a one-sided fixation on economic success and towards the introduction of the idea that environmental and social aims were equally important.

Thus a new strategic understanding was born. If the strategic thinking of the 1970s and 1980s was based on the principle of achieving competitive advantage, in the 1990s it would be specifically about exploiting the broader potentials of a company and would deliberately include the interests of stakeholders. Strategic management means more than employing a sophisticated technique to position oneself ahead of the competition, it means an increase in value for all stakeholders through exploitation of every possible internal and external avenue open to the company. At the end of the 1980s Ciba-Geigy clearly recognized that this was not possible without starting to think in network patterns, and they acted accordingly.

The vision for 2000: economic success – environmental sustainability – social responsibility

What does strategic network thinking mean for Ciba-Geigy and how can they implement it? If we look at Figure 1.1 we see the vision that the company is determined to fulfil and so are given initial clues.

FIGURE 1.1　The vision of Ciba-Geigy

The vision of Ciba-Geigy		
Responsibility for the long-term economic success	Responsibility towards society	Responsibility for the environment
We achieve appropriate financial results through qualitative growth and continuous revision of a balanced business structure, so that we can justify the trust of all those who put their stakes into our company – shareholders, employees, business partners and the public. We will not endanger our long-term future through the maximization of short-term profit.	We are a trustworthy enterprise which is open towards society. With the practice of our business, we aim to make a useful contribution towards the solution of global problems and the progress of humankind. We are aware of our responsibility when making commercial use of new realizations in science and technology. In all our activities, processes and products, we carefully weigh up the benefits and risks.	Taking care of the environment is part of all our activities. We develop products and processes in such a way that they fulfil their purpose safely and with the least possible burden for the environment. We make sparing use of raw materials and energy and make continuous efforts to reduce waste of any form. It is our duty to safely clean up inevitable waste and make it harmless by using technology of the latest standard.

This vision is of course too abstractly formulated to be turned into strategy. It would be put into operation by using the so-called strategic organization which would be carried out simultaneously in varying dimensions (Lippuner, 1993). At the most basic strategic level Ciba-Geigy wants to maintain its leading position in the chemical and biological sector. Expansion would follow in related areas such as the pharmacology of vaccinations and means of diagnosis, but there would only be core acquisitions. First priority would go to internal growth, more than two million Swiss francs would be put aside for research and development. Mergers and acquisitions would only be used to complete a range or to expand the market position, large-scale acquisitions for the sake of size are not part of the plan. Ciba-Geigy considers growth to be indispensable, however the company is aiming for growth which can be supported ecologically. In other words, only products and industries which show a positive risk/benefit ratio and which are less intensive in terms of raw materials and waste disposal would be considered for future profitable development.

This has led to significant directional changes within the various divisions of Ciba-Geigy: stricter alignment to market needs in each area; re-structuring of product ranges in order to improve the maximum value/ environmental sustainability ratio; greater concentration on the geographical areas of North America, Europe and East Asia; and strict alignment of expenditure to the degree of maturity of the business.

In conjunction with its strategic orientation Ciba-Geigy has consistently adapted its organizational structure and its management systems. The complicated three-dimensional tensor-organization has been transformed into a much simpler structure which has fourteen divisions. Wherever it made economic sense centralized functional activities were integrated into the relevant divisions. Local divisions operate in the marketplace under a parent company. A number of small business units and committees support top management in its global task of managing the company. Certain functional activities which cannot be split sensibly are also carried centrally. These fundamental changes led to a number of adjustments in organizational procedures and systems which even now are still being carried out.

For Ciba-Geigy, putting into practice social responsibility means creating opportunities for employee self-development. The key words are 'empowerment' and 'directed autonomy'. Employees are allowed as much freedom as possible and responsibilities are delegated accordingly. This is supported by regular assessment of managerial conduct to which lower grade employees are also invited to contribute. Particular emphasis is placed on a strategic incentive scheme which rewards entrepreneurial initiative.

Using the slogan 'Making it Work' Ciba Geigy has spent six years working on the implementation of this concept. There are signs of initial success, but those at the top feel that it will take a few more years before this change has seeped through to the farthest branches of the company.

Is this strategic reorientation of Ciba-Geigy typical of managerial thinking in progressive companies? There is little evidence to show that this is the case. For most major companies the ultimate goal is achieving optimal competitive advantage. Some may already have realized that the shareholder has to be taken into consideration and do follow a shareholder-value concept. But those companies who have a systemic strategical approach and a well thought-out stakeholder-value concept are still thin on the ground.

The strategic turning point – away from single-minded concentration on competition and thinking that 'anything is possible'

The heyday of strategic thinking based solely on competition was in the 1970s and 1980s. With well-known consultants taking the lead, newly developed tools such as portfolio management and competitive strategies were introduced across the board. The claim of these approaches was that careful analysis of a business and its environment along with expert application of a positioning mechanism would lead, without fail, to a successful strategy. A classic example of the portfolio approach will be examined in depth later on. This approach sets up specific, so-called *norm strategies* for every position in a given matrix and the company has to apply them in order to keep up with the competition. These strategic tools which you can still find around today were tremendously appealing, mainly because they reduced a complex web of interrelations to a few quantifiable ones and pointed the way to a clear-cut solution. The belief was that this relatively simple technique allowed one to take control of the complicated process of strategy finding.

Unfortunately the experience of the last two decades has shown that these expectations were not to be realized. The tools helped companies to realize a variety of strategies and encouraged them to think about their future systematically. But very few companies made an automatic jump from competitive positioning to successful strategy. Paradoxically, it was the very popularity of these strategies which caused their downfall. While the pioneers had at least surprise on their side, more and more companies used the same strategies which became increasingly predictable and gradually lost their impact. Finally a point was reached whereby a company that consciously broke all the rules of the portfolio approach being used by most other companies in the sector was the one that turned out to be the most successful. In defence of these strategic approaches it must be said that at least they prevented huge errors and they did force companies to learn to analyse their market, their competitors and themselves.

The strategic device for staying ahead of the competition also fostered the 'anything is possible' concept. Management was no longer viewed as an art form but simply as a way of implementing the results of business analysis. In many cases the belief in the power of these strategies led to their enforced introduction, regardless of a company's individual circumstances. There was also an almost childlike belief in forecasting, which allowed developmental opportunities to be viewed as indisputable facts.

Perhaps the most damage was caused by top managers believing that strategic planning was nothing other than careful application of a certain technique which could therefore be delegated to professional staff. They in turn developed strategies at their desks without ever coming close to the practical side of the problem. On top of that, those who took over further down the line never considered these strategies to be their own and so were not interested in actually putting them into practice. So in the 1970s and 1980s, hundreds of files were filled with 'strategic exercises' and abandoned in filing cabinets.

Many people did not notice the profound change which began to take shape towards the end of the 1980s. Different people began to question the practice of equating strategic thinking with competitive advantage. Perhaps there were other value potentials a company could tap successfully? Why should a company stare as if transfixed at competitors and try to win a minute share of a market that was already saturated? Instead why not seek out other significant potentials – such as procurement, information management, organization, cooperation, human resources, etc. – which might be under used and which could lead with less effort to successful and effective possibilities? Looking at things from this new angle then threw up the question, what should be the yardstick for successful entrepreneurial action? The main aim of the competitive strategy was to gain competitive advantage. The principal aim of exploiting a company's value potential is to raise the value of the company as a whole.

In the 1970s and the 1980s strategic management was the sole responsibility of managers. More recently investors and shareholders are having a say. From the shareholder's point of view the task of management is to raise the value of the company for the investor. It is immediately obvious that a competitive strategy alone cannot do this. Gradually shareholder interests converge with strategic reorientation of a company towards its value potentials. Yet as the example of Ciba-Geigy clearly shows, shareholders are not the only people who have a stake in the company, the interests of other stakeholders must also be considered. That is why the latest development in strategic thinking is to move away from the shareholder approach towards a stakeholder approach.

These developments lead to new focal points in strategic thinking, which will be studied extensively in the next chapters and which can be characterized briefly under the following headings:

- from competitive advantage to raising the value of a company;

- from strategic potential for success in the marketplace to company value potentials;

- from the shareholder value concept to the stakeholder value approach;

- from strategy development to strategy implementation;

- from strategic patent remedies to network thinking;

- from rigid structures to organizational learning.

This shift can only be understood and evaluated in the light of the development of conceptual strategic thinking over the past two decades.

Stages in the development of strategic thinking

The real cause of the systematic change in management strategy was the profound structural change that happened within the business environment at the beginning of the 1970s – that is, the oil crises. Before then the focus of corporate management was mainly internal. If there was a relatively stable and predictable environment then it was easy to place the optimization of one's own organization at the centre of business activity. The concept of divisional organization which started in the 1920s has been refined over the years and in many companies has replaced the existing functional structure. The increasingly complex internal structures of a company have led to initial experiments with a matrix-organizational structure. It came about as an inevitable result of combining a primary organization structured according to division or function with a mushrooming secondary organization divided according to product or project. Until the 1970s the terms management and organization were virtually synonymous and hardly anybody spoke of strategy or company culture.

The realization that the business environment could be turbulent or even unpredictable led management to move increasingly towards the associated areas outside a business. Question were asked, such as: what economic, social and environmental challenges have to be faced? How can I best tap new markets and methodically gain the upper hand competitively? The first strategical attempts were aimed principally at the individual areas of a company and at the possibility of increasing the market share in these areas. It was still a long time before the focal point of strategic thinking was of the company as a whole and included its interrelation with the environment and the interplay between its stakeholders. These stakeholders are shareholders, management, competitors, business partners as well as society in general.

The transition from the 1960s to the 1970s was marked by a considerable growth in concepts. The first strategic concepts to find widespread application were the product–market matrix, the learning curve, strategic business units, the portfolio matrix and the PIMS principle. The *product–market matrix*, for example, was already developed by Ansoff in the 1960s (Ansoff, 1968). This matrix combines present and future markets with present and future products. This gives four strategic option fields: market penetration, market development, product development and diversification. Executives were particularly fascinated by the fourth field because for so long growth had equalled diversification. This matrix provided the first extensive framework for systematically dealing with market and product development. Even today it remains a popular strategic device.

The next development was the *learning curve* (Henderson, 1968). It declared that an increased market share leads to higher production volume and therefore to lower relative costs. This gives a competitor that freedom in its pricing policy which leads to gains in market share and in turn to higher profits. Initially, this concept worked for pioneering companies, but after it became common practice it actually triggered price wars, as everyone tried to gain an increased market share. In the end it did not help anyone. Nevertheless, this concept did have an affect and management started to look at costs and market share.

The learning curve was followed by the conception of *strategic business units* (Gaelweiler, 1979). Its premise was that the activities of a business in the marketplace had to be segmented and adjusted strategically. One looked for 'companies within a company'. Frequently, they were not identical to previous organizational units and so new boundaries were drawn and resources were redistributed as a result. Without doubt this latest concept increased the autonomy and responsibility of management, but often this focus on the parts caused the operation as a whole to be neglected. Even today, identification of strategic business units remains an important pillar of every strategic approach. This will become clearer later on in the chapter.

Portfolio planning (Henderson, 1968) is closely connected to strategic business units. It positions every strategic business unit in a matrix using the dimensions of market attractiveness and relative competitive advantage, then it assigns a strategic way forward or a *norm-strategy* to each of these positions. The original portfolio approach by the Boston Consulting Group has since been refined in various ways and expanded into additional dimensions. And so it became one of the most popular strategic devices of the 1970s and 1980s and is still one of the tools used by those responsible for corporate strategy. The more extensively it was used, however, the more its limitations became apparent. In particular its one-sided emphasis on the market and competition became clear as well as the limited effectiveness of norm-strategies.

In addition to these theory-based concepts in the middle of the 1970s there came into being the first empirical concept for strategy development and assessment – the *Profit Impact of Market Strategies* programme (Schoeffler *et al.*, 1974). The PIMS programme examined success factors of the strategic approach using data from several hundred US companies (this data bank has now been expanded to thousands of companies, including international ones). The aim of PIMS is to discover laws governing the market and to prepare plans of action. A company should then be able to explain the impact of certain factors on the return on investment of a strategic business unit, to forecast the development of the return on investment by changing certain strategic key factors, to achieve an optimal allocation of resources and to find an efficient method for measuring managerial services. The PIMS principles are still widely used although criticism of the applicability of these empirical conclusions continues. More recently, the question has been asked whether return on investment is the right gauge for assessing strategies.

In the 1980s two new concepts initially supplemented and later on partly replaced the above approaches. They were the *strategic positions of success* and *competitive strategy*. Strategic positions of success are capabilities which enable a company to achieve outstanding results over its competitors, even on a long-term basis (Pümpin, 1987). This makes them different from strategic competitive advantages, which use skilful marketing tactics to raise a company's profile on a short-term basis. The concept of strategic positions of success is still mainly market-oriented but it does increase the range of strategic possibilities by incorporating other potentials such as procurement, financing or the application of human resources. This concept still enjoys unbroken popularity today and will play an important role in later examples.

The implementation of the *competitive strategy* (Porter, 1980, 1985) steered the attention of executives to the determinants of competition and showed how to gain decisive advantage over one's competitors by strict application of certain strategic directives: cost-leadership, differentiation and focusing on market segments. This competitive approach produced actual models of the structure of an industry and led to a better understanding of the dynamics within certain industries. According to this concept special emphasis is placed on the *value chain* of the company. This chain divides the corporate process into separate links and then requires that all individual links are strictly aligned to what is happening within the competition. The competitive strategy approach today is indispensable to the repertoire of a strategically minded executive and as such will have its place in later explanations.

Integrated value management – the new dimension for strategic leadership

Despite enthusiasm for all these concepts of strategic management, towards the end of the 1980s a feeling grew that the market and one's position with regards to the competition could not be the sole measure of success. Every company has at its disposal a variety of further potentials which remain unexplored if there is a one-sided focus on competition. Furthermore, every company as a whole has core competences which can only become effective in the ensemble play if the separate businesses and business units join together. And finally, put together all strategic business unit strategies and you still do not have a corporate strategy capable of covering matters such as investment/disinvestment, financing, restructuring and taxes. That is why there has been a shift in strategic thinking since the end of the 1980s. This shift is reflected in concepts such as value potentials, core competences and integrated value management.

The concept of the value potentials and their multiplication in a company (Pümpin, 1992) works on the premise that a company lays the foundation for successful development and healthy growth by optimally positioning its strategic business units within the competition. However in times of slow growth or stagnant markets a company has to make use of every other and as yet unexploited possibility for development. They could be found within areas such as procurement, logistic and information systems, human resources, reorganization and take-overs, joint venture and restructuring plans. If one succeeds not only in tapping all these potentials but also in multiplying these capabilities then this strategy produces the leverage essential to long-term organic development.

Within the concept of core competences (Prahalad and Hamel, 1990) a company is required to look less towards the competitive abilities of its different business units and to focus more on extraordinary competences to be found right throughout the company. For example, the core competences of Canon lie in precision engineering, precision optics and microelectronics. These enable the company to produce a broad palette of new products and to remain ahead of its competitors. Core competences are the resources of a company. In order to exploit them, all the talents necessary for a specific project are removed from the various strategic business units and put into action together. This orientation towards core competences brings with it a systemic view of the company.

This also happens when *value management principles* are applied, as conceptualized by Rappaport (1986) and developed further by the author (Gomez and Weber, 1989). Integrated value management brings together strategic and financial management. The main aim is no longer gaining competitive advantage but the new objective of raising the value of a company as a whole. Originally raising the value meant increased shareholder value, in its later stages the main focus was on stakeholder value. This strategy should create value for all groups who hold a stake in the company. That this cannot be achieved solely by optimal positioning of business units *vis-à-vis* the competition is quite clear. Therefore investment planning, financial planning, restructuring and taxation planning are to be considered with the same gravity as market position. Until quite recently they were viewed as secondary to strategic planning and were applied only selectively by financial managers. In terms of corporate strategy, however, they are an integral part of long-term planning.

A further refinement of corporate strategy was introduced by Pümpin (Pümpin and Pritzl, 1991), the so-called *owner strategy*. This consists of all measures outside the managerial field of responsibility but within the jurisdiction of the owner. Under this heading I would place the dissolution of a company, going public or non-company financial transactions. These possibilities also have to be evaluated if the potential of a company is to be fully exploited.

Whereas in the 1980s and at the beginning of the 1990s the focus of management theory and practice had been on strategy, it shifted towards organization in the mid-1990s. Key concepts were business process re-engineering (Hammer and Champy, 1993), process organization and decomposition of the value chain (Downes and Mill, 1998). These concepts are still at the forefront of strategic thinking today, but with a stronger focus on implementing strategies.

The relevant strategic approaches and concepts for the 1990s can be summarized as follows: on the one hand the grip on rigorous orientation towards markets and competition is loosened in favour of tapping the various value potentials and core competences, and on the other, the focus is moving away from single business units to viewing the company as a whole, thus integrating strategic and financial areas. The central idea today is to consider the interests of shareholders or investors. But even here there is a shift, as yet not clearly defined but definitely there, and that is the shift from shareholder approach to the stakeholder approach. The example of Ciba-Geigy illustrates this trend very well. So, what are the prerequisites for this strategic thinking?

■ CHAPTER 2 ■

The Components of Systemic Integrated Value Management

The need for a strategic turnaround as shown and illustrated in the Ciba-Geigy example has also been recognized by many other companies. However, it is a long and difficult journey from realization to implementation and the difficulty is then compounded by two further factors. First, the traditional strategic thinking and its tools which we looked at briefly in the previous chapter are still prevalent in industry. They represent the language and the terminology with which strategic questions and problems are discussed throughout a company's hierarchy. The dominant terms are: *strategic business units*, *competitive advantage* and *return on investment*. The vocabulary is less likely to contain terms such as core competences, increasing company value or stakeholder value. That is why the new strategic thinking has first to set up a framework for a company and its environment to be understood systemically.

On the whole, the new ways of thinking strategically can be seen as a step in the right direction. No longer strategic business units but value potentials and core competences of a company are the key. Even re-orientation towards increasing the value of a company and away from competitive advantage is beginning to occur. In its present form, however, too much emphasis is placed on one single stakeholder – the investor or the shareholder. All other stakeholders are considered only by implication. Moreover the desire to take a long-term view is frequently overtaken by the desire for short-term optimization. This is particularly the case in US companies.

The prerequisites for this strategic change go against the grain of traditional strategies. This new strategy is aimed at all legitimate stakeholders and the development of a measure for long-term and healthy development of a company. In order to achieve this, conditions have to be realized in three specific areas:

1   a systemic understanding of the company has to be developed which takes into account the interests of all stakeholders;

2   a clear line has to be drawn between business, corporate and owner strategies and the appropriate strategic methodology has to be prepared;

3   in terms of an increase in the integrated value of the company a yardstick has to be developed to evaluate the success of the strategy.

Systemic understanding of a company

In the pre-industrial age every craftsman was also an entrepreneur. He fulfilled all functions necessary to the survival of his business and in this sense he had to have a systemic understanding of it. When industrialization arrived it brought with it specialization and the partition of labour. The majority of present-day companies follow the functional form of organization, which is a classic embodiment of this development. Teaching posts in the business administration departments of our universities are also divided into functions: industrial production, marketing, finance and accounts, organization, human resources. While this strict partition made good sense in relatively homogenous markets and in a stable environment, it no longer corresponds to today's ever-changing conditions. Increasing complexity and constant changes in the environment require a new way of thinking which can integrate the various functions. In many companies this is proving to be very difficult. The fact that when a company reorganizes, it only reorganizes certain divisions, branches or legally independent units within the company demonstrates this quite clearly. Finding suitable executives also becomes a problem, because until the moment of re-organization the candidates have only been in charge of certain areas such as marketing, production or finance and so do not possess a systemic understanding of their company. This requires a fusion of strategic and financial thinking which is difficult if not impossible to realize, as previously one had been the responsibility of the production manager and the other had been in the domain of the finance director. Until the reorganization the motto had been 'ne'er the twain shall meet'.

The first movement towards an integrated view of a company and the development of corresponding managerial concepts happened at the beginning of the 1970s, at a time when strategic thinking was being developed. The systemic approach played a vital role in all this. It was developed in the German speaking part of Europe by Ulrich (Ulrich, 1968) at the University of St Gallen and was implemented as the St Gallen Management Model (Ulrich and Krieg, 1974). Over the past two decades these approaches have been continuously developed and with the help of industry have been put into practice. Two particular approaches towards a systemic understanding of a company lay the foundation of the following examples: they are the *method of thinking in network patterns* (network thinking) and the *St Gallen Management Concept*. The method of network thinking (Gomez and Probst, 1987; Probst and Gomez, 1991; Ulrich and Probst, 1988, and similarly Senge, 1990) is both a thought process and also a tool to show in a clear and easily implementable way a systemic overview of the complex interrelations in a company. It requires that an executive:

- looks at a problem or business area from the viewpoint of each different stakeholder and outlines their aims and interests;

- assesses the key factors for business success and their determinants;

- assesses the network of these determinants in the form of cycles showing either strengthening or stabilizing effects;

- assesses which determinants are controllable in this network and so determines the starting point for strategies;

- examines to what extent these strategies make use of the company's inherent dynamics;

- monitors the introduction of these strategies by means of an early warning system.

The *St Gallen Management Concept* (Bleicher, 1997) provides a framework for executives who are drowning under the huge range of management theories and tools available to them. It is composed of separate modules (module corporate development: Pümpin and Prange, 1991; module organization: Gomez and Zimmermann, 1992; module management systems: Schwaninger, 1994), but at the same time it provides an overview of all managerial interrelations. The basic concept is to find the distinctions between three levels of management: normative, strategic and operative. One step further on there is a distinction between structure, activities and the behaviour of these three levels. Thus problem areas are constructed which can be logically extricated and defined and as such are easier for management to handle and to resolve. An integrated view of management demonstrates quite clearly that all dimensions have an influence on each other.

Network thinking in management

In 1989 the top executives at Ciba-Geigy AG introduced a change of direction for their company by developing a vision which placed equal emphasis on economic success, environmental sustainability and social responsibility. However clear and convincing this vision was, its implementation was going to be a lengthy process. As a first step the corporate leaders decided that by using the method of network thinking they would be able to make more transparent the complex web of relationships behind this triangle. For this reason, a workshop was set up and attended by a broad circle of executives. Some of the results of this workshop are summarized in a simplified form over the following pages and will illustrate the basic principles of this way of thinking.

To start with, the chemical concern had to clarify which stakeholders and interests they had to take into account. As shown in Figure 2.1, these were investors, employees, consumers, society and the state. Other stakeholders to be considered but not to be listed separately included business partners, competitors and local communities.

So what are the interests and aims of these stakeholders? The investors demand (among other things which apply to all stakeholders) an appropriate return on their invested capital. The employees want interesting work in a 'clean' company. The customer is mainly interested in quality products and good service. Society wants minimum emissions and the lowest possible risk factor. The main priority of the state is its tax revenue and the preservation of jobs. These priorities change in accordance with the different interests and all have to be taken into account when it comes to making decisions.

This step is usually omitted in conventional analysis of business and its environment. It is assumed implicitly that the main objective is economic success and if absolutely necessary the company will also take the investors into consideration. The danger is that if the company's situation is only viewed from an economic angle, as a result only economic factors will show up in the network pattern. The approach shown in Figure 2.1 includes those key factors important to the various stakeholders.

The next step is to place these key factors into a first plan. For example, if we take the stakeholder 'society' then the key factors look

FIGURE 2.1 Stakeholders and their interests

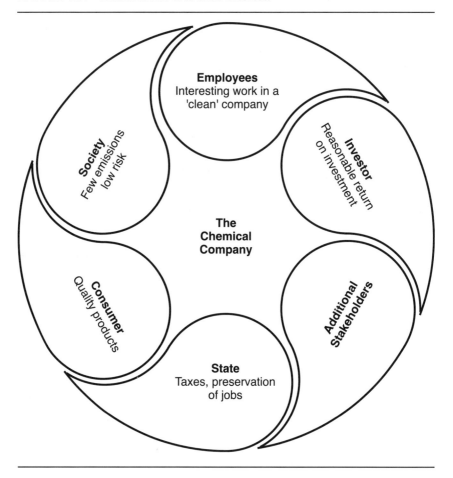

something like this: environmental damage, public health, environmental consciousness, acceptance by society, company image and the side effects of drugs. The same procedure is then applied to all the other stakeholders in order to prepare the raw material for the network pattern.

The development of this network follows in several stages, starting with the central cycle. This is important because a network is not the same as a diagram that simply shows the various determinants. A network consists of interconnected cycles which amplify or stabilize each other. At this point, let us look at the notation as it is used in Figure 2.2. A + sign means an amplifying effect: the *more* sales, the *higher* the profits, the *higher* the investments, etc.; a – sign means a stabilizing effect: the *better* the competitor, the *worse* our competitive position.

FIGURE 2.2   Network pattern of a chemical company

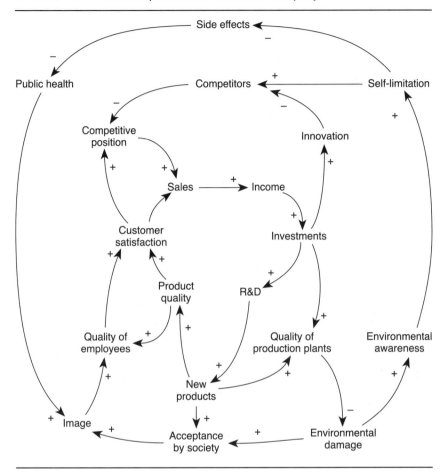

Now let us look at the central cycle, the 'engine' which drives the company as a whole. This cycle reads as follows: the better the quality of the product range, the bigger the benefit for the customer, the more sales, the more profits, the more means available for new investment, the better the research and development, the better the quality of the product range, and so on. The network is extended to incorporate the three further dimensions of the vision. *Economic success* takes into account factors such as competitive advantage, innovation and competitors. If there are more funds available for investment then there are more opportunities for innovation, which in turn weakens the position of the competition and increases one's own competitiveness. On the right-hand side of the network you can see the dimension *environmental sustainability*. The more funds available for investment the better the quality of the production plant, the less harm is done to the environment. This, in turn, leads to a higher acceptance of the chemical industry by society, which leads to a better image, which in turn has a positive effect on the quality of employees which in the end benefits the customer. The dimension of *social responsibility* can be seen on the left-hand side of the diagram. The better the image of the chemical industry as a 'clean' one the more attractive it becomes to potential employees, which increases the quality of the workforce, which in turn has a positive effect on customer benefits and the position among its competitors. If the chemical industry regulates itself responsibly the result is fewer side effects, leading to improved public health, which again improves the image of the chemical industry.

This network only shows a few of the most basic cycles and interconnections – not all stakeholder interests have been taken into account. The network designed by the executives of Ciba-Geigy was of course much more detailed. It also captured the dynamics of this company by assigning to each arrow time dependencies and delaying effects. Normally it takes eight to ten years from making an investment in research and development to placing new products on the market and an improvement in the quality of the product range. Should a disaster happen due to manufacturing equipment not being up to standard, then society's acceptance of the chemical industry immediately hits rock bottom and as a consequence affects the appeal of the company as a potential employer.

Once the network is set up, it is possible to think about potential decisions and disruptions. Different scenarios are then applied to the possible disruptions. How will society's environmental consciousness develop in the future? Will that influence society's acceptance of the chemical industry and what effect will that have on its image? What strategic development possibilities do competitors have? How attractive is the chemical industry to its employees? Will there be a sufficient number of skilled workers? These potential events will be thought out and their effects on the various cycles played through and then, 'just in case', a number of options will be worked out.

In order to make a decision a company has to look first at those factors which are malleable. From these initial factors potential strategies will be developed and then checked within the network against any effects and possible side effects. It will then be clearer to managers what course of action should be taken, so the original model in fact becomes a sound basis for decision making.

I will now set out the design for a non-specific network model suitable for any company. It will show the step-by-step development of the central cycle and demonstrate how aspects of the market and competition, of employees and the societal relationship as well as financial aspects are built into it.

The central cycle is the starting point, the engine of the company as it were, which gets everything moving. An example of this is shown in Figure 2.3.

The happier the consumer the more one can sell, leading in turn to a higher turnover. Usually this means creating a higher operational cash flow which can be invested in research and development. Product quality improves and so does customer satisfaction. All this leads to higher sales and larger turnovers – all of which re-fuels the engine. By adding the considerations of *market* and *competition* to this central cycle, the diagram now looks like Figure 2.4.

If product quality improves this is not only immediately reflected in increased customer satisfaction but also in an improved position *vis-à-vis* the competition. Not only has more been sold but the competitors have been outstripped. Research and development leads to more innovations. Place those together with the new developments of competitors and the industry as a whole starts to look more attractive. This spurs on sales but at the same time breeds new competitors, which in the long term could dampen sales.

FIGURE 2.3   The central cycle ('engine') of the company

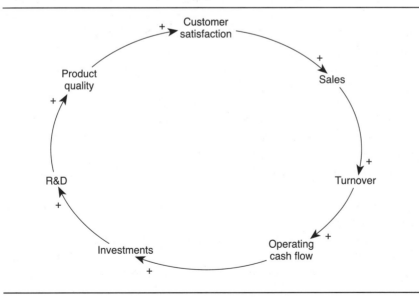

FIGURE 2.4   Inclusion of market and competition

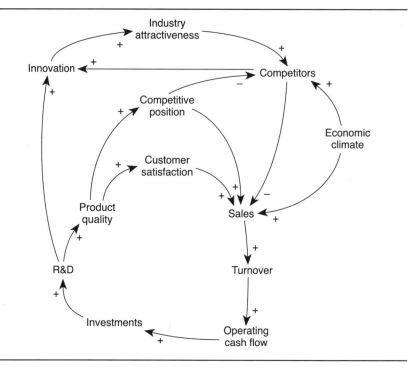

As you can see, all the complex interconnections are slowly coming into view. At least by using this method they can be set out very clearly. The next step is to add employee and societal relations, as shown in Figure 2.5.

The quality of service from staff is crucial to customer satisfaction. But this quality depends heavily on how motivated the staff are. Employees can be motivated by various schemes for promotion, by bonus payments upon achievement of good business results, and in a more general sense by the image of the company, which in turn is dependant on customer satisfaction. At a time when values are changing radically and environmental consciousness is on the increase, a company is constantly being confronted with new demands and new legal regulations, which require both further investment and increased product quality.

As a last step the *financial aspects* of the company and *investors* are considered, as shown in Figure 2.6. A higher operational cash flow leads to a higher available free cash flow, although this will be reduced by investments and taxes. A constant free cash flow and the company's

FIGURE 2.5   Employee and societal relations

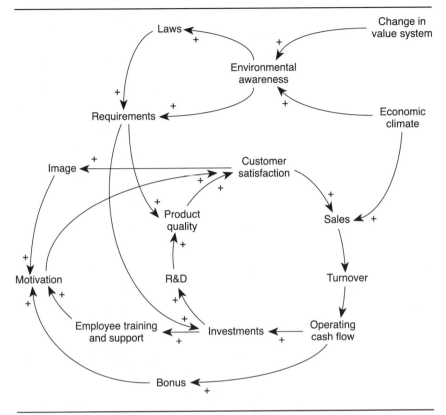

rising end value created by investments leads to a higher company value. This is beneficial to the shareholders and so contributes to the further flow of the company's capital. Investments, however, require additional outside capital leading to higher interest charges but also to lower taxes.

If all the network connections mentioned above are integrated then the picture begins to look like Figure 2.7. All those determinants which are malleable are placed in boxes.

It may look as if this picture has been put together with a great deal of exaggerated complexity. The workings of a company could be portrayed by a much simpler model, capturing only the external factors influencing a company and the internal connections between procurement, production, sales, personnel and finance. Yet there is decisively more information contained in the network above because possible developments can be tracked through several factors and cycles, allowing more accurate consequences to be drawn. Let's take an example: a new

FIGURE 2.6 Incorporating financial aspects and investors

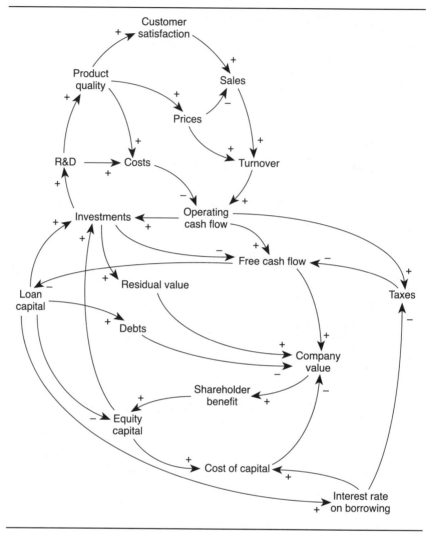

competitor appears on the scene. This will not only have an effect on sales but eventually it will also affect employee motivation as well as benefits to shareholders. In the end, only those who try to understand a company and all its interdependencies can make the correct strategic decisions.

Thinking in network patterns points the way towards a systemic understanding of the company, whether by identifying the interests of stakeholders or by portraying and interpreting the workings of decisive

FIGURE 2.7 Network pattern of the company's total interconnections (the determinants which are controllable, and thus starting points for strategies, are boxed)

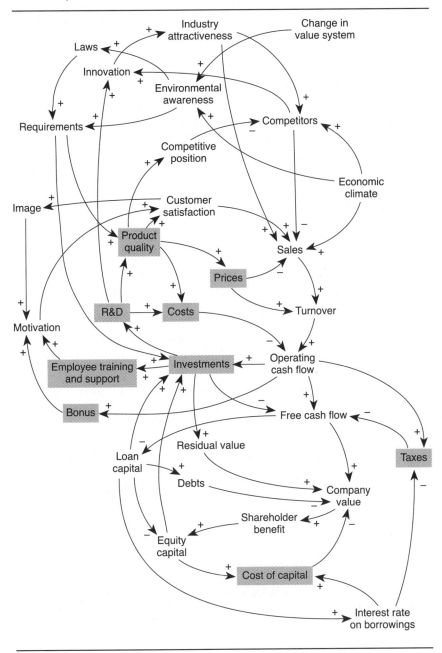

key factors. Now there is another important question to be answered. Can intuition and experience be the only guide to developing such a network? An integrated management concept should also be an important guide when it comes to identifying associated areas and determining factors – especially if it tries to meet the demand for a systemic view. This is in fact what the St Gallen Management Concept aims to do.

Integration: the St Gallen Management Concept

The coordinates of the St Gallen Management Concept are divided into managerial levels: normative management, strategic management and operative management, and integrational aspects: structures, activities and behaviour. The dynamic aspect of corporate development overlies this coordinated system. Figure 2.8 shows the overall structure of the St Gallen Management Concept.

FIGURE 2.8 The St Gallen Management Concept (Source: Bleicher, 1997)

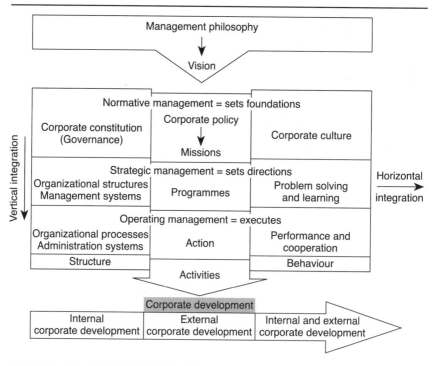

The components of the St Gallen Management Concept can be best shown by working through the coordinates of the referential framework. Subordinate to this framework is the higher management philosophy, the dynamic element is the specified vision and corporate development. The concept marks out the three levels of management quite clearly: *normative*, *strategic* and *operative*.

Normative management deals with the overall objectives of the company, its rules, norms and principles which have to be in place before a company can exist and develop. The company must not only be able to exist and maintain its own identity but it must also have the ability to develop. This is secured by a corporate policy developed out of the vision, which in turn is supported by corporate governance and corporate culture. The *corporate policy* translates the company's vision into basic guidelines and clarifies it by means of mission statements, setting out the aims of the company. *Corporate governance* presents a formal framework enabling basic constraints to be identified. It strives to balance the interests of the internal and external systems of the company and to present them in an economic, ecological and social context. Finally, the *corporate culture* is the so-called soft behavioural dimension. It is shaped by the values, norms and social traditions of the company.

Normative management is directed at creating benefit for the stakeholders. It defines the objectives and the identity of the company within the context of society and the economy and is the internal and external mediator. Normative management is really the basis for all company activities.

The aim of *strategic management* is to create, to maintain and to maximise the strategic success factors and value potentials and to allocate resources to them. It is absolutely crucial therefore to be able to identify new potentials and tap them so that the future survival of the company is assured. The strategic level acts as a regulator for the company's activities. It is put into effect through strategic programmes, organizational structures, managerial systems as well as executive problem solving and learning. The strategic programmes convert the guidelines of the corporate policy into plans of action with regards to the factual and regional performance profile, the design of the value chain and the use of resources. The organizational structures and management systems create a structural framework to implement the strategies. If the strategies are to take off at all the structures have to be capable of change and development, as do the executives with regard to problem solving and learning. Only by integrating these three strategic sections can the company make maximum use of its strategic success factors and its value potentials.

Operative management takes the normative and strategic precepts and converts them into performance, financial and IT processes. In accordance with the modules of strategic management it uses the terms *organizational processes* and *administration systems, actions* and *performance and cooperation.* The operative management can therefore be described as having an executing function.

The aspects of the vertical integration have already been briefly dealt with in the discussions of the three levels of leadership. In the structures part the corporate governance is concretized by the corresponding organizational structures and management systems, which in turn find their operative realization in the organizational processes and administration systems. In the *activities* section the corporate policy is clarified through the strategic programme, leading directly to specific action. Finally, the corporate culture works as the basis for desirable *problem solving and learning* for the executives, which is reflected in the operational level of performance and cooperation.

The interplay of all these modules of the St Gallen Management Concept can be summed up in the words 'corporate development'. This concept delineates the different stages of development from the pioneering company to the growing company, on to the mature company and the turnaround company (Pümpin and Prange, 1991). At each stage different constellations of this interplay are formed and all have to be taken into account when making decisions.

Even to an executive with a specific interest in the subject, the jungle of contemporary management theories and concepts is now virtually impenetrable. The St Gallen Management Concept tries to bring some order and orientation to these theories and to unite their most important concepts. Any executive is able to locate a problem within this framework and then, by using the concepts moving away from that location, find several possible solutions. In the language of network thinking, the St Gallen Management Concept provides the categories and determinants which have to be considered when developing a network. Systemic thinking calls for both network thinking and the application of an integrated framework.

Systemic thinking in practice – the example of 'multi-domestic' management

The management of an international corporation is a multi-layered and extremely complex task. This applies particularly to those companies striving for multi-domestic operation. Multi-domestic companies aim not only for finely tuned, appropriate local action but also for worldwide optimization of their value chain, and at the same time have to keep abreast of global standards in terms of efficiency and quality. A good example of this kind of organization is ABB Asea Brown Boveri AG, whose motto is: 'Think globally, act locally' (Barnevik, 1991). The matrix of ABB has as its dimensions the business areas on one side and the various countries on the other. Woven into this net are 1200 local firms and a total of 4500 profit centres. The local firms employ about 200 people, the profit centres employ on average 50. The firms and profit centres focus rigorously on local conditions, leaving the matrix of business areas and the various countries to concentrate on coordination worldwide.

Systemic thinking and acting are a vital prerequisite to understanding the interrelations of a multi-domestic company and to give a better foundation to decision making. The following examples will show how systemic thinking and the St Gallen Management Concept can be used (further details are available Gomez *et al.*, 1993). In order to understand a multi-domestic company we need the St Gallen Management Concept, or to put it another way, we need a framework which can be immediately applied and which will construct a profile of the strategic characteristics of a multi-domestic company. This profile of characteristics will supply the relevant categories for discussing the managerial problems of a multi-domestic company. The network binds these together into an effective structure which allows decisions and possible disruptions to be played through.

The problem discussed here can be placed on the strategic management level. Nevertheless, in the spirit of the St Gallen Management Concept it also has to be put into the wider context of normative and operative management. At the strategic level, however, it is vital that strategic programmes, management systems, organizational structures and executive behaviour are taken into account. Figure 2.9 illustrates these interconnections.

In the St Gallen Management Concept, the characteristics of a company which acts both locally and multi-domestically are shown as profiles. At the highest *normative* level the locally-oriented part of the company focuses on shareholders and has a uniform structure under strict managerial control. The multi-domestic part of the company is more stakeholder-oriented, its companies are allowed considerable autonomy by means of a holding structure and the management could thus be described as soft. At the *strategic* level, it is necessary to differentiate between the strategic programme, the organizational structures, the management systems and executive behaviour. In the strategic programme local management concentrates on product–market

FIGURE 2.9 Strategic interconnections of the multi-domestic company in the St Gallen Management Concept (Source: Gomez *et al.*, 1993)

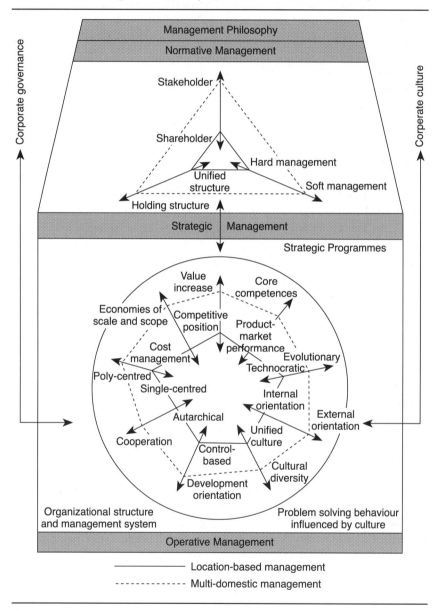

performance and tries to achieve the best competitive position. Cost management plays a central role in this. Multi-domestic management aims to develop core competences and to increase the value of the company; it tries to achieve not only economies of scale but also economies of scope. When looking at structures, local management can be described as mono-centred, autarkical or self-sufficient, and control-oriented while the multi-domestic management is poly-centred, seeks cooperations and sees advantages in being development-oriented.

Finally, we turn to the culture-driven problem solving and learning. Here local management acts as a cultural unifier whose main focus is internal and technocratic, while multi-domestic management works for cultural diversity and acts with an external and evolutionary focus.

By looking at this initial placing of a multi-domestic company into the St Gallen Management Concept it becomes quite apparent what aspects have to be considered when developing a network. There are three stages to constructing this network, as shown in Figure 2.10.

1 *Stage one* constructs the cycle anchored in local markets. It is the engine of the whole network. At its core is the achievement and expansion of local competitive advantages by means of flexible management and optimal customer value.

2 *Stage two* starts with the vision of a multi-domestic company, we then introduce the basic determinants of international management as set out by the St Gallen Management Concept.

   Factors such as strategic core competences, decentralized structures and the diversity of corporate culture play a central role. However, environmental sustainability, risk minimization and social responsibility in terms of the stakeholders are also taken into consideration. Prerequisite to international activity is, after all, the available free cash flows from local business activities to facilitate investment in research and development, in human resources and to allow economies of scale to be achieved.

3 In *stage three* the interactions between local and multi-domestic management can be woven into a network pattern allowing areas of conflict within the multi-domestic company to be identified. These could be between local competitors and the exploitation of global economies of scale, or between a strong corporate culture and local sub-cultures, or between the improvement of local product-market-performance and the build-up of core competences. Furthermore, the interactions allow the risk situation to be assessed, particularly in the problematic correlation between economies of scale (in terms

FIGURE 2.10 Network pattern of the multi-domestic company (MDC) (Source: Gomez *et al.*, 1993)

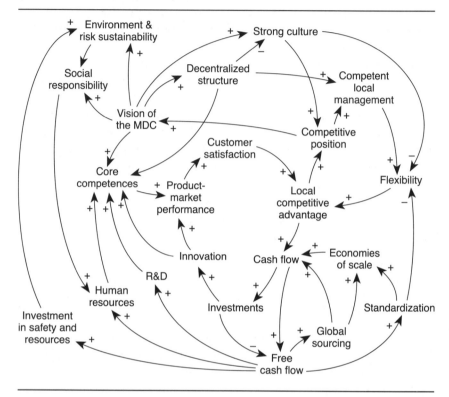

of global sourcing and standardization) and the diseconomies of risk in the whole system.

The network in Figure 2.10 conveys – at a high aggregate level – a systemic view of managerial interrelations in a multi-domestic company. It is also the point at which strategic issues can start to be thought out. For example:

- What effect would a grave environmental disaster have on free cash flows and therefore on the potential for internationalizing the company?

- Does not an enforced growth of core competences weaken them in the long term as it requires an increasingly centralized control of resources? This weakens the decentralised structures, which are the ones responsible for building and maintaining core competences.

This example of a multi-domestic company shows how a systemic understanding of a company can be set up. Of course such a model cannot capture all the facets of corporate activities. But in my opinion its operationability is conclusive. Many so-called systemic corporate concepts are vague and so highly abstract that an immediate practical application is impossible. By using the tools introduced above a systemic understanding of a company is possible without requiring the assistance of specialists or 'translators' of highly abstract thought processes. Thus the first prerequisite for systemic strategic management is fulfilled: an understanding of the company as a whole. The next prerequisite is to define the different strategies so that the company can be clearly and effectively driven forward.

Business strategies, corporate strategies, owner strategies

In the first chapter, I introduced the various stages of development in strategic thinking and showed that the creation of business strategies was until recently key to long-term planning. And so the view was that if you put all business strategies together, i.e. an optimal portfolio of strategic business units, you have a corporate strategy. However, now we know that a whole is more than the sum of its parts, or to put it more precisely, quite different to the sum of its parts. Any company has a variety of further potentials apart from its market potential and these cannot be consistently exploited simply by means of business strategies. These potentials also cover areas previously controlled by the financial director and were never included in the narrower view of strategy.

As an integrated view of a company gradually developed the question arose, how can we measure corporate success? If the yardstick was simply greater competitive advantage achieved through the business strategies, then this yardstick would not be a suitable gauge for the company as a whole. By looking at shareholder value a new indicator appeared: the increase in company value represented by future free cash flows achievable in the future. Thus the components for a new strategic understanding appeared and these are illustrated in Figure 2.11.

This picture was developed further when the owner strategy was introduced. This strategy covers those strategic possibilities open only to the owner but not to management. However, management still has to take these options into account if it does not want a nasty surprise or, to put it more tactfully, if it wants to exploit all possibilities for increasing

FIGURE 2.11   Components for a new strategic understanding

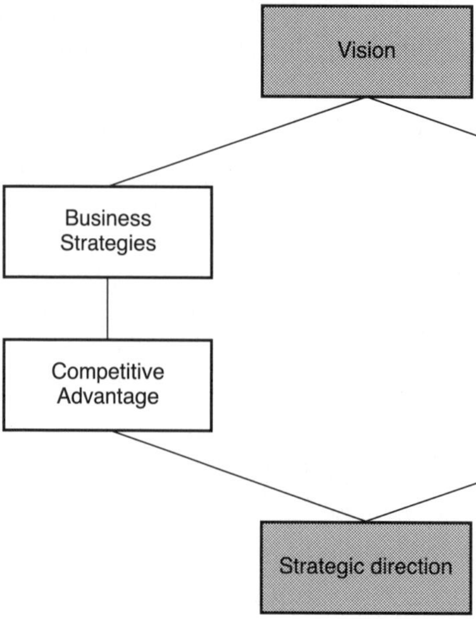

the company value. Management can do so by pointing out these possibilities to the owner.

A systemic but differentiated strategic understanding has to take into account the distinction between business, corporate and owner strategies. At the same time it has to put them into the wider context of the vision, organization and the culture of the company embedded in its environment.

These connections are shown in Figure 2.12, whereby the value increase for all stakeholders provides the yardstick for the success of strategic leadership.

Business strategies for the achievement of competitive advantage

The tools for the development of business strategies are extremely varied as these familiar key words prove: *product–market matrix, strategic business units, portfolio planning, strategic positions for success, competitive strategy*. I will show how to apply these tools systematically in the next chapter when we look at the development of a strategic method of integrated value

FIGURE 2.12 Connections relevant for a systemic but differentiated strategic understanding

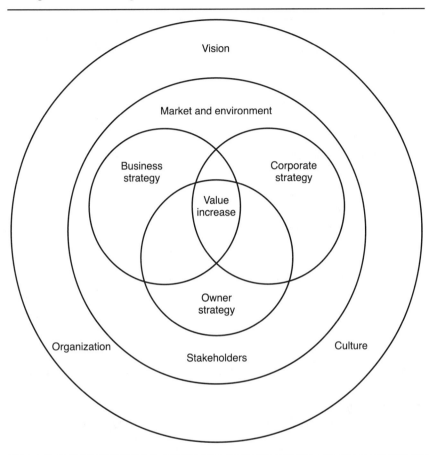

management. For the moment let us aim to understand the basic strategic interconnections. To this purpose I will use mainly practical examples.

The classic strategic tool in terms of markets is the *product-market-matrix* developed by Ansoff. This matrix allows for four possible areas of strategic action, as shown in Table 2.1.

Some of the examples I use illustrate these strategic possibilities. In the areas of *market penetration* we will look at relaunch and unbundling. A good example of a successful relaunch is the bicycle. It has existed for some time now in its present form and sales were naturally much higher at the beginning of the century than over the past thirty years. Yet recently, as a result of a new environmental and health awareness, the

TABLE 2.1 The product–market matrix developed by Ansoff (1965)

	Current products	*New products*
Current markets	Market penetration: ■ intensification of market handling ■ relaunch ■ imitation ■ reducing costs and prices ■ unbundling	Product development: ■ new products ■ new product lines
New markets	Market development: ■ market expansion ■ new client group ■ new channels of distribution ■ new usages ■ new services ■ problem and system solutions	Diversification

bicycle has seen an unexpected boom. This boom was helped along its way by new versions of mountain and city bikes which have sophisticated gearing and accessories.

An example of unbundling would be the car which used to be sold off the peg, a complete bundle as it were. Today when ordering a car the customer can put together his individual car by choosing different accessories. A result of this, for example, is the development of a separate market offering a broad and sophisticated range of car radios.

If we look at *market development* then we touch on new distribution channels as well as problem solving and system solutions. Today, for example, expensive luxury goods are available via mail order. This was unthinkable years ago because it was assumed that customers required expert advice. The same is the case for the large DIY shops – previously an experienced craftsperson was needed. A good example of problem solving and system solutions is the computer industry. At the beginning IBM's success was due to its supplying computer hardware and software. As a result of increasing competition and falling prices it is now more geared towards providing overall solutions such as personnel information systems, production planning systems and management systems, and so on. These are considered to be on a par with hardware and software in terms of service and conception.

Product development and *diversification* are virtually self-explanatory. The latter will be dealt with in relation to corporate strategy in the *Determining cooperation strategies* section in Chapter 3, yet even here there have been many new developments.

The product–market matrix is a popular tool still used by companies to develop sales related strategies. However, it does not stand up on its own as a device to develop business strategies. It does not give any clues as to how to distinguish between businesses and it does not put enough emphasis on market analysis and studying the competitive position.

Strategic business units and *portfolio planning* were the first concepts that tried to do this. It is very rare for a company to be active in one particular region or one market only. Usually companies are active in businesses of different kinds. The starting point for these businesses is therefore to define their identity and zoning. It was for this purpose that strategic business units (or SBUs) were created. An SBU stands for a product–market combination which can be clearly distinguished from other combinations in the same company. An SBU

- sells a specific group of products or services;

- serves a specific group of clients;

- has a well-defined group of co-competitors.

An independent market task and identifiable competitors are therefore the main criteria for distinction. A unit should consist of as few combinations of client groups, client functions and technologies as possible and should barely overlap with other units. In principle an SBU should be able to exist as an autonomous company.

The intellectual division of SBUs serves to produce product-specific and market-specific management and rarely coincides with the company's own organizational structure, whether into departments or groups. This is even the case when the organizational structure has separate divisions or branches. In a large company a division will often contain several SBUs, all very different from each other.

I will describe in detail how to approach the question of delimiting SBUs in paragraph 3.1 below, but here are two examples. This is how Gurit Heberlein, a Swiss industrial company with a turnover of sFr400 million, set up the following SBUs:

- glass and metal adhesive sealing systems for the car industry;

- technical materials (coatings for skis, optical foils);

- medical and dental sector (root canal and anchoring instruments, pressure gauge systems and catheter systems);

- fibre technology (jet systems and component systems);

- Textiles.

The Haefely Group in Basle is another example. It employs 700 people and turns over approximately sFr120 million. Haefely distinguishes between two strategic business units:

1   network components (instrument transformers, carrier frequency instruments, air throttles, network filters, control condensers;

2   control systems (high voltage control systems, testing equipment for electronics, the aviation and aeronautic industries).

The diversification unit of BMW is a third example. It is divided into three SBUs, as shown in Figure 2.13.

After the strategic business units have been identified and zoned the next step is to find their optimal position among the competition. To this end, each SBU is analysed in terms of opportunities/threats and strengths/weaknesses, then positioned in a matrix using the coordinates of market appeal and relative competitive advantage. Figure 2.14 shows this

FIGURE 2.13 Diversification of BMW

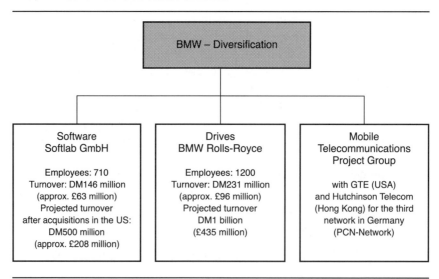

FIGURE 2.14   Relative positioning of SBUs

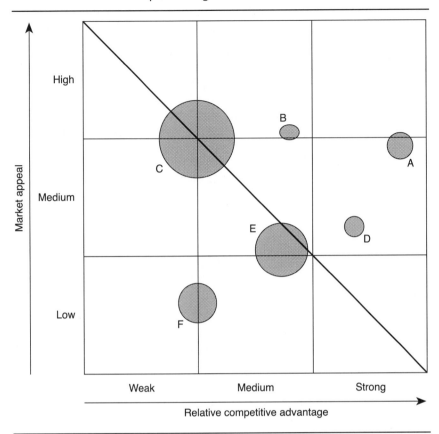

positioning clearly. The size of the circles equals the significance of the business expressed as turnover, cash flows or profit.

What is important about the next step is to use the positioning of the single SBUs to find strategic directions. The coordinate squares and diagonal shown in Figure 2.14 are crucial here. Every activity above the diagonal is considered to be worth promoting: investment and growth strategies start here. The SBUs below the diagonal are suitable for skimming off and disinvestment. If a SBU lies directly on the diagonal its allocation is not so obvious, so selective strategies have to be applied. The nine fields in the matrix above specify the norm strategies for the respective SBUs. Initially there were four fields as proposed by the Boston Consulting Group. They were (clockwise): 'Question Mark, Star, Cash Cow, Poor Dog'. These catchy terms led directly to the respective strategy.

Question Mark meant re-double the effort and/or retreat, the Star was of course to be maintained and developed further, the Cash Cow is to be milked for as long as she delivers and a Poor Dog means think seriously about getting out.

McKinsey increased these four fields to nine fields as shown by Figure 2.15. If we look at the Swiss company Holvis AG we can see how they found their strategic direction using this system. Half of its turnover of more than a billion sFr came from paper production and on top of that there was a small business unit in fleece production. Holvis AG discovered that paper production was an unattractive sector in terms of the market as well as the competitive position. However, the substantially smaller fleece business was settled in an attractive market and had already gained some competitive advantage. So paper was the Poor Dog and fleece a Question

FIGURE 2.15 McKinsey's extension of the BCG matrix

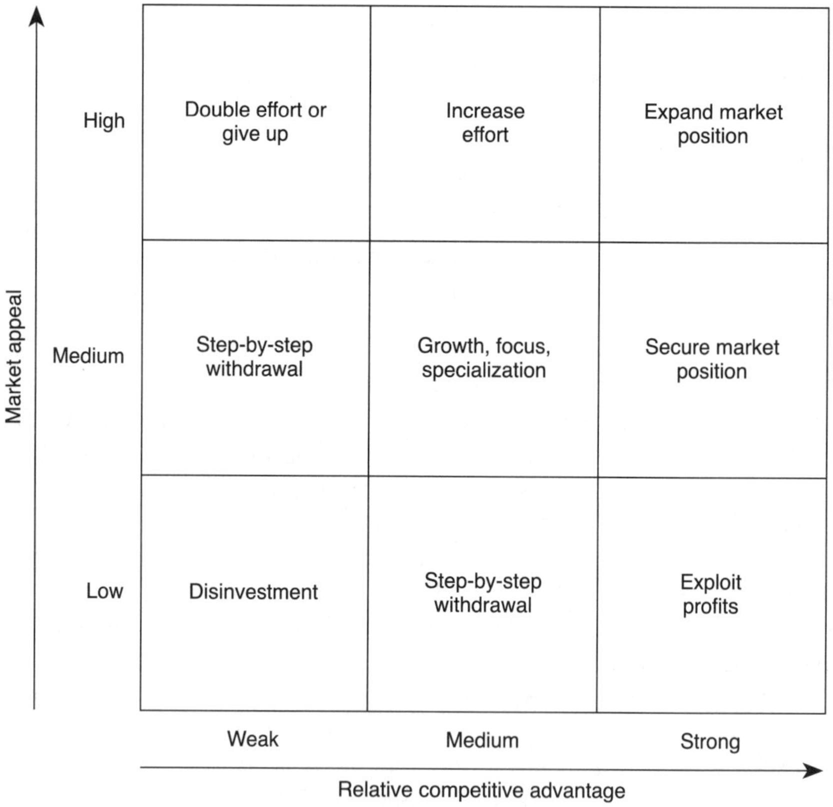

	Weak	Medium	Strong
High	Double effort or give up	Increase effort	Expand market position
Medium	Step-by-step withdrawal	Growth, focus, specialization	Secure market position
Low	Disinvestment	Step-by-step withdrawal	Exploit profits

Market appeal (vertical axis)

Relative competitive advantage (horizontal axis)

Mark. The conclusion to this positioning was that the company should disinvest its paper business and invest in the fleece business. This strategy was fully implemented. Paper production was disposed of completely and an important fleece plant in the US was acquired. Although the company's turnover is down at present, from the perspective of profit and sales this strategy is proving to be absolutely right.

Although the portfolio approach was not able to meet all the expectations placed on it (see Chapter 1) it is still prevalent in corporate practice and is a substantial aid to developing business strategies. This concept has now been developed further and has since added the following portfolios: life-cycle, resources, technology, ecology and country.

The concept of the *Strategic Success Positions (SSP)* was developed at the beginning of the 1980s (Pümpin, 1992). SSPs are abilities which allow a company to achieve above-average results in comparison to its competitors, even in the long-term. They differ from operational competitive advantages which produce short-term gain by means of clever marketing tactics. Every corporate area is basically suitable for constructing SSPs: a company develops a superior product compared to its competitors, or it has the highest profile in a certain market or it applies a superior production technology. The huge success of IBM could be traced to the SSP customer service, Rolls Royce had its SSPs in the areas of image and quality. At Procter and Gamble it was product quality and communications, at 3M it was its ability to be innovative and Benetton was able to respond quickly to the customer's changing needs. SSPs do have to be looked after and developed, however, or their effectiveness can be lost just as quickly. This is what happened with IBM and Rolls Royce.

In determining SSPs a company should try to keep to a small number. Here are some pointers:

In the product and services sector

- The ability to recognize customer needs better and faster than the competition and so be able to quickly adapt the range of products and services to the needs of the market.

- The ability to offer excellent advice to customers and a superior customer service.

- The ability to know a certain material (i.e. aluminium) better in terms of production and application and to master it.

In the market sector

■   The ability to handle a specific market or clients more purposefully and more effectively than the competition.

■   The ability to create and maintain a superior image (quality, for example) in a certain market.

In the corporate activity sector

■   The ability to dominate specific distribution channels best (i.e. direct sales).

■   Through constant innovation, the ability to launch new, superior products onto the market faster than the competition.

■   The ability to tap and to secure superior sources of procurement.

■   The ability to manufacture more efficiently and more cost-favourably than the competition.

■   The ability to recruit and to keep the best qualified employees.

While SSPs were originally market-oriented, their latest development is aimed at the value potentials of a company. Market-oriented SSPs are the quality of Swissair or the image of Perrier. But another SSP is the ability to restructure, as the Swedish company Electrolux did so successfully. Or an SSP directed at the potential of diminishing costs, such as the German retailer Aldi, who consistently beat their competitors with their cost management.

Cost leadership leads us straight to the last concept in the development of business strategies. *Competitive Strategy* (Porter, 1980; 1985) consists of three directions for business strategies: cost leadership, differentiation or focus. The cost leadership strategy seeks to use production costs and overheads advantage to increase the market share with low prices. The differentiation strategy is when a company, through innovation and better service, aims to improve its products and services. The focus strategy is to consistently aim at specific markets, customer groups, technologies and regions. The whole context is shown in Figure 2.16.

On top of these three generic strategies there is a fourth one which is very rarely used. It is the creation of new rules in the marketplace – a new way of dealing is introduced which consciously goes against and recreates the current rules in a market or industry.

FIGURE 2.16   The concept of competitive strategy (Porter, 1980)

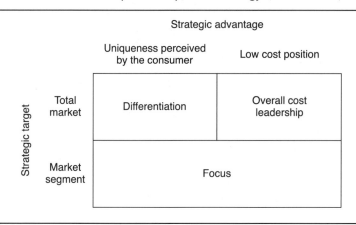

In the development of competitive strategies it is crucial to choose one and then stick to it. The biggest mistake is to mix a little of everything; if you do that you end up with neither one thing or another. You most certainly do not end up with a strategy.

The leading German food retailer Aldi is an excellent example of cost leadership. Its low costs and its uniquely cheap prices are achieved by the fastest turnover of merchandise in the entire German retail industry (eight days on average), by extremely low staffing costs (3 to 5 per cent of the turnover) and by maintaining a consistent tight controlling. The recent blossoming of the Swiss watch industry was due to a consistent cost strategy – and not merely the marketing tactics of Swatch. SMH quickly recovered lost ground from competitors by reducing its production depth, by tightening its product range and by more effective production methods. It was able to regain its leading position in the global market. Asea Brown Boveri demonstrated that it is possible to manufacture cost favourably, even in a country like Switzerland which has very high wages. It built a locomotive plant in Oerlikon near Zurich using the newest production methods.

It is a strategy of *differentiation* or *performance leadership* which made the company Zweifel the market leader in Switzerland for crisps and snacks. The differentiation was not the production of better or even different crisps. It was rather its direct distribution system – a whole fleet of vehicles ensure that the freshness they advertise is not an empty promise. Another example is Ricola AG which produces herb pastilles. The company produces a tiny range of high quality products in large quantities. Its export quota is 80 per cent. An image of Switzerland with beautiful meadows full of flowers is created abroad and enables the company to maintain a high price policy compared to its competitors, which in turn contributes to its outstanding profits. American Express is another example. It has placed itself in the credit card market as an exclusive and efficient product. Image campaigns and special offers such as the 'Shop-Guarantee' have all contributed to this. Thus Amex is able to charge retailers up to 6 per cent commission for a retail transaction, whereas it is only 4 per cent for Visa or Mastercard, and demand from the customer significantly higher prices. The only proviso is that not all shops accept Amex.

The Tetra-Group from Melle/Germany is a good of example of a *niche strategy*. It specializes in food for tropical and ornamental fish. This focus has enabled the company, established in 1950, to gain a present market share of 80 per cent. In Switzerland the Eichhof Group, which was originally a medium-sized brewery, has recently not only re-focused on high-profile top-quality specialist drinks but has also diversified into the household machinery market. It sells special ranges which have potential in terms of future markets and profits. The success of the niche strategy is demonstrated by the positive development of the company in recent years.

The range of tools available for the development of business strategies are highly developed and applied in industry. They are, however, not enough to lead a company successfully into the future. To achieve that, a comprehensive corporate strategy has to be prepared.

Corporate strategies for value increase

Key terms can also be found for corporate strategies but executives are far less familiar with them – this area has only been investigated recently. These new key terms include value potentials, core competences and integrated value management.

Equally important to the context of corporate strategies are areas such as diversification, disinvestment, cooperation, restructuring and financing. This last list shows a trend towards placing strategic and financial management together. However, in order for this to happen a common framework has to be found, it is possible to develop this from the first group of concepts.

Value potentials are latent or extant combinations of circumstances which can be found either in the environment, the market or in the company itself. If these are developed then new possibilities open up for the company. Figure 2.17 shows how to differentiate between the internal and external value potentials of a company.

FIGURE 2.17   How to differentiate between the internal and external value potentials of a company (Pümpin, 1989)

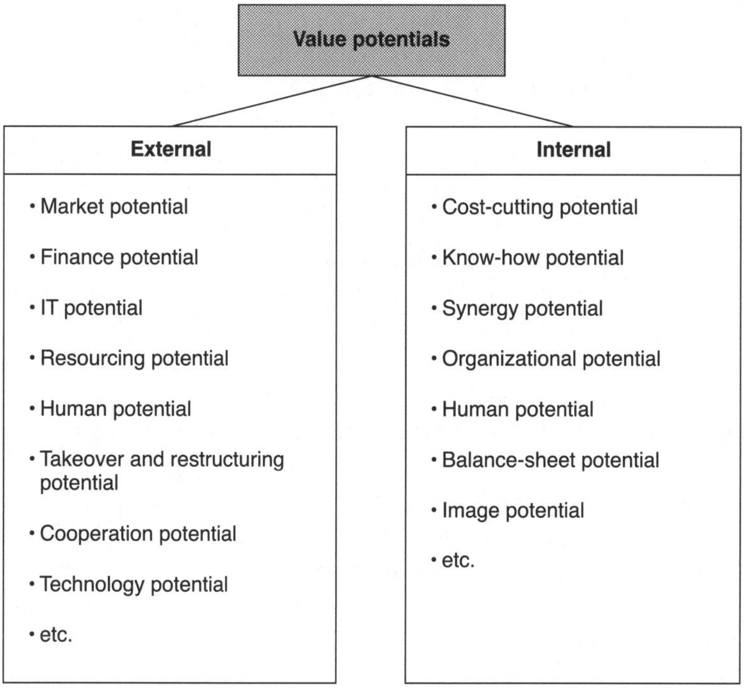

Value potentials	
External	**Internal**
• Market potential	• Cost-cutting potential
• Finance potential	• Know-how potential
• IT potential	• Synergy potential
• Resourcing potential	• Organizational potential
• Human potential	• Human potential
• Takeover and restructuring potential	• Balance-sheet potential
• Cooperation potential	• Image potential
• Technology potential	• etc.
• etc.	

Some examples we are going to look at illustrate the exploitation of such value potentials. Benetton very skilfully uses two potentials at the same time: the IT-potential and the external human potential. By using an integrated computer system the company is able to respond immediately to short-term changes in the market, making it quicker than its competitors. It has a high number of very motivated small businesses at its disposal, as its global network of retail branches are all franchised.

The companies Forbo (floor coverings) and Merkur (retailing), leaders in their field in Switzerland, have specialized in systematic takeovers and thus became leaders in their market sectors. The German company Linde AG attempted by means of comprehensive purchasing to become an international market leader in all its lines of business (production technology, refrigeration technology, technical gases, plant engineering and construction). They have achieved this objective already in the fork-lift truck sector by taking over companies such as Fenwick in

France and Lancing in Great Britain. The corporate strategy of Swissair places special emphasis on cooperating with foreign airlines as the company sees this as the only way to survive in a deregulated environment and a market which is strongly concentrated.

The Swiss machinery company Sulzer made its IT-department legally independent and provides its know-how in this sector not only to its own company but also to third parties. It makes use of its know-how potential in the same way that Siemens did when its central PR-department went independent and became a separate company, MCD (Marketing, Communication, Design) GmbH, which also offers its services to outsiders. The company Dunhill is a good example of a company using its image potential. With a global reputation as a producer of tobacco products it has now very successfully entered the world of fashion.

One-off exploitation of one particular value potential can quite easily lead to increased business activity in the short-term – acquisitions are a good example of that. However, if the dynamics of a company are to be increased in the long term it is necessary to multiply the use of value potentials. A *multiplication* of value potentials has several advantages. For a start it concentrates all the strengths of a company. Coordination costs are reduced by repetition of similar processes, the processes also become simpler and more time efficient. All in all quality improves with ever increasing experience.

There are two basic forms of multiplication, process multiplication and system multiplication (Pümpin and Imboden, 1991). We have already mentioned Forbo AG and so let us look at their process multiplication. Forbo has recently become one of Europe's leading suppliers of floor and wall coverings primarily through process multiplication. A principal element of Forbo's strategy was to take over medium-sized competitors in the region. Through a multiplication of the acquisition process Forbo became highly professional in its methods and in its speedy integration of the acquired firms.

If we want to look at a successful example of system multiplication then we need look no further than the Holderbank Group, which has developed into the world's largest cement conglomerate. Over the years the Holderbank Group has developed a clear idea of how a cement factory should be designed and fitted out. This design was then multiplied all over the world and the company is now the market leader. Through multiplication a company learns to avoid too many mistakes. Inefficiencies and time wasting can also be ironed out.

Multiplications can be of a quantitative as well as a qualitative nature and can be carried out both internally and externally, as closer study of the restaurant chain Mövenpick in the *Defining integral corporate strategies* section of Chapter 3 shows. Mövenpick has multiplied some types of restaurants (i.e. the Marché Restaurants) yet it does not ignore innovations and continually designs new styles of restaurants. Furthermore, although many of these restaurants are managed by Mövenpick itself, others are externalized by means of franchising and licensing.

Another concept which has become increasingly important to the development of corporate strategies is the concept of *core competences* (Prahalad and Hamel, 1991). Core competences are the abilities of a company which prevail right across the separate business units and which enable a company to launch in rapid succession product innovations in different sectors. Figure 2.18 presents the core competences of Canon and their implementation through the development of new products.

Canon's core competences are precision engineering, precision optics and microelectronics. Out of these core competences come a variety of competitive products which can be produced and sold. The elements of Canon's core competences in precision optics are spread

FIGURE 2.18 The core competences of Canon and their implementation through the development of new products (Prahalad and Hamel, 1991)

	Precision mechanics	Fine optics	Micro-electronics
Basic camera	☐	▨	
Compact fashion camera	☐	▨	
Electronic camera	☐	▨	
EOS autofocus camera	☐	▨	▮
Video still camera	☐	▨	▮
Laser beam printer	☐	▨	▮
Colour video printer	☐		▮
Bubble jet printer	☐		▮
Basic fax	☐		▮
Laser fax	☐		▮
Calculator	☐		▮
Plain paper copier	☐	▨	▮
Battery PPC	☐	▨	▮

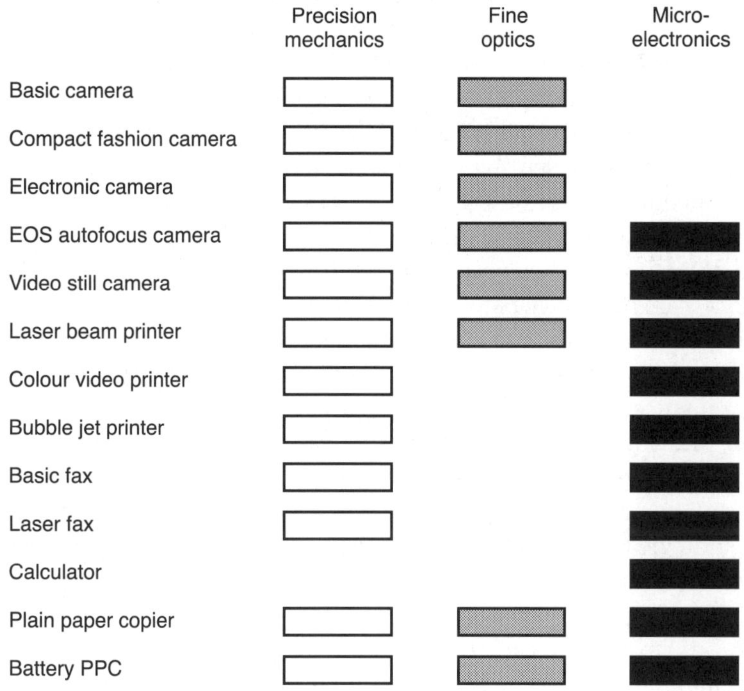

throughout every branch of their business from cameras via photocopiers to semiconductors and mask aligners for the production of microchips. When Canon saw an opportunity for digital laser beam printers it authorized managers of the relevant strategic business units to look into other SBUs and grab hold of every talent needed for the development and marketing of this product of the future. This shows that single SBUs no longer have the right to hold on to their employees and resources. Core competences are resources which belong to the whole company and as such are allocated by the management of the corporate group.

The core competences of Daimler-Benz are, among others, drives and microelectronics. By taking over a number of aviation and aerospace companies Daimler-Benz has accumulated a knowledge of drives which include drive units for cars and HGVs, for helicopters and small planes, even for jets and rockets. This know-how has been mutually beneficial to all sectors and led to several innovations in the drive industry. It also points to the closely woven interlinking of strategy and organization. At the moment Daimler-Benz is organized into different business areas (Mercedes-Benz, AEG, Deutsche Aerospace, debis), there is nothing to stop it reorganizing in the future into a drive division, a microelectronics division and similar competency-oriented units, so that these core competences can be exploited in the best possible way.

The most comprehensive strategic approach at a corporate level is the *integrated value management concept*. It starts by changing the aims of the strategic direction, that is from gaining competitive advantage to increasing the integrated value of a company. Recently, company value has moved into the spotlight because investors are increasingly insisting on an adequate return on their investments. In a public limited company this means a dividend and an increase in the value of shares. The latter can only happen if the company as a whole develops organically and if a balance can be struck between investing in the future and exploiting current markets to the full. Today's managers are still thinking in terms of turnover and market share so they are often influenced by the short-term-oriented incentive schemes. This is especially problematic in markets which are increasingly saturated and can often lead to the incorrect allocation of resources. An optimal value increase can only be achieved when all value potentials are exploited. Among other things this means that strategic thinking has entered areas which used to be in the domain of financial management.

As company value becomes more and more important, two questions arise: how can this value or its increase be determined and how can it be influenced? The question of measuring company value will be dealt with in depth in the *Owner strategies for optimization of value and risk* section later in this chapter, but I would just like to say now that profit and linking indicators such as profitability are not sufficient to determine the value of a company. The future available cash flows generated by the business strategies, corporate strategies and owner strategies will prove to be an appropriate measure.

Another important question in relation to corporate strategy is determining the factors which influence the value of a company. Only when the corporate strategy is put at those points or turns those screws which substantially influence the value of a company does it produce the necessary leverage. Figure 2.19 shows these so-called value generators as specified by Alfred Rappaport in his ground-breaking book *Creating Shareholder Value* (1986).

The five major value generators are:

1   sales growth;

2   operating profit margin;

3   income tax rate;

FIGURE 2.19 The so-called value generators as specified by Alfred Rappaport (1986)

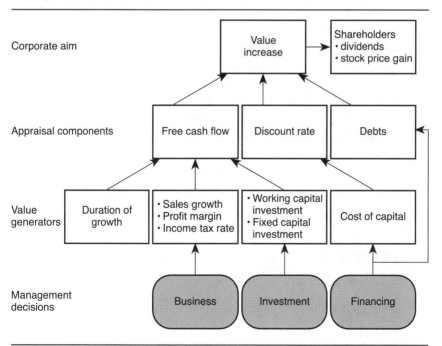

4   working capital/fixed capital investment;

5   cost of capital.

From this list only three of the value generators are already in the vocabulary of conventional strategic thinking – sales growth, profit margins and investments. The cost of capital and income tax rate are normally in the hands of those responsible for finance. A comprehensive corporate strategy can no longer accept such an artificial separation. Every possible value generator has to be put to strategic use in order to increase the value of a company.

Having understood that value generators are the starting point for corporate strategies, we then have to look for other signals in order to continue. These can be found in the value potentials introduced above. If we combine value generators with value potentials we get the Valcor matrix, which was developed by myself and Bruno Weber to help generate corporate strategies (Gomez and Weber, 1989). This has proved itself to be invaluable in corporate practice. This kind of matrix created for a leading Swiss retailer can be found in Table 2.2.

The application of the *Valcor* ('Value-is-Core') *matrix* will be explained in more detail in the next chapter. I will for the moment just raise a few points to illustrate it. It shows that the retailer could in fact increase his sales volume by introducing new business sectors, such as DIY centres or garden centres. The profit margin could be improved either with a value analysis of overhead costs or even by changing the opening hours. Making disinvestments in production plants or in non-essential company assets does help to increase value. Experience shows that better management of working capital can have great results. In order to optimize the cost of capital it is possible to exploit the leverage effect not only on existing business but also on acquisitions, and so using outstanding financial advisors in this area is money well spent. Finally, the income tax rate can be influenced positively either by creating a central purchasing company or by separating wholesale from retail activities. In order to develop a Valcor matrix it is essential to look at five specific areas crucial to the generation of a corporate strategy. These areas are:

- diversification;

- disinvestment;

- cooperation;

- restructuring;

- financing.

TABLE 2.2 The Valcor matrix created for a leading Swiss retailer (Source: Gomez and Weber, 1989)

Value generators/ Value potential	Market	Procurement	Employees	Logistics/IT	Takeover/restructuring
Sales growth	New products Mix-improvement Shops in the shop New types of business	Backward integration	Incentives Training centre New kind of salesperson	Customer support/ services	Foreign acquisitions
Profit margin	Pricing policy Sales promotion Product variety	Central purchasing	Flexible working opening times	Overhead cost Analysis Automation	Reducing overheads Synergies
Investment Working capital Fixed assets	Land analysis Sell and lease back	Disinvestment Production facilities	Outsourcing	Storage, creditor, debtor Management	Sale of non-essential business assets
Cost of capital	Risk optimization of product range	Exploitation of credit standing	Financial specialists	Cash management	Leverage
Income tax rate	Separation wholesale/retail	Central purchasing unit	Tax consultant	Optimal data structures	Goodwill approach

In the current understanding of strategy, diversifications are usually placed under the aspect of a possible realization of operational synergies. Seen in this light the motto is: stick to what you know. From the conventional return on investment point of view it is only those diversifications which build on present activities and abilities that are likely to succeed. They are based on the value chain of the company. From the new value management point of view, however, this theory can no longer be supported. Even conglomerate diversifications which have little in common with the original company can be perfectly successful provided they are founded on a common strategic platform and their success is measured by the value increase of the company (Gomez and Ganz, 1992).

One such example is Philip Morris, who have diversified from tobacco products into the food industry (General Foods, Kraft, Jacobs Suchard). There are virtually no operational synergies between these two lines of business yet Philip Morris has increased its integrated value, as the increase in the value of its shares demonstrates. This is because strategic experience in marketing brand names is viable whatever the product. At the same time, by diversifying, the particular risk of tobacco products can be reduced.

We only have to look at ABB Asea Brown Boveri AG to find an example of *disinvestment*. This company consciously uses disinvestment to increase company value. ABB categorizes all its businesses according to two criteria: what potential do they have for value increase, and is it ABB itself or a third party which can best exploit these possibilities? Businesses that look likely to increase their value and have better capabilities than their competitors remain in the company's own portfolio. ABB disinvests when it feels that a third party is better able to bridge the value gap. The funds gained are then invested in projects which promise a better chance of success according to the perspective of value increase. In this way disinvestments become a very important strategic move.

A further strand of corporate strategies are *cooperations*, which in this context means mergers and acquisitions. While the value increase potential of mergers is difficult to assess, its discovery and exploitation is prerequisite to a successful acquisition. Of course it is possible to interpret acquisitions as part of a competitive strategy and apply the relevant range of instruments to planning the takeover process. But only a small proportion of possibilities latent in an acquisition can be exploited this way. If you look only at those options relating to sales growth and profit margins you are concentrating on one-sided orientation towards increasing market share and on operational synergies. Bitter experience has shown that these are only partially realized after the acquisition. In most cases the value generators of investment/disinvestment and cost of capital and tax management are the ones which produce the greatest leverage and should therefore play a vital role in assessing possible acquisitions. In the third chapter I work out these correlations in depth and introduce a step-by-step approach for spotting the value gaps of potential acquisitions.

Restructuring as a corporate strategy is becoming increasingly important. The 1990s are undergoing a renaissance of seeing organization as a managerial tool (Gomez, 1992). The value increase approach demands that organizations are deliberately changed in those areas which can produce the greatest leverage for generating free cash flows. By placing organization among the value generators it is possible to achieve growth in sales volume by aligning the organization according to core competences and by reducing hierarchical levels in order to improve profit margins. In terms of net working capital and fixed assets it is possible either to increase value through disinvesting businesses as did ABB, or by an organizational divestment of non-essential business assets. In order to reduce cost of capital and to limit the risk organizational units should be decoupled. International group structures are a possibility in order to optimize income tax rates.

If we want examples of a value-led restructuring of a company then let us look no further than Credit Suisse Holding, the Swiss banking group, and the Anova group, which belongs to the leading Swiss industrialist Stephan Schmidheiny. By establishing a holding, Credit Suisse wanted to reduce its involvement in non-banking businesses so that it could re-direct these resources to other sectors. However, the Swiss High Court thwarted this plan by finding the company's argument unacceptable. The Anova Group has many interests in industry. It re-organized its distribution and service sectors in order to reduce any miscellaneous asbestos risks from its Eternit business so that the risk would not prove contagious to other company undertakings. It went on to combine related industrial equities in such a way that any common strategic ground was able to bear fruit. This did not necessarily mean merging these companies.

Finally, we come to *financing*. In financial terms value increase simply means revenue which is higher than the cost of capital. The latter corresponds to the weighted average costs of capital from outside sources and from equity capital and reflects the risks of the chosen strategies. As I will show in the next paragraph it is the equity capitals costs which are always underestimated. Equity capital costs are opportunistic costs. That means they correspond to the rate which could be achieved with another investment which has the same risk profile. It is absolutely wrong to think that equity capital costs are equal to the paid dividend or the reciprocal value of the price/earnings relationship. In truth the shareholder return equals the dividend plus any share price advance. A way to reduce equity capital costs is to restructure the company in order to minimize risk, which is precisely what Philip Morris and the Anova Group did. So then by application of the leverage effect capital structure can be changed, and by putting into action the financial tools of dividend policies and listing on the stock exchange a slowdown can be achieved. Well-directed asset management together with professional cash management can produce the desired effects on outside capital. There are even further possibilities in optimizing the debt mix and by applying some financial engineering.

There are a wide variety of possibilities available to help the management of a company design a comprehensive corporate strategy apart from optimizing the position of its business units *vis-à-vis* the competition. It is nevertheless the case that management's room to manoeuvre is still limited because in the end it has to act on behalf of its investors. If the investors are the owners or have an influence because of a particular set of circumstances, then they too can steer the company in a certain direction. We have to put these in a different category – that of owner strategies.

Owner strategies for optimization of value and risk

In one sense there is no concept and approach for the development of an owner strategy. The idea of putting the owner strategy on a separate level to business and corporate strategies comes from Pümpin (Pümpin and Pritzl, 1991). He views the owner strategy as a 'harmonious overall concept for the management of Strategic Investment Units (SIU)'. A SIU can be a complete company, a minority stake, a commitment package or a venture capital holding, each of which has its own specific objectives and strategies. As Figure 2.20 shows, it is important to achieve a balance between those different interests.

The company may be just one of the owner's many different interests and as a result he may well make decisions which are not favourable to the long-term survival of the company. So you can see it is in the company's own interest to formulate and discuss a possible owner strategy with the management. Under this heading we will look at aspects which contribute to the value increase of the company.

An owner has many choices. The most significant are closure and/or sale of component parts of the company, the accessing of new sources of

FIGURE 2.20 Achieve a balance between different interests (Pümpin and Pritzl, 1991)

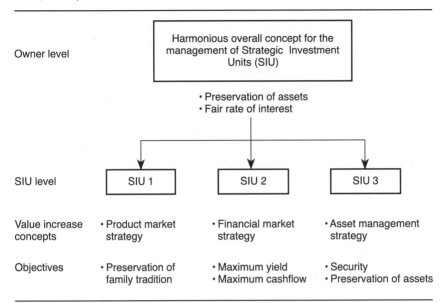

financing such as going public and using non-essential working capital for other purposes. But the owner also has the ability to play with corporate strategies such as diversification, disinvestment, cooperation, restructuring and financing as described above.

Table 2.3 summarizes some of the most important owner strategies according to their value potentials. Only those which concern the company as such are considered.

Let us look at the following examples to illustrate the different features of owner strategies. Klaus Jacobs sold the core of Jacobs Suchard to Philip Morris at an ideal time – shortly before the Iraq crisis. He felt that Philip Morris could achieve a significantly better value increase than he could himself. The price, of course, reflected this thought. With the funds then at his disposal he invested in other companies, including an employment agency called ADIA-Interim. Although it must be said that the latest developments of ADIA-Interim do not yet intimate whether this strategy of disinvestment and investment will pay off.

A more successful example of selling off non-essential business assets is shown by the family who own the Swiss department chain store Oscar Weber. The owners gave up their own department stores which

TABLE 2.3 The most important owner strategies according to their value potentials

Value potential	Owner strategies
Restructuring potential	■ Divestment of parts of company. ■ Decoupling/sale of non-essential business assets (property). ■ Reorganization for tax reasons or to reduce risks. ■ Change of legal form to reduce risks.
Acquisition potential	■ Acquisition and sale of minority shareholdings. ■ Takeover of companies in related or unrelated industries.
Financial potential	■ Going public, going private. ■ Dividend policy. ■ Application of various equity capital devices. ■ Corporate banking. ■ External financial transactions.

were situated on excellent sites, such as the Bahnhofstraße in Zurich, and rented the premises out to competitors. The rent this has yielded far outstrips the trading profits from their own stores.

In England, Hanson plc under the management of Lord Hanson is considered to be a most successful company with regards restructuring. Hanson's partners buy poorly managed companies then dispose of some businesses and lead others back into profit. The result is significantly smaller companies which are profitable. The sale of the individual parts usually covers the cost of buying the company in the first place.

The Swiss industrialist Stefan Schmidheiny continues a tradition which his father had already started with some degree of success. His father could only buy into his South and Middle American Eternit interest as a minority shareholder, yet he always played a dominant role in management. His son has minority shareholdings in several leading companies, such as Asea Brown Boveri, the Swiss watch and clock manufacturer SMH and the retail chain Merkur. On top of that he also has a major shareholding in other industrial companies.

I would like to conclude with the example of Ems Chemie Holding, a medium-sized chemical company. Based on his sound knowledge of the chemical industry its owner Christoph Blocher recognized that some chemical companies were very likely to show stock price advances, so he made some short and medium-term investments in these securities. The result was that he achieved a stock price gain of sFr70 million. Of course, it is outside the managerial remit to carry out such transactions. If, however, management is aware of the owner's intentions and in the case of Ems Chemie, the owner also worked very successfully at an operational level, it can at least prepare itself.

Risk optimization is equally important to the owner as a value increase tool and it can be assessed in two ways. On the one hand a company can be particularly susceptible if all eggs are placed in one basket. It could be susceptible to cyclical influences, product liability, substitution products, environmental or legal requirements. On the other hand risk determines the cost of capital. A company with a high risk factor has to expect a cost of capital significantly higher than others in the same market or industry sector. In capital markets this risk is identified as the beta factor. It is often the case that conglomerates have a high beta factor and thus a high cost of capital as risky and less risky businesses are put under the same roof. If these businesses were to be divested then the separate entities would have a lower beta factor and therefore better chances on the capital markets.

One example is USX. Among other things it consists of the former companies US Steel and Marathon Oil. Icahn, a well-known financier in his own right, took out full-page advertisements in the *New York Times*. In it he informed everyone that a divestment of these two companies would bring about a significant value increase to shareholders as the risk profile of these two companies was so high it had led to the infamous 'conglomerate discount'.

These short illustrations are simply to show the distinction between the different types of strategy. Understanding this is a prerequisite to the development of a comprehensive strategy for integrated value management as set out in the third chapter. Before that we have to look at one more thing. We have to deal with the yardstick of success for these strategies. It is only then that we can judge whether the direction chosen is the right one or not.

Integrated value increase of a company as the new yardstick to evaluate strategic success

Business and environmental analysis, strategic positioning and the development of direct action is usually dealt with in great detail in specialist literature. But strangely enough there is hardly ever any mention of how the success of such strategies can be measured.

One reason for this is the separation of strategic and financial thinking. In most companies it is the job of the line managers to design strategies, leaving the financial managers to assess the results of their implementation in figures. Moreover, the answer to the question, 'What is the yardstick for success?' appears to be quite obvious anyway: the yardstick for success is profit and related factors. The entire business world together with the whole business press thinks solely in terms of profit and profitability – so why pose such a question at all?

If we are going to distinguish between business strategies, corporate strategies and owner strategies according to the criteria set out earlier, then we have to apply distinct yardsticks to each of them. The common yardsticks are shown in Figure 2.21.

Business strategies are assessed according to market share achieved and marginal income gained. Corporate strategy is assessed on profit, return on investment (ROI) or return on equity (ROE). The yardstick for success of the owner strategy is also ROE as well as the total return. Thus it would be quite easy to conclude this section on the yardstick for success. However, recently there has been a growing criticism of using profit and profitability as the only measure. The arguments put forward in this context are set out in the following paragraphs to prepare the way for a reliable gauge for assessing the quality of strategies.

FIGURE 2.21 Common yardsticks to distinguish between business strategies, corporate strategies and owner strategies

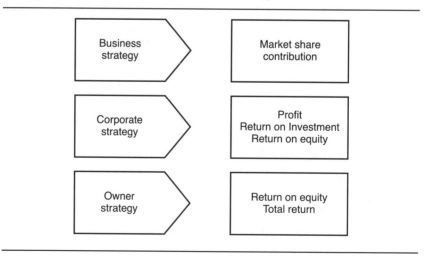

Profit is inadequate as a yardstick of performance

The soundest criticism of profit as a performance yardstick comes from Rappaport (1986). He names five shortcomings and suggests ways to rectify them. The main reason why profit and profitability are so dominant lies in equity law and statutory accounting rules. What is more, this is the language spoken by banks, financial analysts and the business press. And let us not forget that in most companies bonus payments for managers are dependent on profit development.

A shareholder feels that he has invested his money well when profits show a continuous rise and as a result he will award bonus marks to company executives for their professional management. That is why managers are keen to avoid showing irregular profit development or even stagnation. Of course the inevitable consequence of this is manipulation or massaging of results, be it through the setting up and dissolution of reserves, the 'stretching' of investment or profit retention. Other popular methods include changing the periodicity of expenditure and yield. Profits can be manoeuvred within a very broad band if strategies are assessed in this way. It may well appear in the interest of the company to present such a strong image to the outside world, but there is an ever-present danger that by distorting reality errors of judgement will be made.

This inadequacy cannot be attributed solely to using profit as a yardstick for success as such, but to its inappropriate use. Nevertheless, these potential problems have to be pointed out as many managers make decisions based on facts and figures which have been 'polished' for reasons of image. This fact alone would not disqualify profit as a yardstick, but there are other reasons which go against its use as a criteria for orientation. First of all, there is time value of money. Today's pound is worth more than tomorrow's, because it can yield a return overnight. Future profits – and this is what we talk about in strategic thinking – only make sense if they are discounted against the present, a fact which is usually omitted in conventional thinking. Another factor is risk. Profit has a completely different quality depending on whether it was achieved by a rock-solid business or by a high-risk activity. Earning £1000 from a government bond is not the same as earning £1000 from a junk bond – especially if this profit lies somewhere in the future and has not been paid out yet. The risk, small with a government bond and high with a junk bond, has to be taken into account when determining the factor for discounting against the present – otherwise it is like comparing apples with pears.

The next thing to consider is investments. As a rule profits are not available in the amounts that they are declared. Investments in fixed assets and net working capital are inevitable. The latter is often forgotten about. Again and again strategies are justified on the basis of performance calculations alone without essential investments being disclosed.

In conclusion, I would like to touch on dividend payout policy and funding. A reduction in the distribution of dividends brings with it higher auto-financing which can lead to increased profits. These, however, are not automatically effective in terms of value. The use of the leverage effect on funding has the same results. An effective measure for the quality of a strategy has to rectify such 'neutralizing' effects.

Future free cash flows as a measure of value increase

In the paragraphs above I have used the term 'integrated value increase'. If profit is to be replaced then a different factor has to be found which will indicate how in the long term the value of a company has been increased through strategic action. This will take into consideration the objectives of the corporate and owner strategies, all aiming for an integrated value increase. Future free cash flows of a company can be used as a measure which also accounts for the aforementioned inadequacies of profit. Future free cash flows are defined as the operating cash flow minus taxes pending and investments in net working capital and fixed capital. The time-value of money is taken into account by discounting the future free cash flows against the present. The logic of determining the value of a company on the basis of future free cash flows is shown in Figure 2.22.

The present value of a company is determined by the potential of the business strategies, the corporate strategies and owner strategies. Evaluation of a company means to identify free cash flows which can be achieved in the future through the strategies of a company. This view is totally different from conventional valuation techniques which tend to rely on net assets and the past, possibly on the present and on any potential profits for the coming year. This clarifies the tight interdependence of strategic and financial thinking. One cannot exist without the other. But how is it to be interpreted?

The first component is the present value of the free cash flows. These are determined by the planning horizon of the strategies. In written as well as in corporate practise the planning horizon is generally considered to be a period of about three to five years. In many cases such a supposition is not justified. A strategy should be assessed over a period which is sensible for that industry. A computer software company may only be able to make reliable statements concerning the next two years, anything after that time would be mere speculation. Companies in the

FIGURE 2.22   The logic of determining the value of a company on the basis of future free cash flows

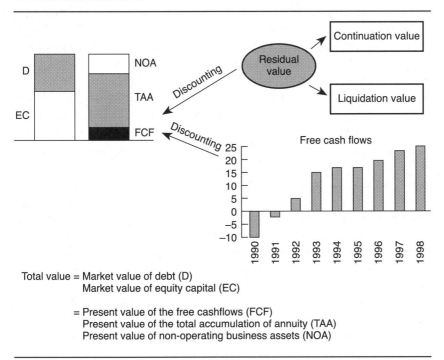

Total value = Market value of debt (D)
              Market value of equity capital (EC)

         = Present value of the free cashflows (FCF)
           Present value of the total accumulation of annuity (TAA)
           Present value of non-operating business assets (NOA)

paper or cement industries, on the other hand, have to invest in production plants and equipment which have a natural planning horizon of fifteen years, so they are able to work within a planning horizon of ten years. This is a direct consequence of the stability of their markets. Therefore the first step towards assessing strategies is to determine the planning horizon. In Figure 2.22 the planning horizon is nine years, showing that we are looking at a rather long-lasting industry.

For each separate year free cash flows from the business, corporate and owner strategies will be assessed. By free cash flows I mean operating cash flow minus investment in fixed assets and net working capital, and minus taxes pending. These free cash flows can only be determined if there is a sophisticated strategic plan and an allocation of future costs, income, investments and taxes for the separate years within the planning horizon. In the example in Figure 2.22 the free cash flows are negative in the first two years before they start to grow. The free cash flows of the separate years are then discounted to the present. The discounting rate is of vital importance.

If this was where the value-determining procedure stopped, only those companies which invest as little as possible and milk their cash cows until the last drop would be rewarded. At the end of the planning horizon the company would logically come to the conclusion that it should go into liquidation. So how can we consider investment strategies which, by definition, would lead to deeper free cash flows within the planned horizon? To do this we need the total accumulation of annuity for the company. In the case of investment strategy, this would be the going concern value. This is determined in such a way that profit after tax for the last year of the planning horizon is accounted for as a perpetuity and discounted against the present. So one works on the assumption that at the end of the planning horizon no more value can be created, so that depreciations and investments break even and the exact cost of capital is achieved. These assumptions can of course be modified if an additional value increase or value decrease can be justified.

Apart from the present value of free cash flows and the present value of the total accumulation of annuity, in order to calculate the value of the company it is necessary to include the present value of non-essential business assets. This is based on the assumption that prior to the evaluation of the strategy, operating and non-operating activities were clearly separated.

A crucial role in these calculations is also played by the rate chosen for discounting to the present. It is identical to the considered average costs of both the debt and equity capital of a company. Figure 2.23 shows how the cost of capital rate is worked out.

The cost of capital is determined by three components (Rappaport, 1986; Gomez and Weber, 1989):

1   capital structure (funding situation);

2   cost of debt after tax;

3   cost of equity capital.

Determining the cost of debt has to be done according to the controlling market and does not pose any real difficulties. Fixing the cost of equity capital is much more demanding. You start by looking at the interest rate of risk-free investments with impeccable credit standing, such as government bonds. By marking the risk up, it is essential to consider and distinguish between the general risk of the company, the market risk premium and the specific risk markup and markdown (systematic risk). The market risk premium represents the profits which investors claim from investments in a certain equity. The general risk of the company is contained in the so-called beta coefficient, which records the volatility of

FIGURE 2.23 How the cost of capital rate is determined

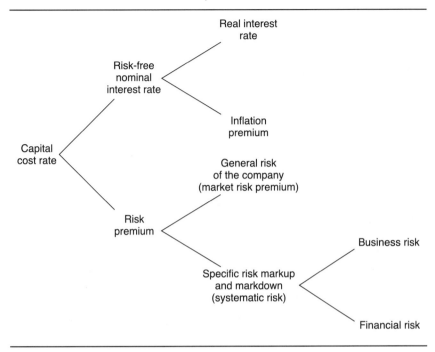

the market price of a company's shares in relation to the market as a whole. A company with a beta coefficient of 1 is defined as having the same volatility as the market. Beta coefficiencies above 1 point are considered to have a higher volatility and those below 1 to have a lower volatility.

Although determining the market risk premium for individual countries is not too complicated because of the existence of historical data, beta coefficients are very difficult to ascertain – apart from in the USA where they are more accessible. On the whole, financial analysts and large banks know the beta coefficient for the most important companies in a specific country, occasionally careful research is needed. The example contained in Table 2.4 shows the components for determining the cost of capital rate for three countries, upon which a large retailing company based their strategies.

These figures vary hugely from country to country so for the development of international strategies it is essential to have a good look at the characteristics of each country. We had to do our own estimate for the beta coefficient because only the UK had a coefficient for the whole retail trade.

TABLE 2.4 The components for determining the cost of capital rate for three countries

Cost of capital	Germany	France	England
Risk-free interest rate (government bonds)			
▪ present	8.5	8.9	9.9
▪ high/low	7.5–9.2	8.8–10.7	9.7–13.2
Market risk premium			
▪ present	1.7	5.1	4.8
▪ historical	4.0–6.0	5.0	5.0
Beta coefficient			
▪ retailing			0.9
▪ estimate	1.1	1.2	1.1
Cost of debt	9.0	10.5	11.2

The formula for calculating the cost of capital rate is as follows:

Interest rate of debt × (1− marginal tax rate) x debt ratio + rate of equity capital costs × equity capital ratio

The rate of equity capital costs is defined as: interest rate of risk-free investments + company specific risk factor × market risk premium. When looking at the cost of debt it is important to take the effect of tax into consideration as it plays an important role. Interest on debt can be deducted against tax, which brings down the cost ratio accordingly.

The example in Figure 2.24 shows how the capital cost rate was calculated for a retailer in Germany, using known historic market risk premiums.

Having looked at the cost of capital in more detail, it is now easier to understand how in Figure 2.22 the total value of the company is composed of the market value of the debt plus the market value of the equity capital. The substantial capital structure does not come from the short-term funding of a transaction nor can the costs be taken from a specific ad hoc funding arrangement. When estimating the cost of capital it is always necessary to work on the premise that a strategy will be financed in the long-term by debt and equity capital.

A practical way of evaluating strategies is to simulate alternatives on a personal computer and play them through so that the effects on the

FIGURE 2.24 How capital cost rate was calculated using known historic market risk premiums

Financial Ratio (equity/debt)	60/40
Cost of debt	
Cost rate (market values)	9%
Income tax	55%
Cost after tax 9% x (1–55%)	4%
Cost of equity	
'Risk-free' investment (government bonds)	8.5%
Market-risk premium	5%
Company-specific premium ($\beta = 1.3$)	1.5%
Cost of equity	15%
Total capital cost (weighted average of debt and equity cost)	
40% x 4% + 60% x 15%	10.5%

company value are immediately apparent. There are various software packages on the market which can carry out the task very well. So let us look at the *Value-Planner* by Alcar (1987) in order to try it out.

The company (see Table 2.5) increases its net income within the planning horizon to over DM1 billion. The profit development looks healthy, too. The figures reflect the expected results of the business strategies, corporate and owner strategies as well as any relevant investment. When these figures are processed using Alcar's *Value Planner* according to the logic of Figure 2.22, the result is the integrated value increase shown in Table 2.6.

The implementation of the strategies should bring about an increase in the integrated value of the company of DM19 million, as illustrated. It lists the accumulated, discounted free cash flows for the years 1995 to 1999 as well as the total discounted value of the company in 1999. Including non-essential business assets of DM100 million, the company value is DM254 million. Debts of DM120 million are then deducted from this figure leaving an equity value of DM134 million. By deducting the shareholder value before implementing the strategies you are left with the integrated value increase.

TABLE 2.5   Development of a retail company

DM million	1995	1996	1997	1998	1999
Net income	826	872	927	982	1042
Operating profit	32.4	33.9	36.5	39.5	45.2
Investments in fixed assets	2.5	2.3	2.1	1.7	0.2
Investments in current assets	1	1	1	1.1	1.2
Capital costs	10.5%	10.5%	10.5%	10.5%	10.5%
Tax rate	55%	55%	55%	55%	55%
Market value of the liabilities					
Non-operational business assets					

TABLE 2.6   The integrated value increase

Year	Free cash flows	Cumulated discounted free cash flows	Discounted final value	Non-operating business assets
1995	11.1	10.0		
1996	11.9	19.8		
1997	−6.6	14.9		
1998	15.0	24.9		
1999	10.0	36.5 + 117.5 + 100		

Total value of the company	254
Liabilities	120
Equity value	134
Equity value before strategy	115
Value increase	19

I have already hinted that part of the evaluation of strategies includes playing through possible scenarios and assessing the sensitivities of corresponding developments. The Alcar software is invaluable here as it shows which value generators have to be changed in order to have the most influence on the company value. In this particular case, as shown in Table 2.7 it is the profit margin, although income tax rate and the cost of capital figure too. Turnover growth and changes in investment have little effect. Now it is a matter of deciding whether the strategic options improve profit margin or are advantageous in terms of tax. On the other hand, there is no point in forcing turnover growth or disinvestments.

The Alcar programme allows for playing through possible developments, and then seeing immediately what effect there is on company value. In this way, it is possible to gradually work out which is the best strategy and then choose only those that have the greatest leverage.

The discounted cash flow method, as this approach is also called, is already part of management practice today. It is almost always used when looking at potential acquisitions. But this method is also becoming more important for evaluating strategies because it allows one to simulate possible strategic options with the help of software such as Alcar's. The following steps characterize this approach for evaluating strategies:

- development of business, corporate and owner strategies;

- quantifying the expected free cash flows for the individual years within the planning horizon, as well as the residual value;

- calculation of the potential for the integrated value increase of strategies using the relevant software;

- determination of the sensitivity of each value generator and assessment of the strategies and their effect on value generators;

- simulation of strategy changes and assessment of their effect on the value of a company;

- choosing the best strategies.

TABLE 2.7 The sensitivity of value generators

A 1% increase in	Enhances the company value	
	in DM million	in %
Turnover growth	0.172	0.128
Profit margin	1.796	1.340
Increase rate of capital assets	(0.216)	(0.162)
Increase rate of current assets	(0.039	(0.029)
Income tax	(0.759)	(0.567)
Cost of capital	(0.664)	(0.495)

I must mention here that it is important to work with different capitalization costs according to the various businesses within a company in order to avoid distortions.

Thinking in terms of integrated value increase and future free cash flows is only just being accepted in managerial circles. The driving force behind this are institutional investors and their clearly formulated aspirations. However, this way of thinking will only receive wide recognition when integrated value increase of a company becomes the criteria for managerial pay and incentive schemes. Such schemes are already fairly widespread across the USA (Brindisi, 1989). The problem in Europe is that there is still too little transparency as far as the determining factors of value increase are concerned. In addition, accounting practice is still almost exclusively geared towards profit and related factors. Progressive companies – and I am thinking particularly of the German conglomerate Haniel here – are starting to reform their incentive schemes. It is clear that a multi-layered model which takes into consideration both operational and strategic aspects will need to be built. As long as accounting rules and the business press stick to profit and profitability as their guiding light it will not be possible to make the radical change to free cash flows. Furthermore, earnings from the integrated value increase of a company cannot always be clearly attributed. This does not help executives who might, for whatever reason, wish to leave the company and who have been following a single-track long-term policy.

In essence, a strategic incentive scheme directed towards integrated value increase should fulfil the following three requirements:

1   *Person-centred scope*: Every executive taking part in shaping the value increase process should be involved. It will be necessary to create a graded system and specific regulations for the overall management.

2   *Incentive*: the aim is strategic premiums connected to operational bonuses. The strategic premium would be fixed in a 'strategic contract' based on an agreed value increase set down at the beginning of the planning horizon. The premium is paid out according to achievement of objectives. The premium sum is aligned to the value increase of a hypothetical joint interest. Operational bonuses are fixed within a framework of the annual budget and intermediate objectives. Bonuses should support the strategy and allow for a number of variables between the respective salaries.

3   *Duration*: The strategic horizon is fixed according to the nature of the business. In order to avoid the total accumulation of annuity being deliberately inflated, follow-on plans should always be tacked onto the initial incentive plans in order to emphasize the importance of the value increase beyond the planning horizon.

Detailed discussion of strategic incentive schemes are not the purpose of this book. But I want to make it absolutely clear that the success of a strategy is entirely dependent on its successful implementation, and naturally incentive schemes play a major part in this.

To conclude this chapter we have to ask ourselves the question whether value increase in the sense of benefits to shareholders should be the principal gauge for corporate success. What about the other stakeholders? I have already described their legitimate interests. Isn't this a raw deal for them?

Integrated value increase and creating benefit for the stakeholders of a company

Who is actually eligible to be called a stakeholder? Stakeholders are those interest groups who can either make some sort of a legal claim on the company or who can put forward their claims so convincingly that the company cannot afford to ignore them in the decision-making process. Apart from shareholders and investors, stakeholders include the board of directors, top managers, employees, the unions, competitors, customers, suppliers, lenders, the state and the public at large. This list could be longer or shorter depending on the nature of the business. The benefits the company has to achieve for these stakeholders must be specified and value generators awarded to enable management to reach their objectives.

A list of these objectives, benefits and value generators has been composed by Janisch (1992) and is shown as Table 2.8.

What is straightforward and compelling in the shareholder value approach, i.e. one aim (value increase of the company), five value generators (sales growth, profit margin, investments, cost of capital, tax rate) starts to become fairly complicated if not downright incomprehensible when it comes to the stakeholder approach. First, one is not forced to determine the aims, benefits and value generators in the same way. The logic of the interconnections is determined less by economic necessity than by subjective choice and the importance of each stakeholder. If we take top management as an example, we see that depending on the perspective chosen, different aims and benefits can be ascribed. It is only

TABLE 2.8 Objectives, benefits and value generators for different stakeholders (Janisch, 1992)

Stakeholders	Main objective/ benefits	Partial benefits	Value generators
Shareholders and investors	Increase of company value	■ Dividends ■ Stock price gain ■ Power	■ Sales growth ■ Profit margin ■ Investments ■ Cost of capital ■ Tax rate
Board of directors	Well-functioning corporate leadership	■ Taking over responsibility ■ Prestige ■ Bonuses	■ Control ■ Delegation ■ Information
Top management	Professional fulfilment	■ Security ■ Success ■ Power/social status ■ Rewards/pay ■ Personal growth ■ Dividends/stock price gain	■ Control ■ Income ■ Sales growth/profit ■ Security ■ Job design
Employees	Quality of life	■ Securing a living ■ Salary ■ Personal growth	■ Income ■ Job security ■ Working conditions ■ Participation
Customers	Satisfaction of needs	■ Market performance ■ Price ■ Security ■ Peripheral services	■ Product quality ■ Price value ■ Product security ■ Quality of supply ■ Image
Suppliers	Maintaining and developing a livelihood	■ Own value increase ■ Independence ■ Security	■ Strength of demand ■ Stable relationship ■ Pricing ■ Turnover/investments
Lenders	Increasing the appeal of investments	■ Return on investment ■ Security ■ Power	■ Cost of loan capital ■ Amortisation ■ Turnover/investments ■ Control

TABLE 2.8 *Continued*

| Government | Welfare | ▪ Economic growth
▪ Procedural justice
▪ Economic stability
▪ Independence
▪ Balance of power
▪ Environmental quality | ▪ Taxes/fees
▪ Tax exemption
▪ Compliance with rules/regulations
▪ Prosperity of private sector |
| Public/Society | 'Fair future' | ▪ Control over economic activities
▪ Justice
▪ Advancement of public welfare | ▪ Donations/ foundations
▪ Information systems
▪ Environmental protection |

possible to judge each strategy in respect of the value generator as each situation arises. This makes it difficult to pass on operational instructions to management. There is of course no problem with the shareholder value concept.

Setting priorities can also be problematic. Of course, one cannot assume that the aims of the different stakeholders are in harmony. So we need a process to negotiate the aims. How to go about it? There is one option that is not very binding but is also not very satisfactory to the stakeholders: a loose commitment by management to take these claims and turn them into a framework for optimizing the shareholder value. This leaves the stakeholders completely dependent on the goodwill of the management and with a justifiable fear that if the situation in the company required it, they would be considered last. At the other extreme the negotiation process could be institutionalized in the sense of a codetermination of the stakeholders. In my opinion, this model does not make economic sense.

So in fact the only serious alternative to a stakeholder management is to establish a forum of representatives from each stakeholder group to discuss at regular intervals with the management issues concerning the direction of the company. This might put management in a tight spot sometimes but it does not open them to legal demands.

So we are left with the problem, how to measure integrated value increase for the individual stakeholder. Here as well there is no clear indicator such as the free cash flows in the shareholder value approach. Janisch (1992) shows that there is a variety of indicators for each individual stakeholder, and it is difficult to know what to recommend as an appropriate selection of indicators. Each management team will have to make its own subjective choice in the knowledge that this will occasionally lead to imbalances. Nevertheless, it must not neglect this task.

Consideration of stakeholder interests as a concept and as a qualitative way of thinking is already beginning to spread. The quantification of these interests and the relevant measurement for the strategies is still in its infancy. A first approach will be presented in the *Evaluating strategies* section of Chapter 3. However visible effort must be made to fulfil the promise of integrated systemic strategies.

■ CHAPTER 3 ■

The Strategic Methodology of Integrated Value Management

Strategic thinking cannot be pressed into a neat scheme. Often it is a brainwave, the grasping of a unique opportunity or simply creative solutions which lead to the successful reorientation of a company. Sometimes it is the patient and committed implementation of an action plan which at first sight looks rather conventional and barely innovative. A good strategist can be an artist or a solid craftsman. The essence of a good strategist cannot be captured easily nor analysed and so is not a suitable model for executives eager to learn.

It is for this reason that business literature has increasingly mystified strategy development. It has also become popular to cite examples of successful companies to document strategic success. A more structured approach to finding strategies is therefore often dismissed as 'analytical', 'staff people work' and 'academic'. Although a step-by-step approach for developing strategies is proposed in the following pages, it comes from the conviction that such an approach does not replace the brilliant idea but instead creates the framework for it to appear. Newton discovered the law of gravity only after long preparation work, even if legend would have us believe that enlightenment was triggered by an apple dropping on his head while he was asleep. Good craftsmanship therefore is the prerequisite for success – although no guarantee of it.

A methodical approach to developing strategies increases the chances of achieving competitive advantage, of increasing the value of the company and of creating benefit for the stakeholders.

Until quite recently it was usual to speak of a single strategist, whether male or female. Now it is increasingly realized that the successful development of strategies is a collective process. The knowledge inherent within the company and the stakeholder groups is too valuable for a single person to claim that he or she knows the golden path.

As we develop a systemic strategic methodology over the following pages it will become clear that this is a step-by-step process using all knowledge available to the company and to the stakeholders. Every single step of the process uses the same method in order to give management a familiar pattern to guide them through the process. In Figure 3.1 we see an overall picture of this method. The circle around the diagram and the connections between the separate steps show that such an approach does not run in a smooth sequence but is in fact a perpetual step-forward-step-back process.

First, I will introduce the basic thought and the methodology behind each single step. This will lead on to the strategic principles to be applied for each step. The process will be illustrated by several examples from corporate practice. At the end of each stage I will again summarize the process with another example of a company which will accompany the whole method. This is the integral strategic study – DELTA.

FIGURE 3.1 The systemic strategic methodology

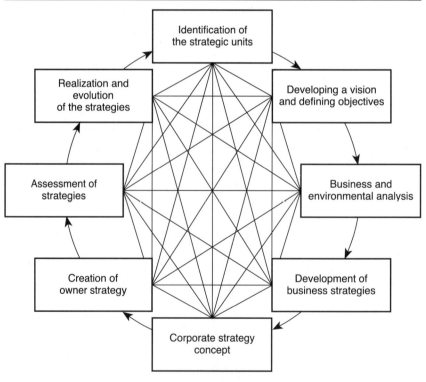

Identifying the strategic units

The need to identify strategically relevant units or areas and to distinguish between them clearly is a natural consequence of the distinction between business, corporate and owner strategies. Each of these strategies has a different sphere of influence and as previous sections have shown, only a clear distinction and a relevant focus will lead to successful long-term direction of the company. Yet strategic units rarely coincide with the existing organizational units of a company. In the age of mergers and acquisitions even the demarcation of the company as a whole is no longer finite. Nevertheless, many companies try to squeeze strategic thinking into the corset of their present organization, allowing management to walk on familiar ground without sending them off into the unknown. But it is precisely a new defining of boundaries and the resulting interdisciplinary way of viewing things that leads to radically new strategies.

First strategic principle

The first strategic principle is: *business, corporate and owner strategy areas have to be clearly demarcated.* Strategic units are usually not identical to organizational units.

This principle becomes clearer if we take a look at the functional organization prevalent in most smaller and medium-sized companies. The organizational units are usually: research and development, procurement, production, sales, finance and personnel. The strategic units, however, cut right across the organizational units. Market coverage is responsible for the marketing of different products, so the development of a general sales strategy would hardly bring about the desired competitive advantages. The integrated approach from research and development through to sales would also be missing. The transition from organizational to strategic business units is not difficult, but it is more demanding to reverse the process at the implementation stage. Even the boundaries of the whole company can no longer be defined as clearly as they used to as mergers and cooperations create shady areas. So in order to start the stategic development process it is essential to clarify what belongs to the company and what interrelations already exist.

From the owner's point of view the company is only one part of his portfolio, so even here boundaries can become blurred if perhaps the owner uses company assets for financial transactions. Therefore it is essential to identify the owner's interest relevant to the company, which requires tact and sensitivity on the part of management.

At the level of the *business strategy,* one has to identify and demarcate strategic business units (SBUs). Figure 3.2 shows how to kick off such a demarcation.

I have already discussed, in the *Business strategies for the achievement of competitive advantage* section in Chapter 2, the demarcation of strategic business units using the examples of Gurit Heberlein, Haefely and BMW. At this point I would like to introduce a more detailed example of a company which is active in the building automation industry. As Figure 3.3 shows the company took the categories set out in Figure 3.2 and filled in their own specifics. They then demarcated those areas to be united in each strategic business unit. The marked areas show that the SBU called 'Building Control Systems' is geared towards very specific customer needs, products, technologies, distribution channels and target groups and consciously excludes all other possibilities. In this case a very distinct demarcation has been made in all categories. It is often sufficient to focus on one category such as target groups and then make a choice.

FIGURE 3.2 Identify and demarcate strategic business units (Schwaninger, 1989)

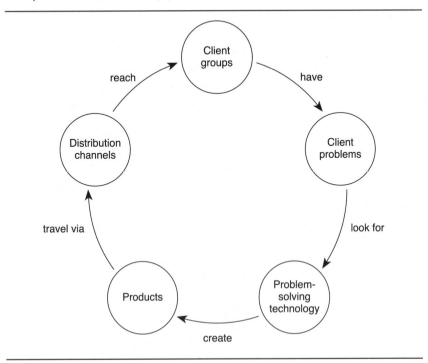

FIGURE 3.3 Company specifics of SBU 'Building Control Systems'

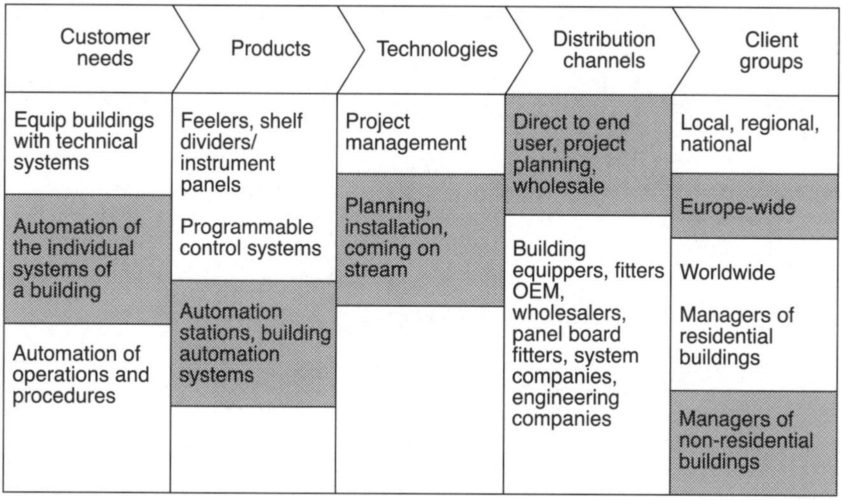

Customer needs	Products	Technologies	Distribution channels	Client groups
Equip buildings with technical systems	Feelers, shelf dividers/ instrument panels	Project management	Direct to end user, project planning, wholesale	Local, regional, national
Automation of the individual systems of a building	Programmable control systems	Planning, installation, coming on stream	Building equippers, fitters OEM, wholesalers, panel board fitters, system companies, engineering companies	Europe-wide
	Automation stations, building automation systems			Worldwide
Automation of operations and procedures				Managers of residential buildings
				Managers of non-residential buildings

Finally, there is also the question: how many strategic business units should there be in a company? Of course there is no general rule. Practical application has shown that it is better to create relatively few SBUs, even if this does mean including some activities which do not fit perfectly in that SBU. The advantage of relatively few SBUs is that the portfolios retain a clarity and the SBUs can be supported in a targeted manner. If a company with some DM100 Million turnover creates twenty SBUs then this demarcation could not be considered very sensible. Using the categories set out above it should be possible to specify about five to seven SBUs. At the level of *corporate strategies* demarcation has never been so difficult. Many companies are interlocked, participating in joint ventures and alliances. So it is important to start with a corporate appraisal by asking the following questions:

- What is the core business of the company?
- Are there any other legally or organizationally independent units which belong to the company?
- Is the company involved in joint ventures or other alliances?
- Does the company have minority shareholdings?

Figure 3.4 lists the alliances of a few selected European airlines to illustrate the necessity of asking these questions.

FIGURE 3.4   Alliances of a few selected European airlines (Müller-Stewens and Hillig, 1992)

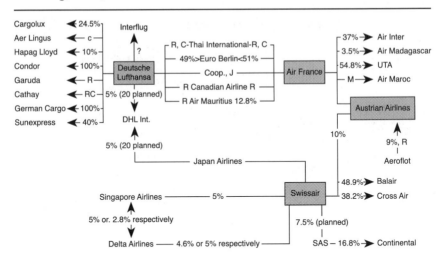

M: Merger in marketing
J: Joint venture
R: Merger for certain routes or markets
C: Cargo
Coop: Further cooperation

Example:
Lufthansa owns 10% of the shares of Hapag-Lloyd.
Furthermore, it has negotiated a cooperation with Canadian
Airlines for certain routes and markets. The same arrangement
exists between Canadian Airlines and Air France.

Only ten years ago it was a simple matter to demarcate Swissair as a company. Today it is an extremely complicated exercise as its various interdependencies are subject to perpetual change. In positioning a company strategically you have to make the demarcations with care in order to avoid developing strategies which neglect possible synergy potentials with alliance partners or even diametrically oppose their interests.

There is yet another element that has to be given particular consideration in the area of *owner strategies* and that is the minority holding. It could make sense for an owner to access potentially interesting companies using such a shareholding and then check them out for possible synergy potential. It is important for management to understand these interconnections in order to make allowances for them when creating a strategy. An example of this can be seen in Figure 3.5 which shows the structure of the leading Swiss industrialist Stephan Schmidheiny's shareholdings in outside companies.

Technology-oriented companies are placed in the section Unotec, which includes two companies dominated by a majority shareholding

FIGURE 3.5 The structure of the leading Swiss industrialist Stephan Schmidheiny's shareholdings in outside companies in the mid-1990s.

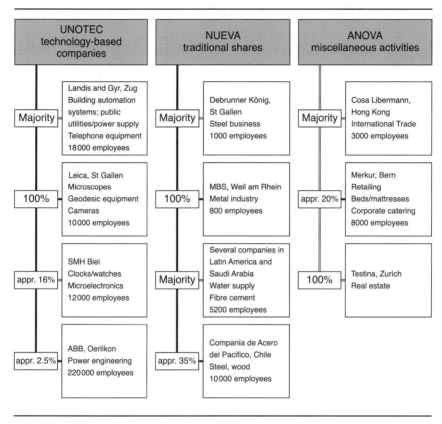

and two minority shareholdings. His shares in the Swiss watch enterprise SMH and the Asea Brown Boveri enable Schmidheiny to discover strategic similarities with both Leica and Landis & Gyr. He can also instigate suitable cooperation possibilities without necessarily fusing the businesses or increasing his shareholding.

In summary, in order to identify and demarcate strategic areas one needs to categorize strategic business units according to customer groups, customer problems, problem-solving technology, products, distribution channels as well as mapping out the share participation or interdependencies of companies. This demarcation is of course only the first step. In the next step of the strategic methodology I will deal with the question of system demarcation in greater depth, determing the strategic area in relationship to its environment and to its interactions with stakeholders.

The step-forward-step-back approach will also come up in the context of strategy finding, and inevitably this question will arise: In developing individual strategies, has the strategic area been demarcated properly?

Strategic study DELTA – Background and facts

At the end of the 1980s DELTA was one of the leading European producers of packaging for industrial goods, with ten companies operating in Switzerland, Germany, Belgium and the Netherlands. 300 million packaging units were sold at an overall annual turnover of sFr250 million. The group was led by a holding based in Switzerland and employed around 1300 people.

DELTA is the result of a directed European strategy which started off as a small Swiss packaging firm with a turnover of not quite sFr30 million. In 1978 the company was taken over by a larger group which at that time did not operate within the packaging industry. The first measure was to restructure as the acquired company was in the red. Priority was given to rationalization, stronger marketing and a clean demarcation of the business. It soon became evident, however, that these measures were not sufficient for a long-term recovery.

Looked at strategically there were two possible directions to go in: either to disinvest or to expand consequentially by merging with similar companies. The latter was chosen. The objective was to build the company up to become the market leader initially in Switzerland and later on in Europe. The only competitive strategy possible was a niche policy as the market was already dominated by integrated paper factories producing large quantities of packaging, which kept raw material costs low. Neither a cost leadership strategy nor a differentiation strategy was possible as packaging is a commodity. The aim of the European strategy was to become one of the leading manufacturers independent of paper factories. The market niches were the individual countries.

The first undertaking in 1980 was to acquire two paper-bag producers in the Benelux countries, fuse them and put them under the umbrella of the newly formed DELTA Holding. This was followed in 1984 by the purchase of a significant Swiss manufacturer. The Swiss companies were separated, creating one company for paper bags and one for plastic bags. This opened up significant rationalization and more targeted marketing possibilities. In 1985 the market in the Benelux countries was developed further. Under Swiss management a 50:50 joint venture was signed with a Dutch company – a majority takeover had not been possible. This completed the first stage of the European strategy. The DELTA group had now a strong foothold in Switzerland and in the Benelux countries and therefore had an excellent platform for their European strategy.

After a period of consolidation in 1986 the next strategic steps were considered, based on the following premises :

- The separation of the paper bag and plastic bag activities in Switzerland and the Benelux countries was proceeding well, but was not quite there yet.

- The search for acquisitions within the EC was focusing on Germany and Spain, where the first encouraging negotiations had already taken place.

- It was necessary to adapt the management and organizational structure of the DELTA group to the new demands. New sources of financing were also essential to this growth.

- The management potential of the group needed to be urgently built up in view of the tasks ahead.

Against this background I will illustrate the integrated value management approach as a strategic study. The framework is the actual development from 1990 until 1994.

The first step is to identify and demarcate the strategic areas. In DELTA's case this meant looking at the company as a whole as well as the individual business units. So let us start by looking at the company as a whole.

DELTA is a 50:50 joint venture between a Swiss and a Dutch group. DELTA Switzerland consists of paper bag company A with 120 employees, plastic bag company B with 185 employees, and paper bag company C with 25 employees. DELTA Benelux consists of paper bag company D with 174 employees and plastic and paper bag company E with 345 employees. In addition, there is an engineering and consultancy company F. The organization of the company is as shown in Figure 3.6.

The management of DELTA Holding is within the Swiss firm, which appoints the director. He delegates the overall management to a management committee headed by the director responsible. The individual subsidiaries are autonomous as far as the operational management goes. In order to document this, they were also made legally independent. Thus there is a clear division of responsibility: day-to-day operations remain with the individual companies and strategic direction of the group comes from the management committee.

In the area of business strategy, DELTA distinguishes between four strategic business units:

FIGURE 3.6 The organization of DELTA

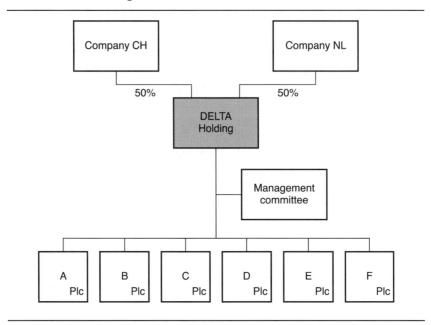

1   paper bags;

2   plastic bags;

3   bottling machines;

4   consultancy/general business.

Criteria for demarcation are quite clearly products and solutions. It made little sense to orientate business activities towards target groups, customer problems or distribution channels. In view of the size of the company subdivision into four strategic business units is appropriate. Of course the SBU paper bags could be divided further, but the similarities in this product group are so broad that a comprehensive SBU is justified.

Developing a vision and defining objectives

The quality of strategy development is heavily dependent on the visions and objectives which lead the strategic process. The second step of the strategic methodology is working them out, whereby the provisional character of such guidelines should never be forgotten. It is often brilliant ideas and innovative thoughts which trigger the strategic process. In turn the process itself modifies, confirms or contradicts the original ideas and allows the visions and objectives to mature. So it does not matter if the visions and objectives are still half-baked at this stage as long as there is a will to work on them. Visions and objectives do have to fulfil one basic requirement, however: in the search for a systemic strategy the interests of the company's stakeholders have to be taken into account. This has been illustrated already and so it can now be formulated as a principle.

Second strategic principle

The second strategic principle is: *Visions and objectives have to take into account the interests of all the stakeholders in a company.*

The development of a vision for the owner or the company and the definition of objectives for the individual business units is a step-by-step process. Even in the early 1970s Drucker (1974) was able to pose those questions which lead the way to developing a vision:

- What *is* our company today?

- *Who is our customer* and how does he view our company?

- What *will* our company be in the future (provided nothing unusual happens)?

- Vision: What *should* our company be in the future?

The last question cannot be answered solely from the perspective of management or shareholders. It has to include the various interests of the stakeholders. The relevant process for this has already been touched on briefly. The following examples should illustrate this even further. This time we will start off with the *owner strategy.*

Figure 3.7 shows which stakeholders have to be considered when formulating the owner's company vision.

The following stakeholders and interests/objectives have to be incorporated when developing the vision:

- financial interests of the owner: security and sustained wealth;

- corporate interests of the owner: maintaining the family tradition, value increase of the company;

FIGURE 3.7 Stakeholders that have to be considered when formulating the owner's company vision

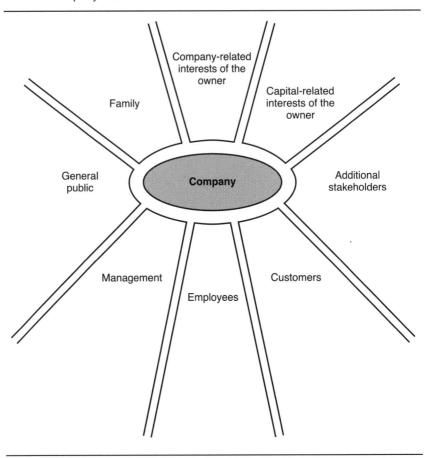

- family: long-term survival of the company, succession;

- public: maintaining the workforce, continuity.;

- management: personal fulfilment, predictability of owner's interests;

- employees: job security, employee promotion;

- customers: quality, good cost-performance ratio.

If we look at Rudolf Sprüngli, the majority shareholder in the leading Swiss chocolate manufacturer Lindt & Sprüngli, we can see what damage can be done if these interests are not considered when formulating an owner strategy. Since the beginning of the 1990s Rudolf Sprüngli has completely disregarded all stakeholders by booting his wife and eldest son out of the company and by sacking top managers en masse. He then shocked both employees and the public in general by marrying his former PA and giving her managerial responsibility. This is the man who at the beginning of the 1980s gave a lecture on the ten deadly sins of a family-owned business, which at the time found widespread recognition and which presented the vision of an owner who took into consideration the various stakeholders. Lindt & Sprüngli is quoted on the stockmarket and with a turnover of nearly sFr1 billion it cannot simply be left to the private interests of an ageing owner, as this could cause widespread damage.

At the *corporate level* let us look at the insurance company Patria to see how stakeholders can be incorporated into the development of a vision. Figure 3.8 sets out the stakeholders of this company, one of the largest in Switzerland.

FIGURE 3.8 The stakeholders of Patria (Brugger, 1991)

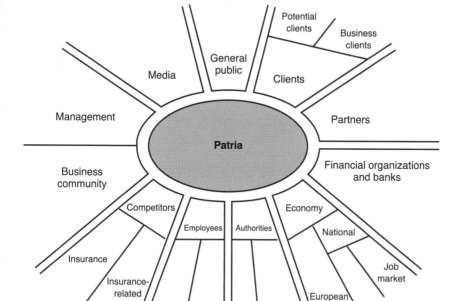

The stakeholders also have to be considered at the level of the *business strategy,* although here the talk is more of objectives rather than visions. If we take the SBU 'Building Contol Systems' as an example again, the objectives of the stakeholders could be defined as follows:

- building operators/general operators: Securing the basic technical functions of the building;

- investors: Earning an appropriate return on investment;

- management: Consolidating the position as number one in Europe;

- environmental protection: Saving energy;

- society: Maintaining Switzerland as an industrial location.

After the interests have been specified it is now possible to work out the vision. A vision is not measured by the beauty of its formulation but by its convincing and motivating powers. Therefore all visions should be simple and clear to every employee. A vision should motivate every employee to give their best, to be ahead of the current situation and to work towards a common goal. Thus it should create a strong sense of unity.

Here are a few examples of visions expressed in one single sentence:

- We want to be the global leaders for fastening systems in the building sector (Hilti AG, Schaan).

- We want to provide the best service in the world (IBM).

- We want to be the best and most successful company in the airline business (British Airways).

And here are a few visions and policies which are a little more detailed and which explicitly take the stakeholders' interests into account. Figure 3.9 presents the vision of the Sigri Great Lakes Carbon Ltd, a subsidiary of the German conglomerate Hoechst.

The significant feature of this vision is that on the one hand it states very clearly what positions are to be achieved and how success will be measured and on the other it makes statements concerning culture and identity. This vision is agreeably different from all those which do not go much beyond: 'We would like to satisfy the needs of our customers.'

The top objectives of Hewlett-Packard present themselves in a completely different way, as Figure 3.10 shows. These objectives mirror the 'HP Way', a corporate culture whose main commitment is to its employees, but also to society.

Other companies prefer to have a relatively short vision from which they construct a detailed and precise model. In Figure 3.11 we have set

FIGURE 3.9   The vision of Sigri Great Lakes Carbon Ltd

Vision
√ Development of a truly global position in Carbon Products with leading quality and customer service.
√ Enhance a top position in electrodes with competitive technology.
√ Leading market position in speciality graphites with technology leadership.
√ Development of profitable niche position with engineering products.
√ Competitive cost position by optimization of European and North American operations.
√ Development of a truly merged international culture and identity at all management levels.
√ Achieve an average percentage return on sales of 5–10% on capital employed.

FIGURE 3.10   The top objectives of Hewlett-Packard

- To achieve sufficient profit to finance our company growth and to provide the resources we need to achieve our other corporate objectives.
- To provide products and services of the highest quality and the greatest possible value to our customers, thereby gaining and holding their respect and loyalty.
- To participate in those fields of interest that build upon our technology and customer base, that offer opportunities for continuing growth, and that enable us to make a needed and profitable contribution.
- To let our growth be limited only by our profits and our ability to develop and produce innovative products that satisfy real customer needs.
- To help HP people share in the company's success which they make possible; to provide employment security based on their performance; to ensure them a safe and pleasant work environment; to recognize their individual achievements; and to help them gain a sense of satisfaction and accomplishment from their work.
- To foster initiative and creativity by allowing the individual great freedom of action in attaining well-defined objectives.
- To honor our obligations to society by being an economic, intellectual and social asset to each nation and each community in which we operate.

FIGURE 3.11 Questions which need to be answered in order to develop a model for the product/market, finance, social and management sector

Product/Market Policy	Finance Policy
■ What is our function in the economy and for the society? What needs do we want to satisfy? ■ What standards do we want to meet with our services (quality, reliability, safety, efficiency)? ■ How do we want to expand geographically (national, international, focused areas, integration)? ■ What market position do we want to achieve (size, importance, reputation, independence)? ■ What principles govern our behaviour towards partners (customers, suppliers, competitors)? ■ What is our technological goal (innovation, quality, capacity)?	■ What are our objectives regarding profit generation and investment (profit objective, efficiency, cost consciousness)? ■ What principles should guide our investing policy? ■ What are the criteria that determine our financing policy (capital structure, capital development)? ■ What rules govern our financial risk policy?
Social Policy	Management Policy
■ What is our basic attitude towards the government? ■ What is our attitude in essential social matters (environment, health, minorities, women in management)? ■ How do we take employees' needs into account (personal growth, remuneration policy, empowerment, co-ownership, responsibility)?	■ What leadership styles are prevalent (delegation, planning, management by objectives)? ■ What organizational paradigms influence our company? ■ How do we realize and foster management development? ■ What is our communication policy?

out some basic questions which need to be answered in order to develop a model for the following sectors: product/market, finance, social and management (Ulrich 1987).

The DELTA model can be constructed following this set of questions and I will now present it together with the corresponding vision.

Strategy Study DELTA – vision and model

Vision: 'We want to be the leading independent European manufacturer of strong paper bags.'
Corporate policy:

- *Product/market*:
    - We want to be champions of productivity and innovation.
    - We are expanding our service organization persistently.
    - We want to expand further by means of acquisitions and joint ventures within the European Union.

- *Finances*:
    - We are aiming for a business cash flow of 8 per cent of net revenue.
    - We want to be self-financing and to remain independent.

- *Social*:
    - We will thoughtfully adapt ourselves to the customs and manners of each country.
    - We empower our management and employees by allowing them to take responsibility for results and by an extensive development programme.

- *Management*:
    - We will integrate the areas of the different countries by allocating the responsibility to one single manager. We will take over management when it comes to joint ventures, with acquisitions we will be major shareholders.
    - We persistently lead by objectives.

What is not represented here is the vision of the owner. That is because it would be difficult to find an owner willing to publicise his personal vision as it might well contain very private considerations. Yet the owner's vision would probably not differ very much from the company's vision.

Now that we have a vision, a corporate policy and the corresponding objectives we have the boundaries within which the strategy development process must develop. The next step in the strategic methodology is to create the basis for strategic development and to prepare the raw material. That is the purpose of the business and environmental analysis.

Business and environmental analysis

In order to find a systemic strategy you have to understand the connection between business and environment. Here business and environment means something quite different to each of the strategies – corporate, business and owner. In terms of the business strategy the 'business' is the strategic business unit and its 'environment' is the industry, the competition and competitors. Included are of course the various stakeholders, in particular management and employees. Corporate strategy requires a profound understanding of the company as a whole and of all its interweaving connections constituted by the various stakeholder groups. To the owner the company is simply one of many fields of operation and this will play a part when it comes to delineating his 'environment'.

Literature on the theme of strategy has developed comprehensive checklists for the analysis of business and environment which are used across the board in corporate practise. However, these checklists are not up to the demands of developing a systemic strategy. In the tradition of good analysis they show up the following areas: environment, competition and corporate factors – but they do not tell us anything about the whole company, i.e. the interconnection of these various factors. In fact they give management the incorrect impression that they have indeed covered the whole field, whereas the result is usually 'data cemeteries', vast amounts of single factors whose importance is not apparent. One single business or environmental factor does not possess any value until it is seen in connection with the others. This puts forward a completely different kind of analysis as required by network thinking. The analysis of business and environment means uncovering all the impact connections of the most important key factors in the strategic arena. By recognizing this we discover the following principle.

Third strategic principle

The third strategic principle is: *Working through one-dimensional checklists must be replaced by the establishment of a systemic network of business and environmental interrelations.*

The process of establishing this network is basically the same whether we are dealing with business strategy, corporate strategy or owner strategy. Differences lie in the detail, as the following example will show. The process can be characterized as followed:

- development of overall objectives;

- determining the key factors of success;

- development of the network;

- interpretation of the interrelations of the network;

- environmental and business analysis;

- setting up of the opportunity/threat and strength/weakness profile.

I will now illustrate this process for business strategy.

Analysis for business strategy

Following steps 1 and 2 of the strategic methodology, the strategic business units have now been defined and the targets for strategic development have been formulated. Now begins the phase of procuring information. This information should provide the basic foundations for the network and is central to the strategic process. Prerequisite to the development of a network is identification of the key factors of success of each business unit. In order to do justice to the systemic view, the key factors are ordered according to each stakeholder and their interests or objectives.

Let us look at the example of a computer manufacturer to illustrate the process of establishing key factors and the ensuing development of a network. Like most of its competitors this manufacturer has had to deal with falling prices and generally weak business development since the beginning of the 1990s. The company decided therefore to build up a new business unit in addition to its present activities. They decided to offer a total or system solutions in the IT sector. The objectives of this strategic business unit could be summed up as follows: 'As providers of turn-key system solutions at a high professional level, we want to achieve a market share of . . . percent and a profit-turnover ratio of . . . percent.'

Details concerning the most important stakeholders and their objectives were registered in order to establish the key factors of success for this new business unit. Table 3.1 shows how key factors were assigned to objectives.

Conventional checklists can offer up ideas while establishing key factors of success. The key factors do not lead to strength/weakness and opportunity/threat profiles on their own, it is also necessary to ascertain the relationships between the key factors which then add weight and

TABLE 3.1   Key factors of success for the SBU IT systems solutions

Stakeholders	Objectives	Key factors
Customers	▪ Turn-key ▪ Quality ▪ Consistency/security	▪ Total solutions ▪ Cost-benefit relationship ▪ Schedule effectiveness ▪ Total quality control
Business partners	▪ Partnership ▪ Business volume ▪ Follow-on projects	▪ Common innovation ▪ Tying down partner ▪ Customer satisfaction with partner ▪ Broad product palette
Management	▪ Market share ▪ Profitability ▪ Growth ▪ Personal fulfilment	▪ Competitive position ▪ Resources ▪ Salaries and wages ▪ Career prospects
Employees	▪ Interesting work ▪ Support and training ▪ Application of abilities	▪ Motivation ▪ Development of abilities ▪ Knowledge of industry and products

meaning to the business unit. The network in Figure 3.12 shows how these interconnections between the key factors (and other important factors influencing the business unit) work. We need to look at this network a little closer in order to see both the areas of influence and the direction specified by the various symbols.

At the centre of the network is the motor of the business unit and it works as follows: the higher the quality of the service performance the greater the customer satisfaction. This leads to more orders, to a higher turnover and greater business success, which again leads to greater available resources and in turn improves the quality of service performance. All around this motor are cycles ordered according to key factors, which have an accelerating or braking effect. These include the employee cycle, the systems solution cycle and the image cycle. The starting point for the employee cycle is the available resources. These resources enable employees to be promoted, which leads on the one hand to improved capabilities and on the other to improved motivation. Both lead to improved employee quality and service performance.

FIGURE 3.12 How interconnections between the key factors work

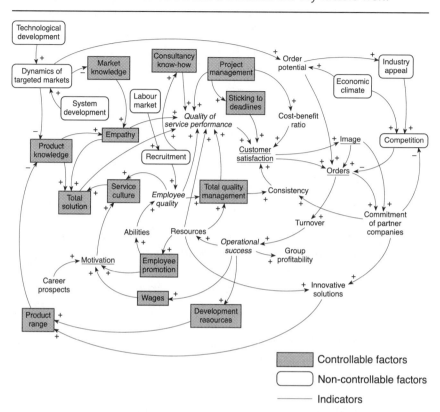

Controllable factors

Non-controllable factors

Indicators

The objective of total quality control is more easily attained if the standard of the workforce improves, in the same way that conditions for the establishment of a service culture is indispensable to systems solutions. In order to offer systems solutions, resources must be found to develop a corresponding product palette. Further prerequisites include an excellent knowledge of the product and the business as well as a keen empathetic understanding of customer problems. If the business unit also has an outstanding service culture at its disposal then the groundwork is laid for creating high quality service performance.

Finally, we come to image, which is dependent on customer satisfaction and is an additional initiating factor for orders. It is also an important consideration when winning and tying down partner companies, so that innovative solutions leading to an attractive product palette can be developed. They ensure the kind of continuity which in the end is the basis of customer satisfaction.

The network shows a myriad of further interconnection which I cannot go into here. So instead let us attempt to interpret the network with regard to its function within the framework of the analysis phase of the business strategy. In this regard the following areas have to be looked at in order for an informative analysis of the strategic business unit to be made:

- general environment;

- industry structure;

- situation *vis à vis* the competition;

- strategic positions for success of the SBUs;

- internal relations.

To interpret the network we need to differentiate between controllable factors, non-controllable factors and indicators. As the name suggests, controllable factors are those particular factors which can be influenced or steered by the managment of the business unit. The non-controllable factors, for example the general economic situation or the competition, cannot be influenced at all. The indicators simply allow the business strategy to be assessed. This means not only the usual factors of corporate success but image development or employee quality as well. In Figure 3.12 the controllable factors shown in the square boxes are principally the key internal factors of the business unit. These show the strategic positions for success and the strengths and weaknesses of the business unit. The non-controllable factors inside oval boxes include the general environment, the industry and the situation *vis-à-vis* the competition. Here it is possible to look at the opportunity/threat analysis. At this stage of the strategic methodology we are not focusing on the indicators but they will play an important role when it comes to the evaluation of strategy.

The objective of this stage of the methodology is to create an opportunity/threat and a strength/weakness profile of the strategic business unit. It is the non-controllable factors which kick off the development of the opportunity/threat profile, in this network represented by the economic situation, the employment market, technological and process development and the competitive position. These factors must be studied in depth and introduced methodically to the process of developing an opportunity/threat profile.

Let us look at the employment situation to see how we can assess the general environmental situation. It is absolutely essential to assess the development of the employment market in order to understand future prospects for recruiting staff. Here, I mean assess, not prognose, as we all know that a prognosis of the future is not possible. Assess means more to look at a number of possible scenarios for the future. There is plenty of comprehensive literature on the development of scenarios (e.g. Geus, 1988; Wack, 1985). Let us look at one particular process which is relatively simple and close to everyday practice. Table 3.2 shows how one basic scenario and two alternative scenarios can be developed for the employment market and includes their opportunity/threat catalogue.

Qualified employees are perhaps the most important factor for success in building up a business for IT and systems solutions. So when developing scenarios the main question is, what is the size of the potential for qualified employees and how many companies will be competing for these specialists? In the basic scenario – perhaps we should call it the probable scenario – the premise is that the market for specialist employees will be tight. Maybe because many computer companies will see systems solutions as the new market. On the other hand, it is likely that the computer sector will recover its traditional business and provide enough resources and that conditions are not right for many consultancy companies to have a long solo run. Therefore one could state that the opportunities balance out the threats.

Alternative Scenario I assumes the pessimistic view that the employment market might dry up completely. Here the threats are in the ascendant, yet there is still the opportunity of exploiting the potential of in-house employees. Alternative Scenario II looks at the whole situation more optimistically and sees no lack of qualified employees in the future. The chance that top system advisors can be employed at reasonable rates is in fact quite high. The threat in that scenario is that follow-on staff will be neglected.

In this way scenarios are developed for the general environment, including technology, society, resources, the economy and the environment. Here it is very important to take the network as a starting point in order to understand the complicated effects of the scenarios on the strategic business unit. If we play through Alternative Scenario I in the network we can see the effects of a dried up market on recruitment and the ensuing chain reaction caused by sinking employee standards, sinking quality of service performance, sinking customer satisfaction and the effect all this has on orders, turnover and corporate success. The scenario is set up and discussed, allowing the dangers to be kept under control.

I have just one more thing to add on differentiating between the basic scenario and the two alternative scenarios. The probable basic scenario is likely to constitute the basis of the development of strategies.

TABLE 3.2 How one basic scenario and two alternative scenarios can be developed for the employment market

Scenario	Developments	Interpretation	
		Opportunities	*Threats*
Basic Scenario 'Tense Labour Market for Specialist Staff'	■ Computer Industry recovers ■ Many computer companies enter the market for Total Solutions ■ Consultancy firms cut back on staff	■ Resources for external recruitment available ■ Possibility of buying in consultancy know-how	■ Top system analysts rarely recruitable ■ Not properly-qualified people in the market place
Alternative Scenario I 'Labour Market completely dries up'	■ Computer Industry still in regression ■ All companies pounce on Total Solutions market ■ Consultancies also enter the market	■ Exploiting the internal employee potential	■ Required competences cannot be brought in from outside; entering the Total Solutions market becomes impossible
Alternative Scenario II 'No shortage of Specialist Staff'	■ Computer industry (sales of hardware and software) recovers ■ Retraining schemes for computer scientists spreading ■ Consultancy firms focus on strategic/organizational questions	■ Sensible conditions for the recruitment of top system analysts ■ Sufficient resources available	■ Internal development of management suffers

Alternative Scenarios I and II, on the other hand, constitute the basis of contingency plans. If we can think through and evaluate possible developments and their effects, then we can prepare measures just in case the unexpected happens. Management would, so to speak, have a plan up their sleeve which they could produce at the first signs of change.

So let us look at some companies which have read environmental trends correctly. In the 1950s the image of BMW was that of a traditional, somewhat old-fashioned manufacturer of motor bikes and luxury limousines. An environmental analysis showed that the trend was growing towards more sporty cars which nevertheless had the comforts of a limousine. BMW set off in this direction and has been eminently successful, although it did take eight years for their changed profile to be recognized by the market. Another example is the medium-sized Swiss furniture company Luethi, which recognized at a very early stage the appearance of individual living design and so managed to place its 'de Sede' range of soft furnishings at the top of the world market. Then there is the Swiss soft cheese company Baer which spotted the early signs of a trend towards environmentally friendly products and production. When the eco-boom hit at the beginning of the 1990s, they were already ahead of their competitors.

Having analysed the broader environment of the business unit, the next step is to analyse the industry in which the competition is positioned. One particular method which has proved itself valid in corporate practise was designed by Porter (1980) and is set out in Figure 3.13.

In order to expand on this basic picture there are various key words which characterize an industry analysis: product lines, consumer behaviour, complementary products, substitute products, growth (rate, determinants), technology (cost structure, real net output, logistics, personnel), marketings/sales (market segmentation, marketing practice), suppliers, distribution channels, innovation (types, sources, rates), competitors (strategy, objectives, strengths, weaknesses). Later, using the DELTA strategic study I, will give a more concrete example of an industry analysis.

The last and final step in the environmental analysis lies in evaluating the strongest competitors in the market place. Porter also developed a grid system for this which is shown as Figure 3.14 (Porter, 1980).

It is not sufficient to consider the present strategies of a competitor as well as their strengths and weaknesses. Future potential strategies and the competitors' own assessment should also be investigated as well as their vulnerability and possible reactions to a concerted attack. Again we

FIGURE 3.13   Method for analysing the industry in which the competition is positioned (Porter, 1980)

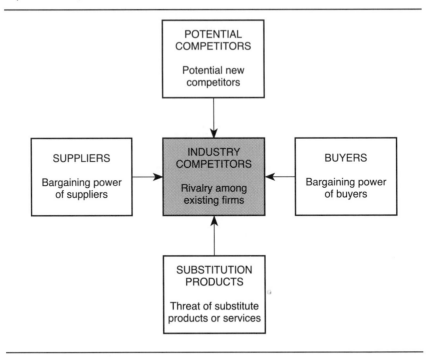

will look at all these connections when we carry out the DELTA strategy study.

Finally, to close this section on the environmental study I would like to mention a few companies which have managed to find their optimal position thanks to excellent industry and competition analysis. The Japanese company Honda is a good example. The objective of Yamaha was to overtake Honda in the motorbike market and to become the global number one. Within twelve months Honda was able to win back their position by means of undercutting and innovation. Yamaha sales fell and they had terrible losses. Yamaha decided they would be happy with second place. This fightback succeeded only because Honda understood their industry and their market very clearly.

The four largest competitors in the German travel market were fighting a difficult battle, made worse by the growing success of new competitors. NUR Touristic, the daughter company of Karstadt, proved to be the most successful with their aggressive pricing policy. At a very early stage they set up their own distribution channels (at present they have

FIGURE 3.14 Grid system for evaluating the strongest competitors in the marketplace (Porter, 1980)

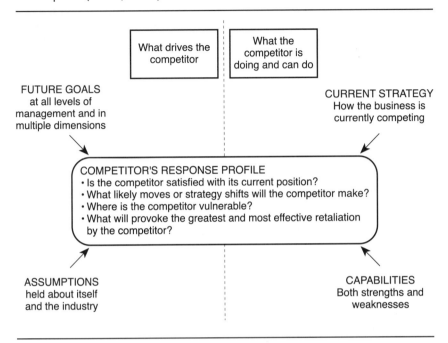

120 travel agencies) which enabled them to combat the increased competition. As their reservation system became more and more efficient they were able to bundle together their own flight and hotel packages into one product palette. It is only possible to understand the decisive factors in marketing and the competition by means of thorough industry analysis. The final example I will mention in this section is a company which did not do their 'homework'. Adidas, the manufacturer of running shoes, did not recognize the trend towards bright startling designs, thus Nike and Reebok were able to take over the lion's share of the market.

The next task is to put the variety of information collected for the environmental analysis into a more concentrated form so that it can be used as a platform for developing strategies. What is needed is an opportunity/ threat profile for the SBU IT systems solutions as set out in Figure 3.15. The title is 'market attractiveness', this is interpreted in the broadest sense of the word and includes the general environmental circumstances.

Having interpreted the environment of the SBU along with its opportunities and threats, we now have to determine the strengths and weaknesses of the SBU. We do this by stipulating the competences or

FIGURE 3.15   Opportunity/threat profile for the SBU IT systems solutions

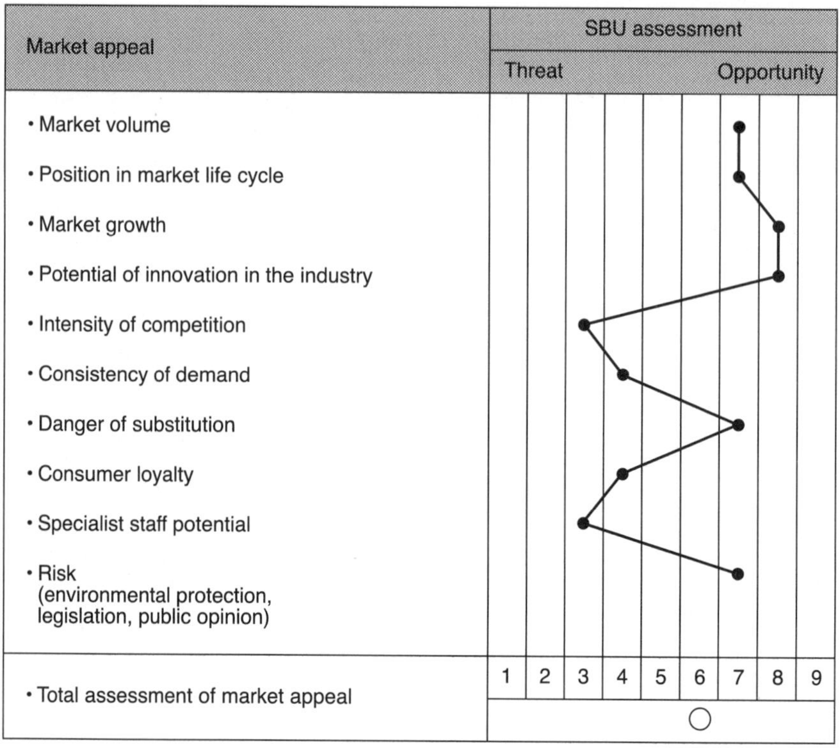

Market appeal	SBU assessment	
	Threat	Opportunity
• Market volume		
• Position in market life cycle		
• Market growth		
• Potential of innovation in the industry		
• Intensity of competition		
• Consistency of demand		
• Danger of substitution		
• Consumer loyalty		
• Specialist staff potential		
• Risk (environmental protection, legislation, public opinion)		
• Total assessment of market appeal	1 2 3 4 5 6 7 8 9	

strategic positions for success necessary to carry the business forward. The features of the strategic positions for success were set out and illustrated in the *Business strategies for the achievement of competitive advantage* section in Chapter 2. We have now to decide what the essential SPSs are. The network in Figure 3.12 answers that question for us. They are in fact the controllable factors shown in the square boxes. If you put together the relevant competences or the strategic positions for success for IT-systems solutions you can assess the strengths and weaknesses, and they look something like Figure 3.16.

On top of the necessary competences covered by the SBU there are other strengths and weaknesses of the business unit that need to be ascertained. The guiding principle is to assess these in relation to the most important competitor or competitors. So it is a matter of determining the strengths and weaknesses in order to ascertain the *relative* competitive advantage. In Figure 3.17 I have set out a cost structure analysis to show

FIGURE 3.16   Assessment of strengths and weaknesses for the SBU

Required competence/SPS	Interpretation	
	Strength	Weakness
■ Knowledge of product	√	
■ Knowledge of industry		√
■ Empathy with customers		√
■ Project management	√	
■ Product range	√	
■ Total quality control		√
■ Innovating power	√	
■ Consultancy know-how		√
■ Service culture		√

how this assessment can be made. The costs are ascertained for each of the value creation steps of the SBU and added in relation to the costs of the most important competitor, A.

Strength/weakness analyses should be carried out for the following areas:

- research and development;

- procurement;

- production, marketing;

- finance;

- personnel;

- innovation;

- management and executive systems;

- organization;

- information technology.

The following examples illustrate the strength/weakness assessment. The Liechtensteiner company Hilti AG, which is the world market leader for fastening systems in the construction industry, achieved their position by having the strongest sales and service organization in their industry and by always being customer-oriented. Being customer-oriented means

FIGURE 3.17   Cost structure analysis (Pümpin, 1992)

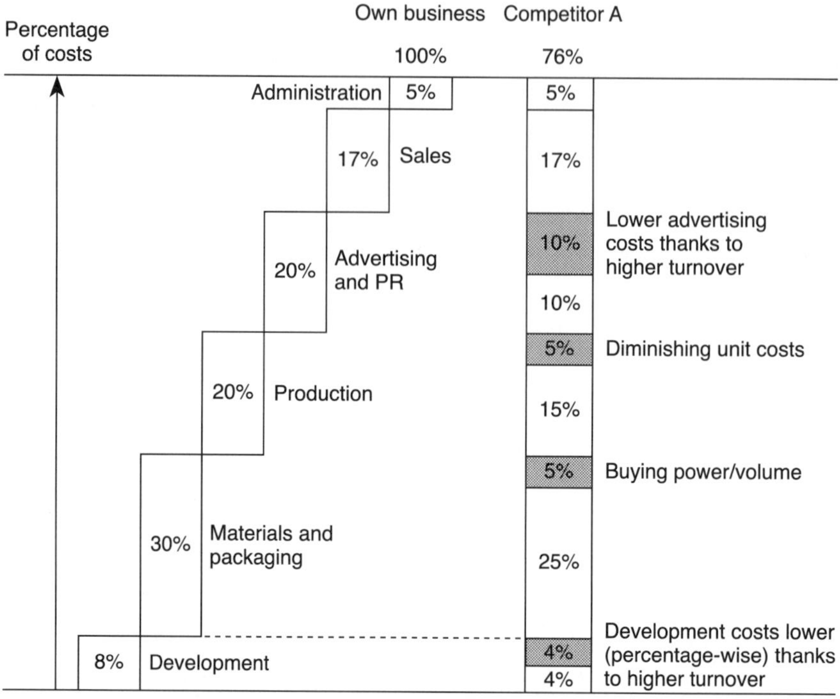

	Own business 100%	Competitor A 76%	
Administration	5%	5%	
Sales	17%	17%	
Advertising and PR	20%	10%	Lower advertising costs thanks to higher turnover
		10%	
Production	20%	5%	Diminishing unit costs
		15%	
Materials and packaging	30%	5%	Buying power/volume
		25%	
Development	8%	4%	Development costs lower (percentage-wise) thanks to higher turnover
		4%	

The cost advantages of competitor A are highlighted per value-added step. In total A's unit costs are 24% less than the company in question.

constantly offering new and improved products in order to resolve customer problems. The medium-sized Swiss company Victorinox achieved their global reputation as manufacturers of Swiss army knives. Thanks to their high quality standards they have established themselves as the largest pocket-knife manufacturers in the world. And finally let me mention the French manufacturer of luxury articles, Louis Vuitton, which gained its leading market position by selling products which had been finished by absolute craftsmen. Without difficulty they manage to successfully combine traditional craftsmanship and the latest technology.

Analogous to the opportunity/threat profile it is now essential to put together a strength/weakness profile. This is illustrated in Figure 3.18 for the SBU of IT systems solutions.

The network in Figure 3.12 shows not only the controllable and the non-controllable factors but also the so-called indicators, which are underscored. The indicators should point out whether the SBU strategy is

FIGURE 3.18   Strength/weakness profile for the SBU IT systems solution

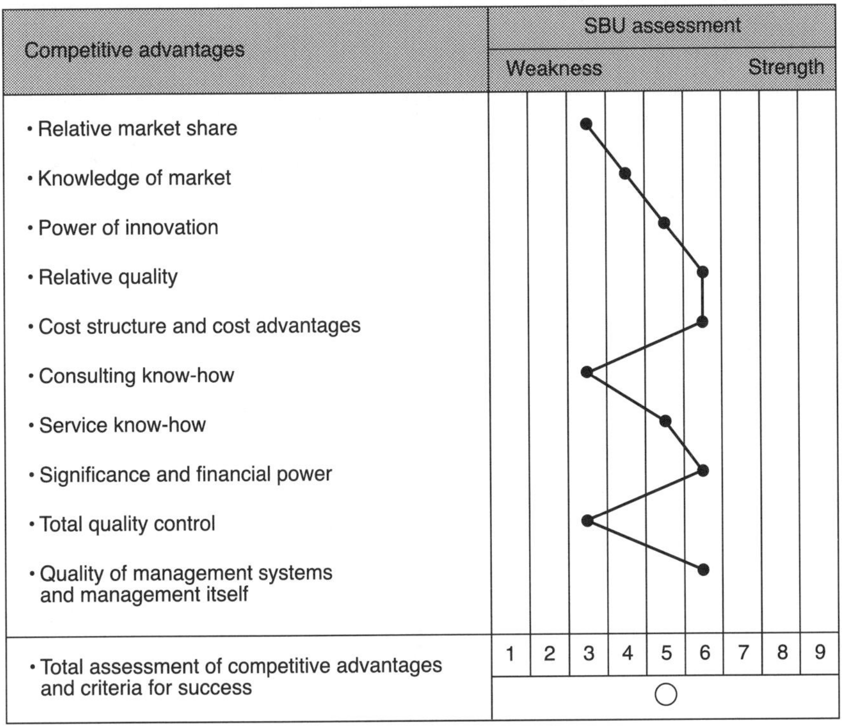

Competitive advantages	SBU assessment		
	Weakness		Strength
• Relative market share			
• Knowledge of market			
• Power of innovation			
• Relative quality			
• Cost structure and cost advantages			
• Consulting know-how			
• Service know-how			
• Significance and financial power			
• Total quality control			
• Quality of management systems and management itself			
• Total assessment of competitive advantages and criteria for success	1 2 3 4 5 6 7 8 9		

likely to be successful or not. As strategic evaluation is to be the subject of a later step in the methodology and is explained in detail in section 3.7, I am not going to study indicators in depth here. I would just like to mention that these must show the quality of an early warning system otherwise the SBU is not able to react to unfavourable developments in time. Therefore it is not only orders on the book or corporate success which have to be watched but also the soft factors which often react early. By soft factors I mean the quality of the service performance and the workforce, employee motivation, customer satisfaction and the image of the SBU, these have to be watched all the time.

Strategic study DELTA – analysis of a business strategy

I am now going to use DELTA to illustrate how to round off the business and environmental analysis and show how it affects the development of the business strategy. To do this I will concentrate on the SBU 'paper bags', whose interrelations were set out as the network in Figure 3.19.

In terms of the environmental analysis (non-controllable factors) this SBU covered three areas: general environmental development, industry structures and most important competitor.

For general environmental development the following scenarios were played through:

- adjustment of structure and reduction of capacity in Europe;

- trend towards small bags and thus increasing consumption;

- upsurge in prices due to the paper manufacturer's position of strength;

FIGURE 3.19 Interrelations of the SBU 'paper bags' set out as a network

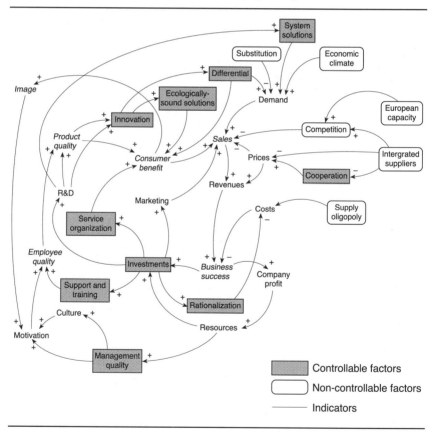

- increased demand due to product differentiation and services;

- large orders increasingly distributed centrally and emphasis on service and quality;

- increased demand because of system solutions;

- ecological demands require new and innovative packaging solutions.

The study of the industry structure was carried out according to diagram 3.15 and suggested in the following solutions:

- Today's competitors and industry structure:

  - too many suppliers: battle to freeze some out;

  - slow market rate growth: over-capacity;

  - very capital intensive: drive towards full capacity operation;

  - low product differential: sales as opposed to price.

- Potential of new rivals:

  - the European Union is allowing trade barriers between countries to come down, international competitors are entering the home market;

  - the most important clients purchase Europe-wide;

  - general sharpening of the competition.

- Suppliers:

  - not enough suppliers, the danger of oligopolitical manipulation;

  - rigid offers and high degree of price fluctuations;

  - possibility of differentiation for integrated manufacturers.

- Buyers:

  - consumer pressure, the product is a commodity and the market is relatively transparent;

  - price sensitivity, above all in the construction industry.

- Substitute products:

  - paper bags are in part being replaced by plastic products.

By analysing leading European rivals according to Figure 3.14 leads to the following characterizations:

- Aims:

  - undisputed number one in Europe;

  - highest possible sales volume of own paper products (integrated manufacture);

  - dissolution of regional protection.

- Strategies:

  - price war;

  - volume growth to full capacity;

  - securing markets by developing strong links to customers (construction industry);

  - acquisition of smaller, independent producers to increase market share;

  - lobbying to bring down regional protection.

- Own estimate:

  - potential for market leadership;

  - achievement of dominant market position only a matter of time.

- Strengths/weaknesses:

  - the integration of the packaging business with paper manufacture is both a great strength (price politics, financial might) and a weakness (need for capacity utilization).

- Satisfaction with own position:

  - only satisfied when leading market position is secured.

- Possible change in strategy:

  - none at present.

- Vulnerability:

  - if the sales market (construction industry) cannot be secured;

  - if regional protection stays in place.

- Defence measure:

  - price war.

All the information gathered on the environmental, industry and business sectors are put together and form the opportunity/threat profile in Figure 3.20.

The internal analysis concentrated on internal strategic positions for success as well as potential strengths and weaknesses with regards to corporate functions. The following strategic positions for success can be attributed to the SBU paper bags:

- specialist products of high quality;

- largest paper manufacturers have their own network of independent manufacturers and distribution organizations;

- secure sales markets exist in certain areas (i.e. the cement industry) via companies belonging to the mother company.

The situation with regards to the corporate functions of the SBU could be summed up as follows:

FIGURE 3.20 Opportunity/threat profile

Market appeal	SBU assessment	
	Threat	Opportunity
• Market volume		
• Position in market life-cycle		
• Market growth		
• Potential of innovation in the industry		
• Intensity of competition		
• Consistency of demand		
• Danger of substitution		
• Consumer loyalty		
• Specialist staff potential		
• Risk (environmental protection, legislation, public opinion)		
• Total assessment of market appeal	1 2 3 4 5 6 7 8 9	

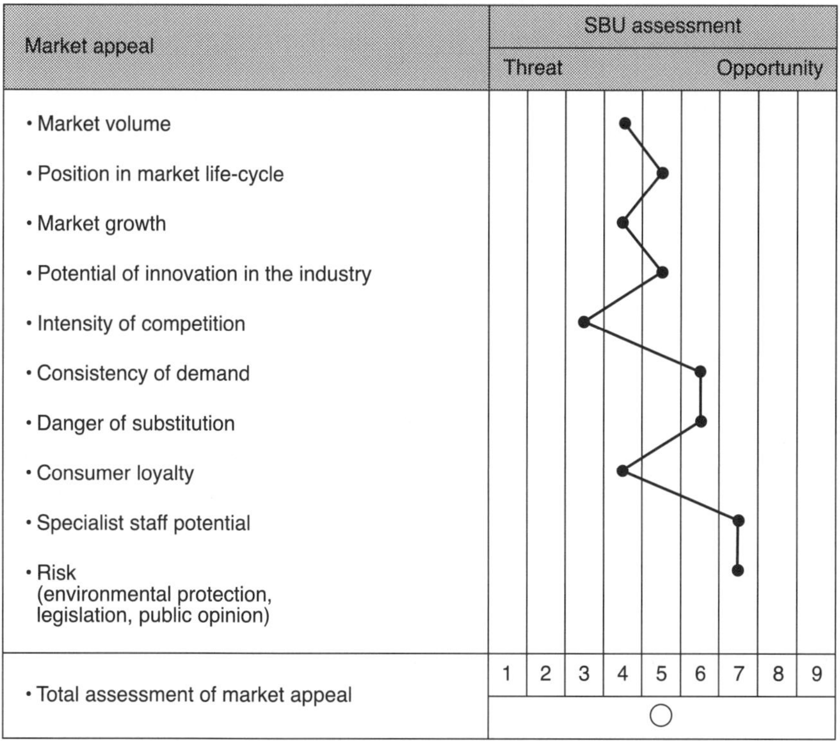

- *Research and development*: not very extensive, occasional innovation in the plastics industry. More of a weakness.

- *Procurement*: not as good as with integrated companies but acceptable thanks to good relationship to suppliers. Still to be considered a weakness.

- *Manufacturing*: in accordance with the vision 'champion of productivity' efficient and cost-effective. Definite strength.

- *Marketing*: good distribution network, partially secured sales market (the cement industry). More of a strength.

- *Finances*: good financial management, excellent cash flow management. Strength.

- *Personnel*: relatively high fluctuations, some difficulties in recruiting staff. More of a weakness.

- *Innovation*: one or two innovations already have a prize from the industry association. Still not distinguished enough. More of a weakness.

- *Management and executive systems*: good management, well developed systems. Definite strength.

- *Corporate culture*: service and client-oriented, still not enough. More of a weakness.

- *Organization*: well organized, autonomous units. Strength.

- *IT*: not clearly defined, thus more of a weakness.

If you put the SBU internal profile together into a strength/weakness profile it looks something like Figure 3.21.

The preparation of an opportunity/threat and strength/weakness profile allows a business strategy to be developed. This development is the subject of the strategy methodology set out in *The development of business strategies* section, earlier in this chapter. Before I come to that I wish to show how the environmental and business analysis can be carried out from the point of view of both the company as a whole and from the point of view of the owner.

Analysis of the corporate strategy

The information essential to the development of a corporate strategy is gathered in exactly the same way as for the development of a business

FIGURE 3.21   Strength/weakness profile

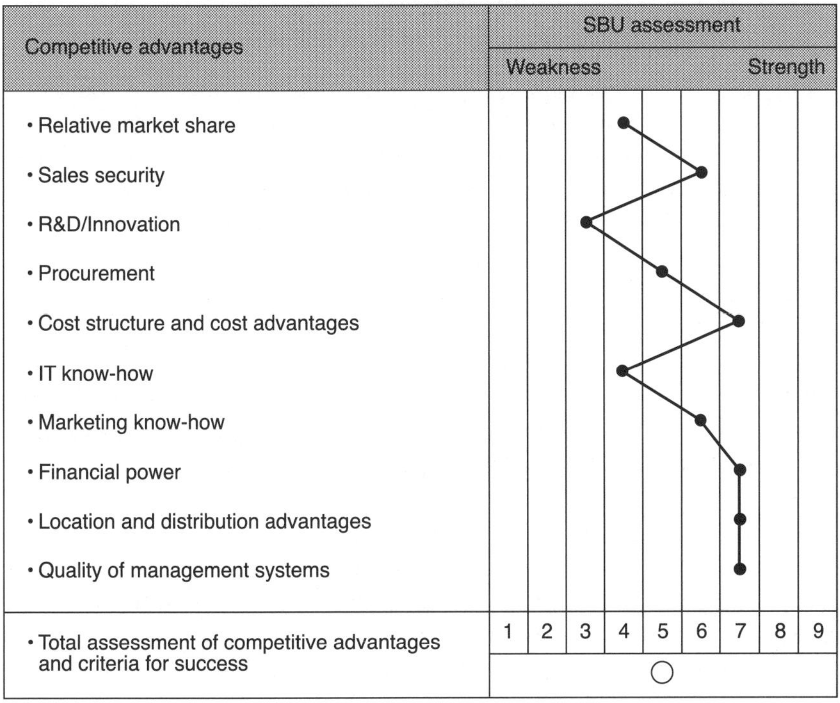

Competitive advantages	SBU assessment		
	Weakness		Strength
• Relative market share			
• Sales security			
• R&D/Innovation			
• Procurement			
• Cost structure and cost advantages			
• IT know-how			
• Marketing know-how			
• Financial power			
• Location and distribution advantages			
• Quality of management systems			
• Total assessment of competitive advantages and criteria for success	1 2 3 4 5 6 7 8 9		

strategy. The starting point is again the vision of the company. After that key factors for success according to the stakeholders of the company and their objectives are determined. They lay the foundation for the next step, which is developing a network for the company, thus demonstrating the controllability of these factors.

Following this, the process is geared towards the company as a whole. The environmental analysis no longer looks at the business sector and the competition, instead it covers the broader environment and particularly the interests of the stakeholders. The internal analysis concentrates on value potentials, core competences and the value chain of the company. Even the so-called 'soft' factors such as the corporate culture are incorporated into this analysis.

An environmental analysis is carried out with the help of scenarios, for example look at Table 3.2 with regards to the employment market. Then the second essential area of the environmental analysis is investigated, that which takes into account the interests of the stakeholders. The beginning of this chapter showed how to identify these stakeholders. So let us examine a concrete example of the inclusion of stakeholders within the framework of an environmental analysis, namely a potential fusion between Krupp and Hoesch. As Figure 3.22 shows, at the forefront of the fusion are the interests of board members and the employees from both companies, various banks as well as national and municipal institutions are also taken into consideration.

A systemic environmental analysis has also to consider other stakeholders, such as clients, suppliers and competitors. It would also be a good idea to think about the future development of other interested parties and to work out corresponding scenarios. In the previous section, I went into this in some detail; now let us turn our full attention to the corporate analysis.

The first priority of a corporate analysis is to identify the value potentials of a company. Value potentials are combinations of circumstances existing in the environment, in the marketplace or in the company itself, which when developed would open up new possibilities to the company. As well as market potential I am talking about financial potential, IT potential, procurement potential, cooperation potential, organizational potential and know-how potential. If the company has at its disposal various, top quality value potentials these are to be viewed as strengths in terms of raising the integrated value of the company. If the value potentials of a particular company are not distinctive enough, then these have to be considered as weaknesses.

The question now arises, how can these value potentials be identified within the framework of a corporate analysis. The answer is, a network. If we take the example of a supplier to the electrical industry to illustrate this point. The company has 800 employees and a turnover of around sFr120 million. It is active in the areas of electrical network components and testing systems. Figure 3.23 sets out as a network the most important interconnections of this company.

The network has been built to show the different cycles grouped around the central motor. In the upper left-hand side of the diagram the general environment is set out and on the right-hand side competition is portrayed. Environmental scenarios can be assessed along with the future development of energy systems, for example, as these will affect market volume and thus future sales. Factors such as environmental awareness, energy saving, replacement demand of the industry, new technology as well as all possible substitutions have also to be considered.

In analysing the situation with regards to the competition, the emphasis is slightly different to that of the business strategy. It is above all a question of value potentials which go way over the market potential. If we look at the network we can see that in the area of competition there is a

FIGURE 3.22 Inclusion of stakeholders within the framework of an environmental analysis – the fusion between Krupp and Hoesch (Müller-Stewens, 1992)

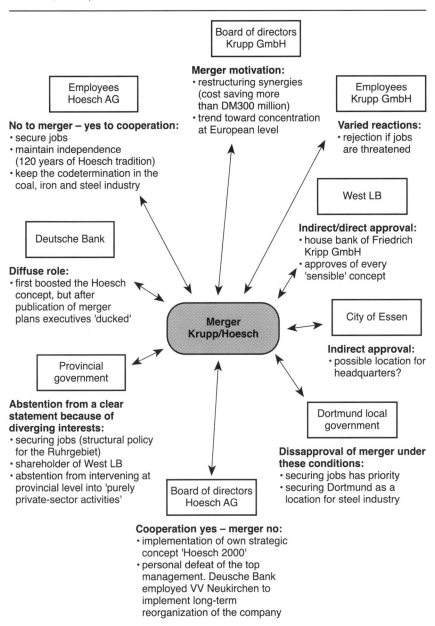

FIGURE 3.23 The most important interconnections of a supplier to the electrical industry as a network

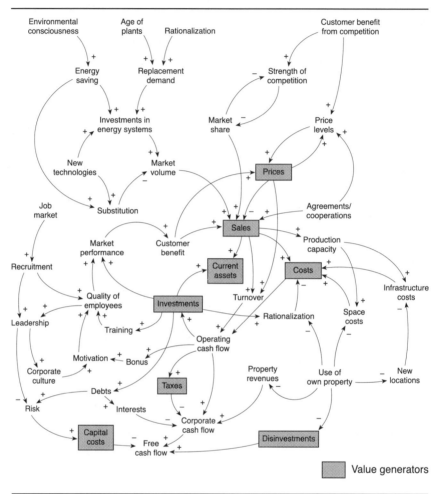

Value generators

cycle which signals cooperation potential. Cooperations with competitors does not simply have a stimulating effect on sales. It has a positive effect on prices in the sector as well as on a company's own prices, which in turn has a positive effect on earnings development. Of course this potential cannot be exploited unrestrictedly, limits are set on the one hand by the strength of the competition and on the other by monopoly trading laws.

If you look at the network for other value potentials, it is a good idea to start with the factors which have been framed. These are growth in turnover (sales), profit margin (price, costs), investments (current assets, investment/divestment) cost of capital and taxes. As Figure 2.19 showed, these are the little screws which have to be turned, in order to increase the value of the company. Each value potential should therefore be arranged in accordance with these value generators.

The value potentials are then briefly worked on in a clockwise fashion (the motor being the central point). The restructuring potential has an effect on cost and disinvestment factors. The company has to ask itself whether it should continue to use its own real estate or get rid of it. The first would lead to lower costs in terms of office space and so to a more favourable cost structure. On the other hand, it wipes out other possibilities, such as choosing more cost-favourable locations and possible rationalization through a complete relocation. The sale of the real estate would also free up cash flows considerably which in turn could be invested into essential business activities.

The financing potential would come to fruition in terms of the cost of capital and taxes. Here it is simply a matter of achieving an optimal financing relationship and lowering of company risk, so that the cost of capital can be optimized. In order to lower the burden of taxes it is necessary for organizational and legal structures to be considered.

Human potential has to be put together with investment. If resources are specifically invested in training and developing the work-force, this not only improves market performance but it also increases motivation. This potential is of particular interest to this company as a good workforce is one of its most important resources.

Finally, let us look at the business logistics potential with regard to the management of floating assets. Important here is just-in-time management and other measures to optimize the inventory.

Determining value potentials by no means exhausts all the possibilities of the corporate analysis. There are two further instruments available, namely determining core competences and analysing the company within its value chain. To illustrate this I am going to look at two industrial companies.

In the *Corporate strategies for value increase* section in Chapter 2, we looked at the concept of *core competences* and in Figure 2.18 set out the core competences of Canon. As part of the corporate analysis it is a good idea to have a shot at determining the required and actual core competences of a company with regards to determining the strategic positions for success. Of course a clear statement of core competences is a central part of the whole strategic process. But already at this point it is possible to find initial indicators.

Core competences are capabilities of a company which cut right across the business unit. They enable it to bring out innovative products in different areas at speed. Exactly what these core competences might be can be shown in the example of a company active in the capital goods sector. This medium-sized company has 800 employees and a turnover of around sFr200 million. It produces welding plants for the manufacture of arms grids, boilers and standard parts for cars. The company relies on three core competences, namely welding, mechatronics and systems technology. While welding could be considered the basic technology, mechatronics consists of a combination of mechanics and electronics and contains the systems technology for total operating solutions in the welding sector. Figure 3.24 shows these three core competences and their corresponding capabilities. The value potentials and core competences already identified in the corporate analysis are considered strengths. It is however possible to make an analysis from the perspective of *required* value potentials and core competences. Then the question is, what are the company's strengths and what are its weaknesses? Although this process is not quite as simple as identifying strategic positions for success, value potentials or core competences can appear quite unexpectedly and could well be new to that sector. What is *required* might not always be known beforehand.

Another tool useful to corporate analysis is the value chain (Porter, 1985). The value chain divides up a company into its strategically relevant activities. Main activities are separated from support activities. The main activities can be divided into procurement, logistics, production, marketing/sales and service/distribution/business logistics. If necessary these can be divided into even smaller sub-divisions. Support activities are usually divided into company infrastructure, human resources management and research and development. For each individual step a strength/weakness profile is made within the framework of the corporate analysis.

The use of the value chain as an instrument of analysis can be shown in the example of a medium-sized company; a supplier to the print industry and a manufacturer of high-quality components for printing presses. One characteristic of this company is its readiness to deliver to a large number of very small customers. Service/distribution/business logistics therefore plays an important role. Figure 3.25 picks out this particular arm of the value chain of the company and presents its strength/weakness profile.

On the basis of the corporate analysis it should be possible to recognize the basic 'logic' of the company. What is missing are the psychological and social aspects, in other words, a glimpse of the corporate culture.

We now have to ask the question, what makes up the personality of a company? Every company has its own identity which makes it

FIGURE 3.24 Three core competences and their corresponding capabilities in a welding technology company

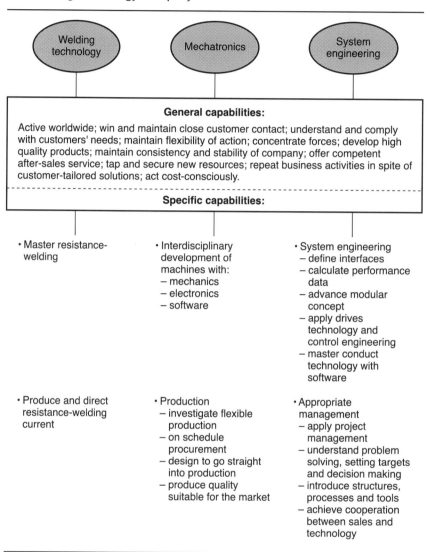

different to other companies. It is not easy to analyse this personality, in fact it is really an intuitive understanding. Let us look at concrete examples. Ueli Prager built up Mövenpick from small beginnings to a gastronomic corporation which is unlike any other company in Switzerland or Germany. Mövenpick stands for quality, originality and reliability. There is barely another gastronomic chain which has

FIGURE 3.25 Value chain of a supplier to the printing industry with a strength/weakness profile for service/distribution/logistics

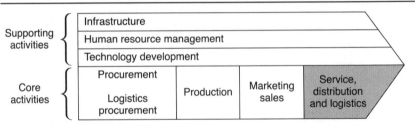

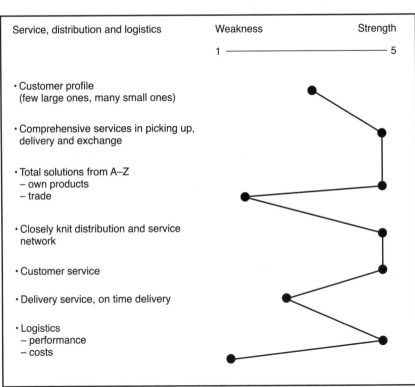

anything like as strong a personality. Then there is Benetton, which came virtually from nowhere and yet now has shops on nearly every high street in Europe. Benetton has a distinctive image, a personality. We must not forget Coca-Cola either. Its excellent marketing and communication strategy means that it always knows exactly how to market its profile.

It is personality which adapts the workings of the company to the outside world. It is an external expression of the internal corporate culture. It expresses itself in fundamental value presentations and standards which are at the heart of economic trade. It consists of 'soft' factors tightly bound together as opposed to formal organization. Usually the corporate culture bears the stamp of a particularly charismatic person or perhaps the alignment to a particular strength. A cost-oriented company is clearly different to an innovation-oriented company and personalities such as Ueli Prager leave an indelible mark.

One possible way of determining the corporate culture during this phase of the analysis is to build a network as shown in Figure 3.26. The further a factor is away from the central point, the stronger the impression this factor has on the corporate culture. In this case it is customer-orientation, employee-orientation and innovation-orientation.

A good example of employee orientation is the company Hewlett-Packard. The workforce and its development is at the forefront of this company's culture, the so-called 'HP-Way'. It is immediately noticeable on entering the company that all work areas have been especially fitted out so that ideas can circulate and employees are comfortable. To see how

FIGURE 3.26   Profile for determining the corporate culture

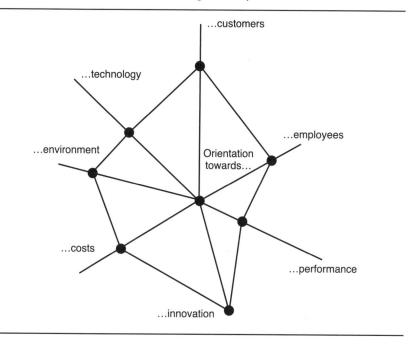

a change at the helm of a company can affect its culture we need only look at the computer company Apple. In 1983, Steven Jobs passed on the highest responsibility to John Sculley. Under Jobs' management Apple was oriented towards innovation, technology and the workforce. When Sculley took over the orientation started to lean markedly towards the customer and service. It is an extremely difficult task to judge the culture of a company. Yet the corporate analysis must not swerve away from this task. The external (personality) and internal (orientation of the culture) must be determined. It does not matter how factually and convincingly the strategies have been worked out, if they go against the corporate culture they will fail.

Strategic study DELTA – analysis of the corporate strategy

So DELTA has to follow two different analyses at this stage, it has to determine its value potentials and their multiplication possibilities and it has to assess its personality and corporate culture.

In addition to positioning its individual business units within the competition, including how to exploit its sales market potential, DELTA also concentrates heavily on the following value potentials:

■   Procurement potential:

– There are two main objectives here, to increase the purchase volume of paper in order to achieve better conditions and to secure supply. To this end only contracts which offer preferential treatment clauses will be signed, cooperation with paper factories will be actively sought; DELTA will aim for a decentralized purchasing policy accessing different European countries, co-operations with other paper bag manufacturers as well as tax favourable solutions.

■   Employee/management potential:

– The aim is to close all loopholes by having a targeted plan for management and a considered plan for employee development, which will build up strategic reserves of personnel and encourage employees towards entrepreneurial thinking and trading. The slogan is 'Management not administration'.

■   Acquisition/restructuring potential:

– The company's European presence can be increased by taking over other companies within the paper bag sector. This will be a good counter-balance to the integrated paper bag manufacturers. The know-how is already available to restructure these companies.

- Business logistics/IT potential:

  - There are still too many applications of IT and business logistics which have been put together any old how. Considerable improvements could be made in this area through the introduction of modern production planning systems, management information systems and accounting applications.

Two value potentials lend themselves perfectly to DELTA:

1 Acquisition/restructuring potential:

  - DELTA already has considerable experience of acquisitions and restructuring companies. The main characteristic of paper bag manufacturers in Europe is that kraft paper bags and plastic bags are viewed as one. DELTA has worked out how to disentangle these two and realize cost improvements. What is more, as they understand the process of acquiring such companies they can effectively multiply it.

2 Procurement potential:

  - In order to optimize purchasing DELTA has already built up several cooperations with other bag manufacturers and paper factories. The know-how gained through this process can be multiplied for further alliances without much extra expense. The most important factor here is that this know-how is not specific to a particular country but can be applied all over Europe.

With regards to the *personality*, DELTA has not yet succeeded in creating an unmistakable identity. The starting point is simply a profile of the company as the largest independent manufacturer of bags or perhaps (after further acquisitions) as the single largest supplier covering the European arena. The product and the service do not exactly lend themselves to a personality profile. The culture of DELTA is defined by two slogans 'Champions of Productivity' and 'Service'. Bearing this in mind, the culture network of the company could look something like Figure 3.27.

Having gathered all the information to study the company as a whole, the final step in the process of this strategic methodology is to look at the environment and the company from the owner's point of view.

FIGURE 3.27   The culture profile of DELTA

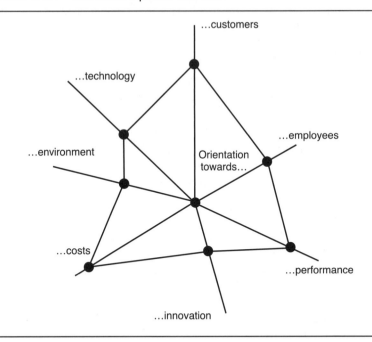

Analysis of the owner strategy

There are various interrelated aspects that a company has to bear in mind while collecting information in preparation for the development of an owner strategy. I have already shown that the owner can position his company strategically in ways which are not open to management. These are the subject of the following examples, not financial market strategies nor asset management strategies but what environmental factors does the owner have to consider and what value potentials can he exploit to increase the integrated value of the company.

In exactly the same way that we started by looking at the vision of the business and corporate strategies, we also start by looking at the owner's vision of his company. Building on the vision, the owner then has to ascertain his key factors of success, placing particular emphasis on the considerations of the various stakeholders. As Figure 3.7 shows, these then have to be assessed in connection with his financial market and asset management interests as well as the claims of his family.

Key factors help to develop the owner's network relevant to a particular company. Figure 3.28 shows the network of a majority shareholder in a medium-sized Swiss industrial company.

The emphasis of the network is placed on the company relevant strategic levers for the owner strategy. Environmental factors and factors based on the stakeholders' interests are only shown at the edge of the diagram. This is because the environmental analysis can be taken from either the business or corporate strategies.

What is of interest here are the owner potentials relevant to the company. These are framed in Figure 3.28. From the company's point of view the question is, how can the exploitation of the owner potentials develop into either opportunities or threats. Figure 3.29 puts together an opportunities/threats profile for the company in question.

FIGURE 3.28 The network of a majority shareholder in a medium-sized Swiss company

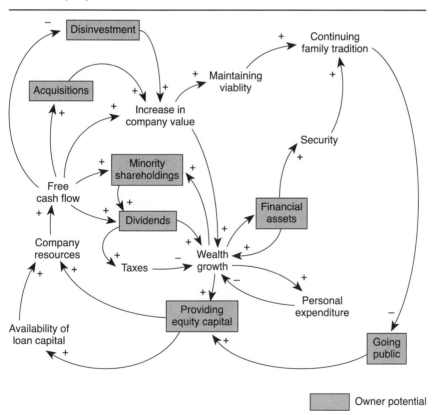

FIGURE 3.29 Opportunity/threat profile for the medium-sized Swiss company

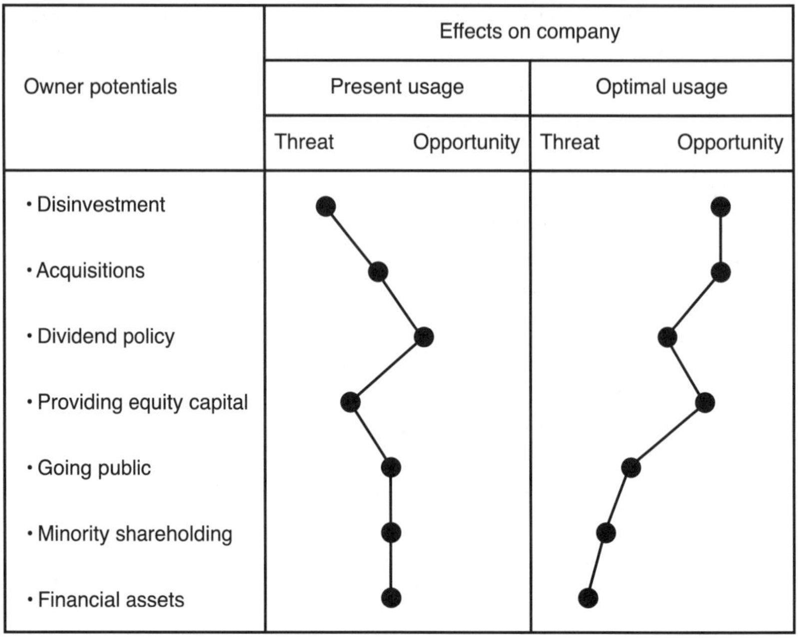

Owner potentials	Effects on company			
	Present usage		Optimal usage	
	Threat	Opportunity	Threat	Opportunity
• Disinvestment				
• Acquisitions				
• Dividend policy				
• Providing equity capital				
• Going public				
• Minority shareholding				
• Financial assets				

The owner is even today loath to disinvest the less attractive parts of the company, which could be interpreted as a threat. If this problem is tackled systematically it is possible to turn it into an opportunity. The situation is somewhat better when we look at acquisitions, yet even here quite important possibilites lie dormant. The present day dividend policy is considered to be favourable to the company. If the policy was changed this could lead to its weakening, although it is possible to hold the negative effects in check. The allocation of equity capital is also to be considered a deficit. Furthermore, going public is considered to be of no advantage to the company. Minority shareholdings and financial assets are not so important to the owner. On the other hand, if money set aside for the company should then be placed in foreign investments, this could prove particularly dangerous.

The owner should not take risk evaluation lightly. The company would like the owner to place as much funding as possible at its disposal. But a clever owner does not place all his eggs in the same basket, particularly if a company is seen to carry a relatively high risk whether due to the industry or the volatility of the market. It is for this reason that management has to look deeply into the question of risk when considering future strategic direction.

Strategy Study DELTA – analysis of the owner strategy

The management of DELTA considered which potentials the owner should exploit and what risks he should aim to divest. The following owner potentials were identified:

- acquisition potential (either companies in the same or different industries);

- joint venture potential;

- financial engineering potential;

- restructuring potential (with disinvestments possible).

These potentials can be exploited in different ways, as I aim to show with the development of the owner strategy. With regards to risk, according to DELTA the owner has to attempt to balance out the following problems:

- dependence on paper suppliers;

- endangering the environment with plastic bags and other plastic products;

- isolation due to the opening up of Europe.

Exploitation of the acquisition potential would help reduce dependence on paper suppliers as well as help in avoiding isolation through the opening up of Europe. One example looked at was the possible acquisition of an integrated paper manufacturer in Spain. This would not only secure raw material sources but enable the company to get a foothold in an EU country. With regard to ecological problems, the exploitation of the restructuring potential would help as the paper bag and plastic bag activities could be separated in preparation for the disinvestment of the latter, thereby reducing the risk from environmental regulations. It is worth mentioning that the owner has several companies from different sectors in his DELTA portfolio and so from an overall consideration has already spread his risk.

Now we have gathered this information on the potentials of the owner's interests we possess the raw material necessary for developing strategies. You could even say that we are now in possession of the pieces of a puzzle, the next step in the methodology is simply to put the pieces together to make a picture. However, this analogy does not quite follow. It is not the case that analysis of information is automatically followed by a certain strategy. Strategy development is more of a creative process than that, a creative process which can at least be steered by practical and proven guidelines. The next sections introduce them.

The development of business strategies

If there is any area of strategic corporate management which has been fully documented in terms of its tools and its literature, then it is without doubt the area of business strategy development. The relevant key words often come under different headings: product–market matrix, portfolio strategies, competitive strategies. I do not want to introduce and describe these approaches again. What I want to do is give practical examples on how to go about developing business strategies.

Let us start with the breakdown of present strategic approaches as set out in Table 3.3, including structuring recommendations for strategy development.

While portfolio strategies, competitive strategies and product–market strategy were already introduced and illustrated in the *Business strategies for the achievement of competitive advantage* section in Chapter 2, I have several comments to add to the synergy strategy and the integration strategy. Synergy strategies deal with a quite specific section of business dealings and focus all energy on this section. An example would be a buyer-oriented strategy with the emphasis on the skier and his/her needs – skis, shoes, clothes, accessories; or alternatively a function-oriented strategy which offers a palette of products based on lighting for example. Integration strategies enable an improved market position to be attained by means of placing together value added steps. Forwards integration would be looking for a cooperation with a suitable sales organization for a manufacturing business unit, while backwards integration means acquiring perhaps a supplier of raw materials.

So how can one develop business strategies based on the interrelations set out in Table 3.3? If the analysis was striving simply for the two dimensions of market attractiveness and relative competitive advantage then it goes without saying that the only possible strategy would be the portfolio strategy. The connection between information sourcing and strategic application is not as clear with the other tools. That is why a process is necessary which identifies a sensible way forward for each

TABLE 3.3 Breakdown of present strategic approaches

Strategies	Details
Portfolio norm strategies:	
■ Disinvestment strategy	■ Disposal of parts of the company to release resources for more promising areas
■ Skimming off strategy	■ Maintain market position and generate high cash flows without further investment for as long as possible
■ Investment strategy	■ Expand the market position through a directed investment policy
■ Segmentation strategy	■ Concentration of resources and investments in attractive markets in order to establish a competitive position
Competitive strategies:	
■ Cost leadership	■ Achieve production and overhead costs advantages over the competition and increase market share via low prices
■ Differentiation (performance leadership)	■ Distinguish company's products and services from those of the competition through innovation and service
■ Focus on market niches	■ Consistent orientation towards certain markets, target groups, technologies, sales markets, regions
■ New rules in the market game	■ Introduce a 'new game', consciously violate and re-create the rules of both market and industry
Product/market strategies:	
■ Market penetration	■ Stronger involvement in the market, i.e. reducing costs or prices and other measures for better control of market
■ Market development	■ Tap into new client groups, create new uses and purposes for products, services, channels of distribution and problem/system solutions
■ Product development	■ Develop new products and product ranges
■ Diversification	■ Break into new markets be it through own expansion or acquisitions

TABLE 3.3 *Continued*

Strategies	*Details*
Synergy strategies:	
■ Technology orientation	■ Focus on products and services which are based on the same technology or are produced with the same equipment
■ Customer orientation	■ Offer all products to satisfy a certain area of need for one client group (i.e. all products for skiing)
■ Function orientation	■ Offer a wide range of products for one specific function (i.e. lighting)
Integration strategies	
■ Forward integration	■ Gain direct access to the market via creation of an in-house sales organization or by fusing organizational steps
■ Backward integration	■ Strengthen one's own position by securing procurement sources and create cost advantages by fusing pre-sale operational steps

possible strategic approach. This also helps avoid the frequent and dangerous automization of strategic development, which often happens with the portfolio strategy. As the name suggests, a strategy promising success can be clearly attributed to a particular present position within the dimensions of market appeal and relative competitive advantage. In practical application, however, this promise cannot always be fulfilled. On the other hand, if we work through several strategic approaches to see what direction they are heading in, we are presented with a surfeit of ideas. This furthers the creative process and is the forerunner to the success of all strategic management.

Table 3.4 looks at the example of the SBU 'IT systems solutions' and illustrates the process of choosing strategic directions.

Based on the opportunity/threat and strength/weakness profile it would be best in terms of the portfolio application for this SBU to strive for an investment strategy. In terms of the competitive strategy, differentiation would appear sensible. An advantageous competitive position can be built up by better quality or different product features *vis-à-vis* the competition. Cost leadership or niche positioning would not prove as successful here. The product–market strategy points up quite clearly the development of a market. The desire is to change from being a supplier of hardware and software to being a comprehensive supplier of system solutions. The synergy strategy shows that customer orientation would be best. All resources must be concentrated on finding made-to-measure turn-key problem-solving for the customers. Finally, in terms of

TABLE 3.4 Strategic directions for the SBU 'IT systems solutions'

Approach	*Strategic directions*
Portfolio strategies	*Investment strategy:* building up a market position
Competitive strategies	*Differentiation (performance leadership):* distinction from the competition
Product/market strategies	*Market development:* from a supplier of hardware and software to a supplier of system solutions
Synergy strategies	*Customer orientation:* tailor-made, 'turn key' problem solutions
Integration strategies	*Forward strategy:* cooperation with suitable consultancy companies

integration a forward strategy is what is required. A cooperation with a suitable consultancy firm would be indispensible to achieving the desired level of orders and competent employees.

The next step in the strategy development procedure is to settle on one approach, to decide on one particular direction and to work out the fine details of this direction. It is even possible to combine two approaches, for example here it could be the investment strategy with a differentiation strategy. However, it is not a good idea to continue the process with such a broad spectrum. One would only get bogged down and possibly damage a clear strategic position. So a fourth strategic principle can now be formulated.

Fourth strategic principle

The fourth strategic principle is: *Strategic business units have to be positioned on the grids market attractiveness and relative competitive advantage. From this position a strategic direction must be pursued single-mindedly.*

Determining the strategic direction

In the SBU IT systems solutions the company decided on a portfolio approach. This decision could almost have been made earlier on in the information procurement phase, when the market attractiveness and relative competitive advantage profiles were determined. On the basis of the insights from Figures 3.15 and 3.18 we can establish the actual position in Figure 3.30. The strategic business unit has settled itself down in the midfield position, albeit slightly to the right of the diagonal and therefore in the tying up of funds zone. The business is still relatively unimportant, symbolized by the small diameter of the circle. If a growth strategy is applied to the SBU IT systems solutions then the target position is on the upper right-hand side of the matrix. As the development should also lead to an expansion of the business it is symbolized by a larger circle. The SBU's development is not dependent on its own initiative with regards to the development of the relative competitive gain. It is also due to the expectation that the market for such systems solutions will become more attractive.

Let us look at the general interest publication of a large Swiss publisher as another example of the positioning of a strategic business unit on the portfolio matrix. For decades the *Illustriertes* had been an indisputed favourite with the public, but in recent times its circulation had gone down in the face of a trend towards specialist publications.

FIGURE 3.30   The portfolio of the SBU

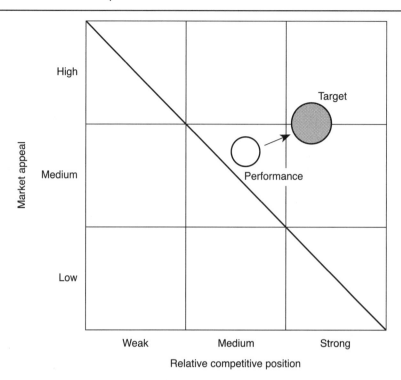

Above all, it was the level of general conversation on television which had led readers to seek out specialist knowledge from the printed press. The publishers of general interest publications have been forced to use new methods not only to retain their old readers but to draw in new readers. This meant that the publication had to find its clear strategic position within an environment that was in the process of social change and was characterized by the appearance of new media.

This positioning is critical as not only the changing environment but also the company's internal interests had to be considered. What is significant is that the publishing house offers its products to two completely different markets, namely the readership market and the advertisement market. So both these markets had to be fitted into the portfolio matrix. The result is to be seen in Figure 3.31.

If one takes the standard strategies from Figure 2.15 the motto is 'Secure the market position' for the readership and 'Build up the focus of activities' for the advertisement market. Thus a basic direction is set for

FIGURE 3.31 Portfolio position of the SBU 'magazines' in the reader market (△) and advertisement market

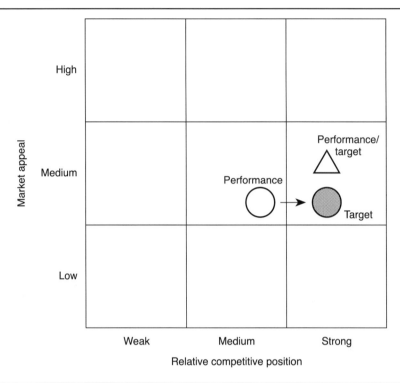

the publishers to follow. What these directions were in terms of strategy and specific measures is dealt with later on.

The first signs of the market positioning of a strategic business unit by means of the portfolio matrix appeared in the 1970s. Since then this tool has found wide acclaim and is viewed as the absolute strategic approach. The matrix continued to be developed and set off in different directions. The country portfolio, technology portfolio and environmental portfolios were all developed. Figure 3.32 illustrates a combination of all such portfolios (Hahn, 1990).

In order to make the market portfolio, the technology portfolio and environmental portfolios all compatible it was necessary to mark the axes in a similar way. In the market portfolio it was market attractiveness and relative competitive advantage. This changed slightly in the technology portfolio to the appeal of the total technical and economic advantages gained by using the relevant technology. The other axes shows the

FIGURE 3.32   Combination of portfolios (according to Hahn, 1990)

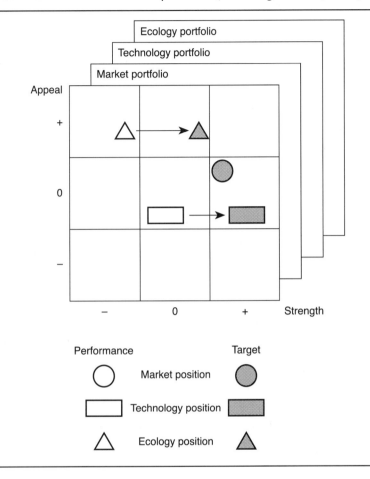

relative strengths of the strategic business unit in comparison to the competition. The environmental portfolio defined appeal as the advantages to be gained from behaving in an environmentally friendly way and incorporating this in product manufacture, product use and product disposal. Here the corresponding public awareness should not be underestimated. The actual environmental sustainability of the manufactured product can be seen as a strength.

If we now put the three portfolios together we can ascertain the actual/target positions. In Figure 3.32 a strong market position is shown in a market of average appeal. This portfolio position is an optimal one as a further increase in market appeal cannot be expected. The present technology position is somewhere in the middle. This shows that the technology being used has not many advantages, there are sufficient resources available although these are slightly below average in comparison to the competition. A better target position could be achieved by building up the resources available for technology. The environmental position can be summed up as follows: there is great potential in an environmentally friendly company management but this potential has not been fully exploited yet. In this case a better position could be achieved gradually and the environment could become a strength.

The product–market matrix is the second most important approach for strengthening the strategic position of a business unit. It was presented in Table 2.1 on p. 34. I would like to show how this matrix can be used to find strategies by looking at a supplier to the print industry whose value chain is shown in Table 3.5. This table lays down possible strategic directions for every field in this matrix.

The company's traditional business was manufacturing printing rollers. There were three possible directions: market penetration, market development or product development. Market penetration was headed by the idea of copying the competitor's process for manufacturing printing rollers. The possibilities of market development included market expansion into the textile and wood sectors, the availability of system solutions (comprehensive service/replacement demand) and perhaps the offer of new services such as printing roller cleaning. Product development included the promising alternative of entering a new market by offering rollers for copying machines and well as ceramic rollers. In the fourth field of the product–market matrix we find potential new products and markets. Nevertheless diversification, as the *Determining cooperation strategies* section in this chapter will show, is not an aimless entry into

TABLE 3.5 Product–market strategies of a supplier to the print industry

	Current products	*New products*
Current markets	**Market penetration** ■ process imitation in traditional fields	**Product development** ■ rollers for copiers ■ ceramic rollers
New markets	**Market development** ■ rollers for the textile and wood industry ■ comprehensive demand for servicing and repairing ■ cleaning agents	**Diversification** ■ plastics industry ■ medicinal/orthopaedic technology

any promising sector. The decision has to be based on present strengths and capabilities. The outstanding capabilities of this particular company lie in its ability to manufacture precision products that require an excellent knowledge of the basic material. This suggests the possibility of diversification into specialist areas of the plastics sector as well as medicinal and orthopaedic technology. The brief could be even wider spread as long as strategic similarities with the present business are at hand. From this perspective it would not be a good idea for this company to enter the financial services sector or the insurance sector.

So now we come to the final approach that I want to consider here, and that is competitive strategy. In Figure 2.16 on p. 41 I introduced the three 'generic' strategies which can help a business unit to achieve competitive advantage. They are: cost leadership, differentiation and niche marketing. I would like to show the practical application of this approach within the European arena on a sunglasses manufacturer. What strategic alternatives are at the disposal of this business unit of a larger international corporation are shown in Figure 3.33.

Due to their unique lenses this particular manfacturer had held an excellent market position for years. However, this was being chipped away at by the innovatory power and marketing capabilities of the competition. A new direction was essential. All three strategies had potential. In the sense of niche marketing, the company could concentrate on selling within the price range of $30–60. That would mean avoiding both the cheap end as well as the luxury/designer end of the spectrum. In terms of differentiation, the originality of the polaroid lenses still offered something to customers which the competition could

FIGURE 3.33 Strategic alternatives at the disposal of a sunglasses manufacturer

		Strategic advantage	
		Customer perception	Cost advantage
Strategic target area	Total market	**Differentiation** Uniqueness of the Polaroid lens	**Cost leadership** Creation of a secondary brand for price-leadership
	Market segment	**Concentration on market niches** Focus on price range $30–60	

not. All the company's activities should cluster around this benefit. Cost leadership is in the end only effective if there is a secondary brand name – for example, the secondary brand of the Bordeaux-Chateaux – which is related to the original product but which is sold at much lower prices.

A further example is the SBU Building Control Systems shown in Figure 3.3 on p. 75. The SBU is active in the larger market of building automation but decided to concentrate on one particular part of the market, namely Control Systems. So here in the sense of the competitive strategy we are talking about focusing on one market segment.

Development of alternative strategies

Once the possible strategic directions based on the proposed approaches have been determined we have taken a great stride forward. However, the process is by no means over as these directions now have to be concretized. The SBU Building Control Systems and the SBU general interest publication will show how we go about this.

Figure 3.34 lays out the alternative strategies open to the SBU Building Control Systems.

FIGURE 3.34   Alternative strategies open to the SBU 'Building Control Systems'

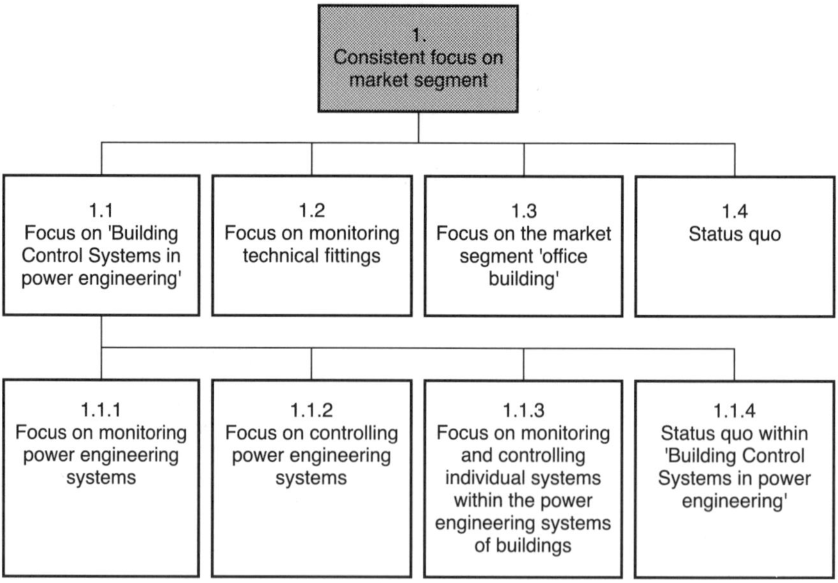

The starting point is the single-minded concentration on a market segment. There are four possible alternatives, alternatives 1.2 to 1.4 will not be followed. Alternative 1.1 is the one we will go on and it is then sub-divided into four possible areas. Alternative 1.1.4 is the one that is finally chosen for further development.

Figure 3.35 shows the alternative strategies for the SBU 'general interest publication'. According to their positioning in the portfolio matrix in Figure 3.31, the strategy for the readership market is: secure market position. This can be achieved quite simply by strengthening certain segments, by concentrating on quality or simply carrying on in the same way. Alternatives 1.2 and 1.3 drop out of the race, so which segments should be strengthened? There is a choice here between strengthening those segments which are already strong or strengthening all segments across the board.

The next step can be taken independently or by amalgamating with another company publication. Here, the SBU decided to opt for a strategy which took them along an independent path.

FIGURE 3.35 The alternative strategies for the SBU 'general interest publication'

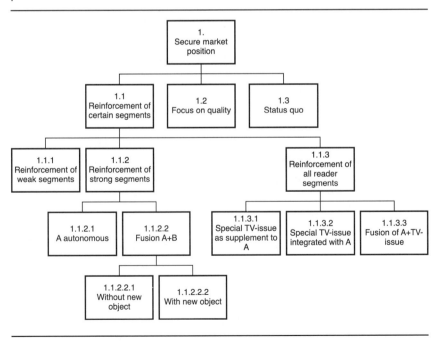

Strategic study DELTA – development of business strategies

As I set out in section 3.1, DELTA is active in four different areas: paper bags, plastic bags, bottling machines and consultancy/general operations.

Cost leadership is not a possibility when discussing possible competitive strategies. The integrated companies, i.e. the combined paper manufacturer and packaging company has such a huge advantage that cost management simply could not be achieved. We are left, therefore, with performance management or differentiation and the determining of a niche market. DELTA decided on the following strategies:

- paper bags: differentiation;

- plastic bags: niche policy;

- bottling machines: niche policy;

- consultancy/general operations: niche policy

DELTA was quite correct in deciding on a differentiation policy in the area of paper bags as they have a know-how advantage over their competitors in the strong paper bag sector. Only a niche policy is possible in the plastic bag sector as here we are talking about a typical commodity market. The areas of bottling machines and consultancy are just too small to consider anything other than niche marketing. If we place the four business units into the portfolio matrix, the picture looks something like Figure 3.36.

The surface area of the circle shows the relative importance of the individual businesses. The most important business unit, paper bags, finds itself in the middle with regards to market attractiveness as well as relative competitive advantage. The corresponding strategy will be to maintain the present position, using a differentiation approach. Further growth through favourable acquisitions is also a good idea. With regards to market attractiveness as well as competitive advantage the business unit plastic bags is in a position which can only suggest withdrawal in the long term. Even if the proposed niche strategy was successful it would scarcely be possible to improve its position substantially. Bottling machines and consultancy are both quite small sectors but on the basis of their positioning on the grid they deserve further attention, because either market attractiveness (bottling machines) or competitive advantage (consultancy) call out for further development. The business unit paper bags is the key orientation.

FIGURE 3.36 Positioning of the four Delta SBUs

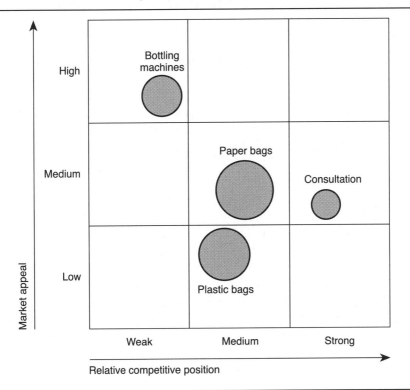

Of course, the differentiation strategy must be formulated in detail. Here are some key ways to achieve this:

- orient towards products with know-how advantage (strong paper bags);
- intensify research and development to raise the level of innovations;
- become champions of productivity;
- offer system solutions with corresponding advice;
- raise flexibility within production.

By developing alternative business strategies the company has taken an important step towards its future. The alternative strategies now have to be assessed and the best one chosen. This process is set out in the *Evaluating strategies* section of this chapter.

Beforehand, corporate strategies and thereafter owner strategies have to be developed, as business strategies alone are not sufficient for a comprehensive strategic orientation.

The conceptualization of corporate strategy

It is far more difficult to develop a corporate strategy than it is to define the strategic direction of individual business units. This is not simply due to the fact that the range of instruments available for developing a business strategy is broader and has seen more corporate practise than say the corresponding approaches for corporate strategies. When developing corporate strategies it is necessary to take into account more deciding factors than simply market considerations or the competition. Not only do the various stakeholders demand what is theirs by right, but consideration has also to be given to financial and tax aspects – and yet the line managers do not have the necessary experience. If the integration of strategic and financial thinking is ever to become a reality then management has to take this on board.

Figure 3.37 shows those areas covered by the corporate strategy. These should connect up all the examples in this chapter.

Three main themes come to the fore when developing a corporate strategy. They are integral corporate strategies, restructuring strategies and cooperation strategies.

FIGURE 3.37   The areas covered by the corporate strategy

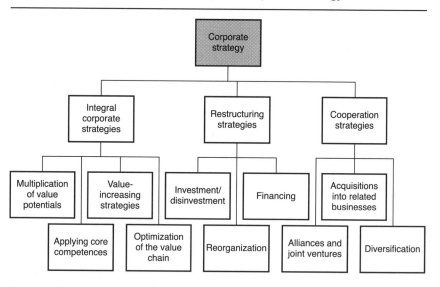

The *integral corporate strategies* concern the company as a whole and view it on a stand-alone basis. We start with the findings from the *Analysis of the corporate strategy* section, earlier in this chapter. Key words here are value potentials, core competences, strength/weakness profiles on the basis of the value chain. Four strategic approaches will be discussed:

1   multiplication of value potentials;

2   value creating strategies;

3   employment of core competences;

4   optimization of the value chain.

When it comes to *restructuring strategies* the question is: how can the value of specific sectors of the company be raised through targeted measures? The following possibilities present themselves:

■   investment/disinvestment of fixed assets and net working capital;

■   reorganization of the company or some of its individual parts;

■   optimization of finances and taxes.

Finally, when we come to *cooperation strategies* we no longer consider the company on a stand-alone basis but instead look into the value-increasing potential of cooperation. This suggests the following possibilities:

■   alliances and joint ventures;

■   acquisitions in related areas;

■   diversifications.

Put all these together and you have the fifth strategic principle.

Fifth strategic principle

The fifth strategic principle is: *strategic reorientation of a company means surpassing all barriers: melting strategic and financial thinking into one; questioning all existing structures; considering cooperations with other companies.*

Defining integral corporate strategies

To start developing comprehensive corporate strategies we need to look at a company's value potentials. These were already defined in a previous step of the strategic methodology and now have to be exploited to the full. Two strategic approaches place the value potentials at the centre of the process, namely the multiplication concept and the value creating strategy. The following practical example will clearly illustrate both these approaches.

The multiplication concept, originally set out in the *Corporate strategies for value increase* section of Chapter 2, turns into the principle of multiple use. One objective is the concentration on a company's strengths. Above all constant repetition reduces the effort of coordination, simplifies all processes and saves time. It is also taken as read that ever-increasing experience brings about improved quality. The multiplication concept approaches multiple use systematically and assesses processes, systems, products/services, know-how/capabilities as well as image/goodwill/brand according to their potential. An excellent practical example of this process comes from Pümpin and Imboden (1991), which researched the multiplication possibilities for the restaurant chain Mövenpick. Table 3.6 ties all these possibilities into a neat bundle.

Although this figure is self-explanatory, I would like to pull out one particular aspect and explain it more fully. Recently, Mövenpick fought and won the ice-cream war in German-speaking countries. Initially, it was simply a delicious dessert which contributed to the pulling power of Mövenpick restaurants. Yet in line with the multiplication concept the question arose as to whether sales could not be further increased by retailing the product from different outlets (for examples street stalls) and by selling through retail outlets. A decision was also made to offer an unlimited selection of flavours. The question then arose as to whether it would be better for Mövenpick itself to push this through its own production and distribution or whether it should consider licensed production and distribution. Thus a large number of strategic options were opened to the company, all of which could be used quite adroitly.

However, Mövenpick was slightly less successful with its multiplication in an area which is not set out in Table 3.6. Investment in the global expansion of a Mövenpick hotel chain did not prove to be so happy. This lack of success was not due to an unsuccessful multiplication policy but to the fact that the hotel business has little in common with the usual activities of Mövenpick. What is more the hotel business requires absolutely specific know how and very long-term thinking.

The supporting pillars of *value creating strategies* are built on value potentials. The central pillar is the Valcor matrix which we have already looked at in Table 2.2. The Valcor Matrix (Gomez and Weber, 1989) combines corporate value potentials with value generators to increase future free cash flows. Based on the logic of the value creating approach,

TABLE 3.6 Possible multiplication strategies for Mövenpick (Pümpin and Imboden, 1991)

Multiplication Objects	Different kinds of multiplication					
	Who?		How?		When?	
	Internal	External	Quantitative	Qualitative	Simultaneous	Successive
Processes *food distribution*	Via Mövenpick catering companies via own shops	Via food retail	Using one distribution channel	Varying from one distribution channel to another	Simultaneous tapping of all distribution channels	Gradual tapping of distribution channels
Systems *system catering*	Silberkugel City Silberkugel Motorway Cindy Marché City Marché Motorway	Franchising of restaurants in the Far East	Using one style of restaurant in different locations	Varying from one style of restaurant to another	Simultaneous opening of different restaurants	Gradual opening of different restaurants
Products/services *Swiss premium ice cream*	Swiss Premium Ice Cream: own production and distribution	Licensed production and distribution	Sticking to one flavour Sticking to one product	Varying from one flavour to another Varying from one kind of product to another	Simultaneous global introduction of Swiss premium ice cream	Gradual introduction country by country
Know-how/ capabilities *restaurant management*	Own company Temporary management Consultation	Licensed companies	Using the same management structure	Varying from one management structure to another	Simultaneous application of management capabilities	Gradual application of management capabilities
Image/goodwill/ brands *brand name Mövenpick*	Restaurants Hotels Ice-cream Salad dressings Salmon Coffee	Licensed companies Licensed products	Using the same brand name for each product	Varying the brand name: 'Mövenpiccolo'	Simultaneous transfer of brand name	Gradual transfer of brand name

value generators are always the same: sales growth, profit margins, investments, cost of capital and tax rate. It is the value potentials which have to be mass tailored for each individual company. These are derived from the network developed in the analysis step of the strategic methodology. Again if we look at the supplier to the electrical industry in Table 3.7 we can see that the starting points of the network are the value potentials set out in Figure 3.23. If these value potentials are then combined with the value generators, each interface offers up strategic options.

Strategic development cannot be described in any way as automatic. The creation of a Valcor matrix demands not only excellent knowledge of a company but also considerable creativity. Table 3.7 shows the result of this creative process for the supplier to the electrical industry. According to the results of the analysis, five value potentials present themselves to this company. They are restructuring potential, financing potential, IT and business logistics potential, human resources potential and cooperation potential. But which particular strategic options are yielded by the individual potentials with reference to the value generators? Some fields of the matrix can be commented on briefly. In order to increase turnover in the area of restructuring there is the possibility of placing together all electronic activities and then allowing this area to become independent. If we look at a possible holding construction, this could be in the form of a legally independent sub-contractor. In order to strengthen its position the company should seriously consider taking over competitor A – in the area of electronics this could help the company achieve that market share which would secure the 'critical' mass of the company. In order to improve the cash flow margin the company could go for computer-integrated manufacturing as well as flexible working hours and quality circles. Outside the company there is the possibility of coordinating with selected competitors in order to gain a certain freedom within the pricing policy.

Optimization possibilities include fixed assets as well as working capital investments. When it comes to industrial plants the disinvestment of certain real estate would not only free up funds but also open up rationalization possibilities to re-conceive production. In terms of working capital optimization possibilities include just-in-time management to be arranged with suppliers as well as reallocation of the production planning system. If we look at cost of capital we see a very far-reaching measure, the possibility that the company could go public. In order to optimize the tax situation the development of new structures within the company need to be discussed, particularly the idea of turning the present divisional structure into a holding structure. To a lesser

TABLE 3.7 Valcor matrix of corporate strategies for a supplier of power engineering

Value potential / Value generators	Restructuring potential	Financing potential	IT and logistics potential	Human resources potential	Cooperation potential
Sales growth	Autonomy of core competence 'Electronics'	Granting more favourable payment targets/ conditions	Networking customer service IAS-System	Incentives for sales force, client-oriented training	Takeover of competitor A to gain market share
Profit margin	Merger of testing activities	Hedging against currency risk	Computer integrated manufacturing (CIM)	Flexible working hours, quality circles	Agree pricing policy with selected competitors
Investments working capital/ fixed assets	Disinvestment of the estates X and Y sale of components division	Sale of property and leasing back	Reducing working capital through PPS	Strategic personnel planning	Arrange just-in-time operations with suppliers
Cost of capital	Going public	Improvement in relations between investors, conservative profit distribution	Software-aided cash management	Separation of treasurer and controller, banking contacts	Exploit leverage potential of takeovers
Income tax rate	Holding structure	Increase in percentage of loan capital	Tax planning programme	External tax specialist	Tax advantages through cooperations in the former eastern part of Germany

extent, more intensive cooperations with companies in the former eastern part of Germany could offer tax advantages.

The Valcor matrix is eminently suited to generating possible corporate strategies as a sort of structured brainstorming. It also facilitates the discussion of strategies which are often taboo within the existing setting of certain corporate cultures. The matrix enables everything to be looked at objectively, as it is clear from the very beginning that it simply offers a list of strategies from which a choice can be made. In making a choice both the corporate policy and the stakeholders' interests must be considered, as set out at the beginning of the strategy process. On the other hand, the strategies will be judged on their potential to generate future free cash flows, which makes many of the suggestions obsolete. I will set this out in detail in the *Evaluating strategies* section of this chapter.

If value potentials stand at the centre of the first two approaches in the development of corporate strategies, then core competences and the value chain of the company are approaches three and four. The *core competence approach* aims to use every capability of the company right across the business units and to enable product innovations in different sectors to be carried out at speed. Figure 3.24 illustrated the example of a capital goods company. It shows how core competences can be outlined as well as which general or specific capabilities are required in the area of these competences. Figure 3.38 looks at this company again and shows its every product innovation and how each one arose and will arise in connection with its core competences.

The three core competences of the company are expanded in such a fashion that step-by-step integrated solutions can be offered. While the competence welding leads to components and the competence of mechatronics leads to machines, the competence of systems technology makes the production of turn-key plants possible. These core competences have been moved to the different strategic business units of the company, so to integrate them means taking the point of view of the company as a whole. Today the company is organized according to the logic of strategic business units. But now structural changes emerged which could lead to a reorganization according to core competences. The company has received considerable strategic input from this re-direction and created several product innovations – something which would not have been possible with the previous structure.

The last approach to developing corporate strategies is the *value chain based operating procedure*. As Figure 3.25 illustrated, in the analysis phase of the strategic methodology a strength/weakness profile was set up for every single link in the value chain. Now strategies or – on an operational basis – measures will be assigned to the individual positions

FIGURE 3.38 Core competences and product innovations of an investment goods company

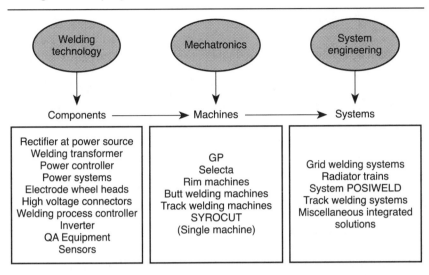

in this profile. Figure 3.39 looks at the supplier to the print industry and shows how the process works. This particular link in the value chain is looking at the area of service, sales and business logistics. The client structure is considered to be mediocre, which would make carrying out an ABC analysis worthwhile. The exchange service was considered to be positive, as were the concentrated sales and service networks and also customer service. The company's own products were considered to be excellent when it came to total solutions; however, this was not the case with commercial transactions. So the company's own products are to be promoted, commercial transactions, on the other hand, should be suspended. The delivery service and ability to stick to the deadlines were considered to be problematic, the price-performance-ratio with regard to business logistics was also found wanting. In this case the introduction of a PPS and a value analysis would bring about the desired improvement.

Another possible procedure based on the value chain could be developed in support of Figure 3.17. In that Figure the company's cost structure according to value-added steps was compared to that of the competition. On the basis of this comparison it is possible to develop strategies which lead to a cost optimization of the individual links of the value chain. This procedure could be interpreted as bench marking, in that the company's own performance is compared with the best in their sector leading to the development of a corresponding set of measures.

FIGURE 3.39   Strategies of a supplier to the print industry based on their value chain

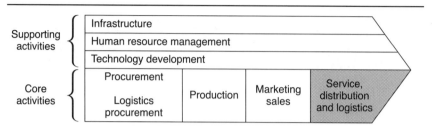

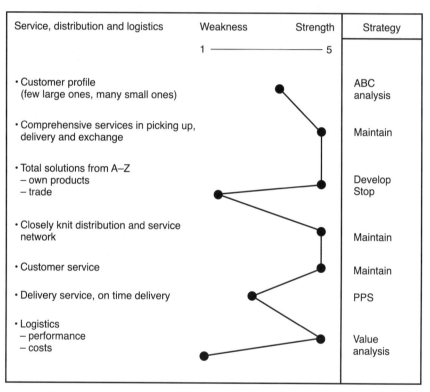

When seeking strategies using the value chain method the boundaries can often become confused between strategies and operative business. In the strictest sense an ABC analysis, a PPS and a value analysis cannot be described as strategies. However, it is not possible to avoid such a blurring of the edges as the value chain takes such a detailed look at the various areas of the company.

The multiplication concept, the value creating strategy approach, the core competence concept and the value chain approach all offer a fully developed range of instruments with which one can develop corporate strategies. Yet I have to say that not all strategic potential at this level is used up. There are further possibilities which I will tackle later on under the heading 'Restructuring Strategy and Cooperation Strategy'. Before we come to that, however, we must apply the processes mentioned above to the DELTA study.

Strategic study DELTA – development of a corporate strategy

At the corporate analysis stage, DELTA proved to have value potentials in the following areas: sales market, purchasing, human resources and management, acquisitions and restructuring as well as business logistics and IT. DELTA chose the value creating approach as a strategic concept and developed a corresponding Valcor matrix. This is set out in Table 3.8.

The individual strategies speak for themselves. It is interesting to note that here the so-called 'soft' factors also prove themselves to be useful, namely the aspects of the workforce and management. Whether these strategies will actually prove to be successful in terms of increasing the value of the company will be discussed in the *Evaluating strategies* section of this chapter.

Development of restructuring strategies

The whole point of a corporate strategy is to increase the value of a company. As Figure 3.40 shows, integral corporate strategies represent an important but not necessarily only possible starting point for the company to achieve this goal.

If we start with the present-day value of the company, the first step is to realize the value increase potential of the business strategies. The second step is to define the strategic direction based on the previously introduced integral approaches. Yet this does not exhaust the whole range of value increasing possibilities. There are other possibilities, such as restructuring or cooperations with other companies.

There are three main paths for *restructuring*, according to the logic of integrated value management thinking:

■ investment/disinvestment of fixed assets and net working capital;

■ reorganization of the company or some of its parts;

■ optimization of financing and taxes.

TABLE 3.8 Valcor matrix of DELTA

Value potential Value generators	Sales market	Procurement	Employees/ management	Acquisitions/ restructuring	Logistics/IT
Sales growth	Specialist products/ system solutions	Backward integration (paper production)	Incentives programme	Further takeovers of European companies	Improvements in marketing/ distribution/ organization
Profit margin	Optimisation of product range	Central purchasing	Quality circles	Reduction of production depth	Introduction of PPS, MIS, DB-calculations
Investments: – working capital – fixed assets	Closing down field warehouse	Just-in-time operations	Strategic personnel reserves	Sale of non-essential business assets	Use of second-hand machines
Cost of capital	Optimization of customer credit standing	Cash management	Maintaining good relations with banks	Leverage capital	Application of sensitivity models
Income tax rate	Central trading company	Central purchasing association	Tax specialists	International group structure	Computer-aided tax planning

FIGURE 3.40   Strategic approaches for increasing the value of the company

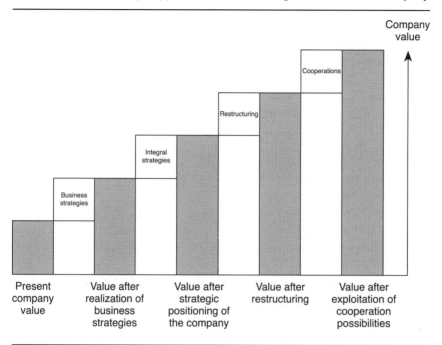

In Figure 2.17 on p. 43, I introduced value generators as the starting point for corporate strategies. One of the most important executive decisions is the establishment of an *investment policy*. From that the importance of the value generators 'investment in fixed assets' and 'investment in net working capital' can be established. As practical experience has shown it is investment policy which has a great leverage effect on the value of a company. That this lever is not used as effectively as it could be has many different reasons. In comparison to the USA, where disinvestment of those parts of a company which are considered to be under-achieving is quite normal, we find it difficult in Europe to come to terms with such disposals. A disinvestment is often interpreted as a confession of defeat or of managerial weakness. So many European managers continue with a forward-moving policy despite all signals pointing to the necessity of a parting of the ways.

Another reason for this is the yardstick used to measure the success of the individual parts of a company. If I refer you back to the examples in the *Integrated value increase* ... section of Chapter 2, the problem is caused by judging success based on the criteria of a profit-oriented return on investment (ROI). At first glance any business activity can seem to have a positive ROI, but if we look again in terms of value increase the positive quickly becomes a negative. An undifferentiated focus on the usual profit margins can lead to resources being misplaced or to a failure to make disinvestment decisions vital to the survival of the company.

One of the obstacles to a good disinvestment policy is the fact that in Europe there is no clear distinction between operations and non-operative activities. These must be differentiated before developing and carefully assessing thought-out measures to increase the value of a company. Often candidates for disinvestment can be found which then frees up resources for the main business.

Based on value management considerations, investment and disinvestment decisions can be objectified to form an essential part of a corporate strategy. That I speak here of investments and disinvestments shows that all investment decisions need to viewed from the same perspective. However, investments usually mean acquisitions in terms of the company as a whole, so I will turn to this subject in the next section: *Determining cooperation strategies.*

First, let us look at Alusuisse-Lonza (Haerri, 1991) as an example of a company which has lined up its investment and disinvestments policy according to value management thinking. After the Swiss conglomerate sustained a loss of nearly sFr700 million following a weakness in the aluminium market, its new management decided to restructure. The objectives were:

- reduction of a one-sided dependence on the aluminium business;

- separation from those areas which were not bringing in an adequate return;

- disinvestment of those businesses for which Alusuisse-Lonza was not a natural owner;

- adjustment of the management structure.

One part of the project involved a major investment-disinvestment decision. In their portfolio Alusuisse-Lonza had a US-based manufacturer of automotive parts which they had acquired in 1980. The question arose whether Alusuisse-Lonza should continue to be active in this industry – which would require additional investment of US$100 million over the next three years – or whether they should part from this company and diversify into another industry. It was a simple choice between a forward strategy and a disinvestment, the latter of which would free up resources which could then be allocated elsewhere.

As an alternative, Alusuisse-Lonza considered entering the packaging industry. Table 3.9 show a comparison of the industries that were considered.

At first glance, Business A looks the more attractive, but the pendulum swings towards Business B if we look at the ratios. The scepticism set out in the *Integrated value increase . . .* section in Chapter 2 points towards profit and profit-related factors as a yardstick for corporate success as well as consideration of the considerable future investments demands closer inspection. And more detailed evaluation reveals the following: the stagnant, relatively small market offers few chances of growth and the essential expansion of redistribution channels means going into an area that Alusuisse-Lonza knows very little about. What is

TABLE 3.9 Comparison of investment/disinvestment alternatives of Alusuisse-Lonza (Haerri, 1991)

	Business A (car accessories)	Business B (packaging)
Turnover (Mio $)	900	230
Earnings before interest and taxes (% of turnover)	5.1%	4.5%
RONA (% of net assets)	12.0%	9.1%
Market appeal	Market size $5 to 6 billion Stagnating market	Market size $100 billion Growing market
Competitive position	A is market leader Necessity of developing new distribution channels	Alusuisse-Lonza is technology leader
	No direct relation to other Alusuisse-Lonza activities	Related to other Alusuisse-Lonza activities
Inventory/sales ratio	3 times per year	8 times per year
Investment requirements	100 Mio $	

more, car accessories are not a core business of the company. The packaging business on the other hand is distinguished by a large expanding market, it shares many common factors with the present day Alusuisse-Lonza activities and requires a lower working capital as its stock turnover is very fast.

On the basis of these considerations Alusuisse-Lonza decided to sell the automotive parts business and to invest in the packaging industry. Although at that time the first business appeared to be more attractive financially, from the strategic point of view the second business was undoubtedly sounder. This decision based on value management considerations proved to be invaluable to Alusuisse-Lonza. Since then the company has invested further in the packaging sector, enabling packaging to became the third most important area of this company, alongside its aluminium and chemical activities.

So what then is the system used to develop an investment/ disinvestment policy? The first step is to look at the individual business units and see whether they, together with their strategies, would increase the value of the company as a whole. The *Evaluating strategies* section of this chapter will look at this procedure in detail. On top of this direct approach a tool has been developed in corporate practise which facilitates the search for candidates for investment/disinvestment and this is set out in Figure 3.41. It was this tool that ABB Asea Brown Boveri used to examine all their businesses in order to see which should be developed in future and which should be disposed of. The central question in the process is: are we the natural owners of this business?

FIGURE 3.41 Determining the 'natural proprietor' as a basis for investment/disinvestment decisions

Relative capability to realize potentials for value increase	Best owner	Maximizing cash flows (minimal investment)	Medium priority (investment)	High priority (investment)
	One of many	Liquidation (disinvestment)	Disposal (disinvestment)	Disposal or development (disinvestment/ investment)
		Low	Medium	High

Potential for value increase

In order to determine the natural ownership the value potential of the business has to be investigated and then the relative capability of the company to exploit this potential has to be judged. If the value potential is high and the company dominates this business better than any other, then it obviously has a high priority and is a candidate for investment. If the value potential is low but at the same time the company is considered best suited to running it, then the business should be viewed as a cash cow and supplied only with minimal investment. If the value potential is middling to low and a third party has a better capability profile, then a disinvestment cannot be avoided. And let us not forget that if the potential is extremely low then hardly anyone will be interested in the company. In this case the best option is liquidation.

The situation with a company that has a high value potential but which a third party would be better off owning is much trickier. The question of disinvestment has to be taken very seriously – perhaps a clever investment policy could build up the necessary capabilities. If the above considerations on investment/disinvestment raises questions about other parts or businesses of the company, then the question must also be asked from other perspectives. One concerns operational formulation of questions on working capital management and the other questions the existence of the company as a whole and looks at the possibility of breaking it up.

Working capital management means optimizing investments in new working capital. On the whole, this way of increasing the value of a company is not used often enough and it is only very occasionally mentioned when strategies are discussed. When the future effects of strategic alternatives are under discussion it is mainly profit development and investment in fixed assets which are considered. The effects on net working capital become submerged or are neglected altogether. Yet this factor can be a decisive influence on the value increase. Here the following questions come to the fore:

- How do we structure our cash management in the conflicting areas of liquidity and interest loss?

- What are the basics of our debtor management?

- How can we keep our stock of goods low without affecting customer satisfaction?

- How can we improve our terms when it comes to suppliers?

One approach to help the value generator 'optimization of the net working capital' is the just-in-time principle. Here the stock of goods is delegated back to the supplier. One example I can quote is the car industry. Suppliers leave their lorries circling around outside the factory area until they are called away by radio. This shifting of the goods onto the street creates a cost curbing (and thus a value increasing) effect for the car manufacturers. From the macro point of view however these practices should be questioned carefully, especially if the company is pursuing a stakeholder approach. Not only must the suppliers suffer consequences that are out of all proportion but the environmentally damaging effects of the 'travelling warehouses' also have to be considered.

The most extreme variation on the disinvestment theme is the break up of the company. Within this there are further possibilities: the creation from one company of two independent companies with different briefs and the division of the company into individual business units in order to put them up for sale. I am not going to go into this approach now as it really is part of the owner strategy and will be dealt with in section 3.6.

When investment/disinvestment strategies are developed one is in fact taking the first step in the direction of restructuring the company. The next step is the *organization* of the company – in all its structuring as well as its processing aspects. The adequate organization of the company is not only an indispensable precursor to conversion, it also represents an important value potential. The first function of the organization is discussed further in the *Realisation and future development of strategies* section of this chapter, when implementation of the chosen strategies is discussed.

First of all I would like to consider organization as a value potential. In what way can a company exploit this value potential? Table 3.10 shows us. The value potential of the organization is compared to the company's value generators in accordance with the principle of the Valcor matrix set out in Table 2.2.

Unfortunately, the allocation of organizational measures to the individual value generators cannot always be done so precisely, often one particular measure is a moveable feast between different areas. The decisive factor answers the question: where can the greatest leverage effect be achieved? A good example of this is time management. Time management is an organizational concept to speed up all processes from development through to delivery to the customer. Its main purpose is to eliminate any 'dead time' during which the product cannot create any value or is simply stored somewhere. As a general rule the production of goods and services, i.e. the really value creating activities, only takes up 5 to 10 per cent of the whole processing time. That is why carefully carried out time management can make huge savings. This also means that products and services get to the customer much faster, which is a powerful competitive tool.

TABLE 3.10   Organizational corporate strategies

Value potentials Value generators	Organization
Turnover growth rate	■ Time management ■ Core competence organization ■ Market-related alliances ■ Profit-centre organization ■ Multi-domestic organization
Profit margin	■ Lean production ■ Overhead cost value analysis ■ Target costing ■ Horizontal organization ■ Dismantling hierarchies (flat organizations)
Investments (WC, FA)	■ Just-in-time management ■ Outsourcing ■ Divesting non-essential business assets ■ R&D/product alliances
Cost of capital	■ Holding structure ■ Risk-optimizing legal form ■ Corporate banking
Income tax rate	■ International group structure ■ Central trading and purchasing firms

Top executives at Hewlett-Packard believe that a few months delay in placing a newly developed computer onto the market has a more serious effect than say massively overdrawing on the development budget. That is why the right place for this organizational measure is at the top of the matrix. To have a product in the marketplace before the competition means the ability to generate turnover and to increase market share. The corresponding cost advantages in terms of production have a much smaller influence on the value increase of a company. Stalk and Hout (1990) point out that using this concept in different industries can mean a quantum leap for a company. Matsushita was able to bring down its production time for washing machines from 360 hours to two hours; Harley Davidson no longer requires 360 days to manufacture a motor bike, it needs only three; and in 1995 it will take Toyota only three days to deliver a car fitted exactly according to the customer's specifications.

Another value generator in line with the concept 'turnover growth' is the core competence – organization. By building up the the core competences a company can be organized in such a way as to direct all available know-how towards the development of new products and services in these areas. For example, if we work on the basis that Daimler-Benz's core competence is drive motors for various vehicles and planes then this know-how, which is spread throughout the company, can be activated by managers at any given time and used to launch new products. In Figure 2.18 I showed how Canon was able to use its core competences of precision optics, precision engineering and micro electronics.

Marketing alliances are another measure with an effect on turnover. Companies which have little in common often enter into cooperations in order to develop new markets or to have quick access to distribution channels. An example of this kind of marketing alliance is the cooperation between Mannesmann-Kienzle and the Digital Equipment Corporation. The former specializes principally in computer systems for small and medium-sized companies whereas the emphasis of the latter is on official bodies, large conglomerates and universities. DEC hopes that this alliance will enable them to gain a foothold in the lucrative medium-sized company market segment, in particular in the former East Germany. Mannesmann can offer DEC a fully developed marketing network in Germany and at the same time they will profit from the technological know-how of their new partners. In this case the structuring principle is symbiosis; each company profits from the other without losing their own identity. In the next section I will go into alliances and similar cooperations in more detail.

In most cases it is also value-increasing for a company to single-mindedly orientate itself towards a profit-centre organization. On the one hand, the autonomization of business activities enables turnover and cost to be specifically targeted and on the other the building up of 'companies within the company' develops individual initiative, which in the end reduces everything down to a better running of the business. Bühner (1990) goes one step further and proposes a transition from profit centres to value centres. The yardstick for success is no longer profit or return on investment, but the achieved free cash flows and thus the coverage of the capital costs. The German conglomerate Haniel is one of the most advanced companies in this regard. Yet even Haniel discovered how difficult it is to draw a clear line between areas of operation and to agree tailor-made cost of capital rates. The management of Haniel are convinced, however, that this alignment has considerably promoted thinking in value terms within the company.

The multi-domestic form of a company is also related to turnover and turns the principle 'Think globally, act locally' into a reality. The perfect example of this is of course the much-vaunted Asea Brown Boveri. This company does everything to find the optimum market position for each of its 1500 local companies and its 4500 profit centres in order to get as close to as many customers as possible. The coordinating structures of the worldwide matrix organization are of a supportive character and should help the whole to become more than simply the sum of its parts. This organizational form opens up considerably larger turnover potential than more centralized company structures which do not take the basic principle of customer access seriously.

Profit margin is another important leverage factor in using organization as a corporate strategy. At the centre is professional cost management. The concept which has been used the longest and is perhaps the best known is the overhead value analysis, which is also known as zero-based budgeting. The aim is to reduce heads of steam which build up during the good times and to remove cost build ups. In order to do this emphasis is laid on the relationships between the parts of the structures being examined – in accordance with the principle of network thinking. The targets are the functions and processes whose cost-performance ratio needs to be examined. The first question that has to be asked is: what is fundamentally necessary to fulfil a particular function or to adequately carry out a particular process. It is not just a matter of cutting back anything that is unnecessary, it is also a matter of priming functions which are crying out for expansion. A good example of such a new direction is the MOVE Programme of Swissair. Over the years the Swiss airline expanded its personnel quite liberally until they reached a point where intensive competition made slimming down essential. Swissair took to the task with alacrity and the result is that today internal conditions are better than ever enabling them to survive deregulated competition.

More recently other concepts and processes have been developed which continue the tradition of the overhead value analysis and integrate new aspects. Key words here are: business process re-engineering; target costing, flat structures and horizontal organization. In each case it is a matter of increasing efficiency by reducing bureaucracy and by targeted cost management. As an example of this approach we will look at *horizontal organization* which heads in the same direction as *business process re-engineering* as set out by Hammer and Champy (1993).

According to Ostroff and Smith (1992) the main classification criteria are not the hierarchically ordered units of a company but rather the processes which make their way horizontally through those units. Every single important company process has someone responsible for it, who looks after it from beginning to end. Such a process could be the ordering process. The optimization criteria here is to guarantee a smooth and speedy passage from receipt of the order through to delivery to the customer. In the US several companies have already organized various units according to this principle, among them Motorola and du Pont. And it is self-evident that this process enables different aims to be achieved, for example closeness to the customer, reduction of hierarchical levels or the motivation of those responsible for the process.

When it comes to investments it is important to differentiate between measures to optimize fixed assets and to optimize net working capital. Measures to optimize net working capital were presented in previous sections. In particular it is the just-in-time concept which has to be assessed, as it requires a number of structural and processing adjustments. In the organizational concept of optimizing fixed assets there are two approaches I would like to discuss here on top of R & D and production alliances, which I will be dealing with later. These two approaches are outsourcing and spinning off of non-operative business assets. By outsourcing I mean services which were previously carried out internally but which will in future be contracted externally.

There is an interesting variation on this theme – a company sector is made independent but the parent company still has access to their services in future. Let us look at the example of Sulzer Informatics. The IT department of this important Swiss engineering company was made legally independent and was divested. Sulzer still gets its IT services from this company, although it pays the market price for them. Sulzer Informatik on the other hand also services third parties who are delighted to use the know-how potential of the former IT department of a conglomerate. Even outsourcing kills several birds with one stone. Not only does this reduce investment intensity but it also promotes management. In market terms both sides gain.

It is here that corporate divestment can open up the way to new perspectives and can steer management towards asking key questions about a company. If, for example, the general importer of a leading German make of car uses its own real estate in central Zurich as a show room and what is more, uses it very intensively, then from the value management point of view this could not be seen as optimal. If the showroom was moved to the edge of the city and the real estate rented or even sold then considerable funds would be freed for operational business. It is often a company's traditional outlook which stands in the way of such considerations.

Cost of capital is the next focus of the corporate strategy relevant to organization. The examples used in the *Future free cash flows as a measure of value increase* section of Chapter 2, all lead one to surmise that one way of increasing the value of a company is to reduce company risk and thus bring down the cost of equity. The possibility of achieving optimum loan capital costs is an added bonus. The problem of risk is particularly marked for conglomerates. If a company with a high risk profile is absorbed into the portfolio of a conglomerate then the total profile is geared towards this weakest link. The expression 'conglomerate discount' means that investors must reckon with the possibility of one company's unfavourable developments affecting all the others.

Philip Morris is a very good example. Recently this company has developed away from purely tobacco goods and is now a multi-faceted conglomerate. Today Philip Morris has a strong presence in both the brewing industry and the food processing industry. One important indicator of this turnaround is the new chief executive of the company. For the first time the chief executive's previous experience was not in the tobacco industry but in the food industry. Despite this development the cost of equity is still very much geared towards the cigarette industry. This is because in the eyes of investors there is still the possibility that a tobacco product liability case could affect all the other companies.

A high cost of capital always means low value increase. Different companies have tried to gain a handle on this problem by means of organizational and legal constructions. However, the most effective solution is to break up the conglomerate, a solution which does not appear opportune to Philip Morris – for whatever reason. There is another possible way out: keep the holding structure but make the individual parts of the company legally independent units.

In a slightly different connection the high expectations of holding structures were dampened somewhat last year in Switzerland. The Credit Suisse Bank group built up a holding structure whose expressed purpose was to offset the underlying of equity guaranteeing applicable to banks, at least for those companies which were not active in the banking sector. The Swiss Federal Appeal Court, however, was not of the same opinion and would not allow CS-Holding to release a company such as Elektro-watt from its equity guaranteeing. Despite this setback it is still an excellent idea to develop organizational and legal structures which bring about a relaxation in the cost of capital.

Recently, many companies have gone over to the idea of setting up their own corporate banks, thus bringing the experts in optimum financing under their own roof. Of course this avenue is only open to the largest conglomerates who have the necessary means to fund such a step. Perhaps other companies will also be able to learn from the experiences of these front-runners.

Another approach in this mould is the corporate tax rate. There is a range of possibilities here in the shape of international group structures as well as the tax favourable construction of central trading and purchasing companies. These possibilities are nothing new but in general they were never fully exploited. Tax considerations have up until now rarely been coupled with value potential considerations. But it is precisely a clever tax construction which can lead to much greater value increase, particularly with regard to acquisitions than say, increasing market share through much hard work. There is no point in setting out examples of international tax constructions as many of the large conglomerates have such clever and complicated structures that it would be impossible to add anything new. What is more, one requires such a specialist knowledge to understand and discuss these structures. So a value increase strategy in this matter could be to place a tax specialist on the management team.

As well as all the possible organizational corporate strategies there is a third category of measures which falls into the area of restructuring, and these come under the heading *financing and tax optimization.* For financing read optimization of the cost of capital. This has a major effect on increasing the value of a company. As I have already shown, a value increase is reached when the achieved free cash flows overtake the cost of capital. The lower the cost of capital, the greater the prospect of new strategies increasing the integrated value of a company. So how can such an optimization of the cost of capital be achieved?

The development of strategies starts with the cost of capital's determining factors:

- capital structure or financing ratio;

- cost of debt after tax;

- cost of equity.

The following example will show how the cost of capital can be influenced by the financing ratio:

- Cost of debt:

    - market interest rate   8 per cent

    - corporate tax rate   35 per cent

    - cost of debt rate after tax   5.2 per cent

    - cost of equity   12 per cent

- Cost of capital rate within financing ratio:

    - loan capital/equity capital 30:70   9.96 per cent

    - loan capital/equity capital 60:40   7.92 per cent

So exploiting the leverage effect means changing the financing ratio in favour of debt/equity. This can have an important influence on the cost of capital. At the same time one must watch out because increasing debt/equity can raise the financial risk again and thus increase the cost of capital. The most important thing is to mix and match for the best result. Possible ways of reducing equity capital include no longer carrying forward profits, dividing off real estate, sell and lease back operations or reducing capital. It is ideal if such equity capital reductions prove to be tax advantageous.

Table 3.11 sets out those strategic possibilities that directly influence debt and equity capital.

As I explained in the *Future free cash flows as a measure of value increase* section of Chapter 2 in some detail, the equity costs reflect to a great extent the risk profile of the company. Equity costs are higher if the risk in comparison to the whole market, the sector and the most important competitors is higher. Earlier, I mentioned 'conglomerate discount' in connection with organizational measures to increase the value of a company. If the portfolio of a company contains parts which have higher risk factors than other parts then the capital markets orientate themselves towards that risk category. I will mention again the widely diversified cigarette industries. Because of the risk profile of tobacco the product liability risk is always measured according to that. One way of reducing capital costs is to change the company's structure so that an optimal risk portfolio is developed.

Ways of doing this are, on the one hand, new organizational and legal constructions and, on the other, separating off the units that have a

TABLE 3.11 Financial strategic approaches for optimizing cost of capital (Weber, 1990)

	Determinants	Action
Cost of equity capital		■ Portfolio for optimum risk
	■ Company structure	■ Leverage capital, reduction of
	■ Capital structure	equity capital
	■ Financial tools	■ Listing on stock exchange, placement
Cost of loan capital		■ Asset and cash management
	■ Cost of capital	■ Debt mix, financial engineering
	■ Financial tools	■ Exploitation of tax differences and
	■ Legal forms and structures	privileges

particularly high risk factor. The key term here is portfolio optimization and many companies are increasingly turning their attention to this end.

Changes in the capital structure can also help bring down the cost of equity, as the table shows. Companies which have highly stable cash flows and a high break-even point are particularly suited to an above average level of debt thus making use of the leverage effect. The criteria for determining the desired financing ratio can be quickly derived from a more dynamic way of looking at things. In place of balance sheet figures and financing based on present lendings we look at market value, potential and risk assessments. Banks have also taken this into consideration and been converted. They do not simply take note of available securities but also consider the strength of a company's strategies.

Finally, I must mention in connection with cost of equity a third circumstance which is particularly relevant to Switzerland. It is to do with the usual equity tools. Registered shares are more expensive ways of creating equity than bearer shares. This is because registered shares are usually dealt with at a much lower market rate than bearer stock, the reduction can be as much as 25 per cent. This knowledge seems to be spreading as rules governing restrictions of transferability are eased and shares are sold back or supplied with options on stock. In this connection we can look at transactions carried out by Asea Brown Boveri Switzerland or Nestlè. The latter is a good example of how targeted placements on different capital markets and with different investors can be very advantageous.

Even the cost of debt can be affected by using the correct financial tools chosen from an ever increasing selection. Although loan capital is always 'on top' as it were, its application can be determined by the volume of capital tie ups or it can be placed where its tax-deductive capabilities have the greatest effect. Of course, the legal form of the company and its various parts, where it is based as well as its interrelations, all play a role. Servicing funds is important when it comes to optimizing costs. Capital requirements can be managed by multiple use and liquidation of non-operational assets through to cash management for minimizing the liquidity funds. Ever more sophisticated instruments are joining the usual loan financing for borrowing. These include zero bonds, swaps as well as currency and interest rate options, to mention just a few. Nowadays one talks about 'financial engineering'. Of particular interest is the external indebtedness of countries with high income tax rates. As the cost of debt after tax is relevant to the calculation of the whole cost of capital, as far as possible debts should be turned from tax-privileged holding companies, domicile companies or other companies into completely income tax-liable companies with high tax rates.

This brings us to another way of influencing the value of a company, namely *tax optimization*. It is unavoidable that all important business decisions have tax consequences, i.e. cash flow reducing consequences. Those managing a company have the strategic task of keeping fiscal consequences to the bare minimum and of avoiding superfluous tax burdens. I am talking about measures which either avoid taxes or delay them, perhaps the legal form or structure of a company. If used together with business activities and managerial requirements a company can be constructed in such a way that national and international tax duties fall away, and so all available tax benefits are fully exploited. It is worth mentioning here the construction of internationally active companies, the Swiss holding company benefits and the varying optimization possibilities extant within German legislation. It should be noted that the German tax law closely followed US tax law in terms of being amenable towards leveraged buyouts. Do not forget either that unincorporated trading companies such as GmbH & Co. KG can have very interesting tax constructions.

On top of integral corporate strategies there is also a selection of restructuring strategies which will increase the value of a company. Even then the potential for corporate strategies has not been exhausted. There is a broad field of further strategies available which I am going to discuss under the heading 'cooperation strategies'.

Determining cooperation strategies

The one thing that binds together all the corporate strategies introduced so far is consideration of a company as an independent unit fending for itself. The integral corporate strategies such as the restructuring strategy aim to strengthen the company on its 'stand-alone' basis. Yet every single company is able to increase its value either by cooperating with other companies or parts of other companies and it is quite possible to lay down the different stages of such a cooperation.

The loosest forms of cooperations in terms of commitment are alliances and joint ventures. The reasons behind a loosely binding cooperation with a partner include easy access to the market, gaining know-how or learning new capabilities. Alliances do not require reciprocal participation or even integration of new areas, they can also be set for a fixed period. This kind of cooperation is winning an increasing number of admirers. This is because mergers often require the surrender of some part of a company's corporate personality and frequently have national economic barriers to overcome. Alliances, on the other hand, have the many advantages of working together without the disadvantages of a strong commitment.

The next rung up the cooperations ladder is the acquisition of companies in a similar sector – companies are acquired which fit in with present business activities. The choice is based on an analysis of the acquiring company's own strengths and weaknesses as well as consideration of possible additions to the value chain. This means that a company's own know-how is immediately available to increase the value of the newly formed association. If there are any problems then they are usually to be found in the area of corporate culture, particularly if the management philosophy of the two companies are very different.

The most difficult kind of cooperations are diversifications into foreign sectors. In this case companies which have nothing in common with the traditional business of the company are acquired and absorbed. The possibility of these cooperations failing is very high. However, it would be wrong to damn all diversifications which have nothing to do with the traditional business of a company, although this damnation can be heard everywhere today. As I intend to show, well-prepared diversifications can be very successful if strategic common ground between the companies can be found.

I will introduce and illustrate the three kinds of cooperation strategies starting with the loosest one, an alliance.

What are the motives behind *strategic alliances* and what value-increasing potentials can they exploit? Bronder (1992) put together the connections as shown in Figure 3.42.

There are five basic motives behind a company's decision to enter into a strategic alliance, and all aim at the value generators of turnover growth, profit margins and investments. How long growth lasts is another important factor. This is a time benefit, as the mutual research and development efforts expand the length of time the value increase grows. The value increase effects of alliances were already set out in Table 3.10. However, I am going to look closer at these basic motives to reveal their value increasing effects.

The first aim of an alliance is a time benefit. Time has become the deciding weapon in terms of competition. A shorter product life-cycle requires faster development and quicker market entry. Even the shortest delay in placing a new product on the market can lead to considerable loss of profit. In many cases alliances are indispensable in raising the response speed of a company. Such amalgamations can lead to a jump in sales, particularly if the competition has not launched a similar product. Even the profit margin can be improved because the first supplier gains a

FIGURE 3.42 Value increase through alliances (Bronder, 1992)

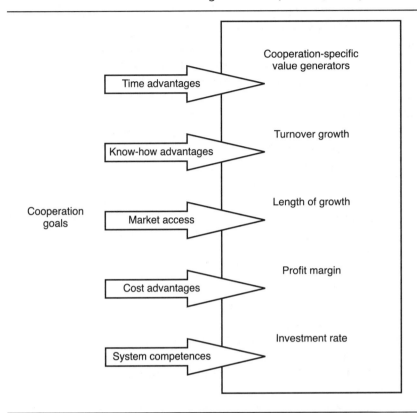

monopoly income. There are examples of gaining time benefits via alliances in the pharmaceutical and the semiconductor industry, as Bronder (1992) showed quite clearly. The British pharmaceutical giant Glaxo was one of the first in their sector to enter into alliances in the sales and marketing areas in the USA. Thus it was quickly able to catch up with the five year time advantage of its competitor Smith-Kline and to become the market leader in the area of gastro-intestinal medication.

Today the semiconductor industry is firmly in the hands of the Japanese. Despite this, European and US companies are constantly trying to break the stranglehold. Individual companies on their own do not have enough weight to succeed. In 1990 Siemens and IBM formed a strategic alliance to develop a 64-megabyte chip with the intention of starting production at the beginning of 1995, each bearing half of the R & D costs. By working together each of the cooperation partners expected to shorten development time by up to two years.

Know-how advantages are a further central motive for entering into alliances. Often the risks of an acquisition are considered to be too high because of the danger that the best experts might wander off. Know-how alliances aim to be mutual learning processes. A lack of knowledge in a particular technology or competence can be caught up. Again if we look at the pharmaceutical industry Glaxo is an excellent example. In 1990 a research alliance was set up with the US company Gilead and the Canadian company IAf Biochem. An alliance with the US biological company Icos was planned for 1992. The cooperation is carried out in areas of treatment stipulated by Glaxo. Specialist research groups concentrating on these areas will reduce development time considerably.

A third reason for alliances is market entry. Either high barriers of entry or protectionism from other countries can make a direct entry impossible. The turnover potential cannot therefore be fully exploited. It is possible to overcome these barriers by means of strategic alliances. An example of this is the US aviation industry. After US internal deregulation all indigenous airlines were considered to be equal. Foreign companies however were not allowed in, nor were they allowed to acquire an interest in a US airline. Under these circumstances an alliance was an ideal solution. Swissair joined forces with Delta Air Lines. The latter had a very strong presence in internal US air traffic but had a very weak presence in international traffic. Together these companies were able to offer a strong combined presence which brought additional turnover and market share to both parties.

A fourth motive behind alliances is cost advantage. The linking of activity fields of the value chain can result in scale effects and experience curve effects. Such cost advantages were surely one of the reasons behind the alliance between Siemens and IBM in the semiconductor sector. Both companies expect degressive effects from this cooperation as well as an essential high turnover of units. In the household goods sector it is worth mentioning the alliance between Bosch and Siemens, neither of whom could have survived on their own. As opposed to Electrolux which managed to build up a leading market position via acquisitions, Bosch and Siemens tried cooperation in order to attain the critical bulk.

A final aim of alliances is to increase core competences, particularly in the area of systems competence. Companies often have individual core competences at their disposal but find it difficult to put them together as a complete package. If we look at track transport technology it is clear that new high-speed trains could only be developed and produced sensibly as a complete system. Even the largest companies were unable to put together a total packet on their own, and so alliances were formed between ABB and Thyssen for example, and between Siemens and Krauss-Maffay/Duewag.

When looking at the value increasing effects of alliances one should not be blind to the downside, namely costs. Bronder (1992) talks about coordination costs, and then divides them into initiation costs, agreement costs, control costs and adjustment costs. Initiation costs include searching for information on purchasing a suitable cooperation partner. Agreement costs include the intensity and duration of talks until agreement is reached with a partner. Control costs originate from taking possession of and keeping to the cooperation agreement. Adjustment costs include adapting to a changed environment and to new corporate conditions. All these costs reduce the value created by an alliance. That is why it is best to specify them beforehand and avoid unpleasant surprises.

By *acquisitions,* as opposed to alliances, I mean a stronger intervention in a company which had previously been independent. By the time an acquisition has been fully integrated it will be clear whether the companies suit each other or not. I mean not only from the strategic and structural point of view but also at the corporate culture level. There is one essential difference between acquisitions in a similar industry and acquisitions in unrelated industries. Let us first look at those takeovers which have a direct connection with the business of the acquiring company.

As in all other corporate strategies, the acquisition of a company in a related industry should realize value potentials. In this case it is not a matter of the potential of one or the other company, rather it is a matter of the potential of the cooperation. For the company taking over the real question is not what can the new acquisition do for us? Rather the question has to be, what advantages does the company taking over bring to the new partner which enables them to work better together than on their own? From this perspective Porter (1987) differentiated between three different kinds of acquisition activities:

1   Joint implementation of horizontal synergies:

   – Starting with their own value chain, candidates are required to amplify their individual links optimally so that synergies can appear.

2   Transfer of know-how:

   – The company will look at acquisition candidates on the basis of their core competences and strategic positions for success, which they will then be able to improve by transferring know-how.

3   Exploitation of the restructuring potential:

   – The company will acquire companies which are ailing, under-developed or in a bad state or which contain a particular value-increase potential. The company sees its task as making the acquisition candidate successful by means of restructuring, by changing the management, by means of new strategies or by placing resources at its disposal.

Porter also laid down a fourth possibility: portfolio management. In this case a company acquires attractive healthy firms which will continue to be managed by their previous management team. The new purchase will keep their extensive autonomy and will be managed by means of targets. This direction, however, is more relevant to the activities of an investor and has less to do with the objectives of a corporate strategy.

If we now put these three approaches into the larger context of the acquisition as a means to increase value, then the interrelations can be set out as in Figure 3.43.

The vision of the company kicks off every acquisition process. This vision already helped break new ground in terms of expanding the present portfolio of strategic business units, the specific arrangement of the value chain as well as the targeted development of strategic positions for success and core competences. The portfolio of strategic business units and the value chain are the natural starting point for acquisitions in related industries. They make possible the development of horizontal strategies and determine the search for candidates with horizontal synergies, as I will show later. If this search does not produce the desired value potential then an eye has to be kept open for candidates for a know-how transfer. Again the starting point can be horizontal strategies or if these are not forthcoming, fields of activity with appeal. These can be derived from the strategic positions for success and the core competences.

A third possibility are candidates with restructuring potential, here the link is again appealing fields of activity. If candidates have been traced, their value increase potential determined and if the value increase comes up to expectation then the acquisition can go ahead. Of course the process does not run quite as simply and as smoothly as is suggested here, there are a number of traps which have to be watched out for – principally of the corporate culture variety – as Gomez and Weber (1989) showed.

The search for candidates suitable for a transfer of know-how and for candidates with restructuring potential follows roughly the same pattern as the search for integral corporate strategies based on core competences and restructuring strategies. The search for candidates with horizontal synergies has its own rules. Let us look at the acquisition process of a retail trade company to clarify what I mean.

During the second half of the 1980s the Schmidt-Agence AG was the undisputed market leader in the Swiss CTN business. By CTNs, I mean

FIGURE 3.43 Guide through the acquisition process

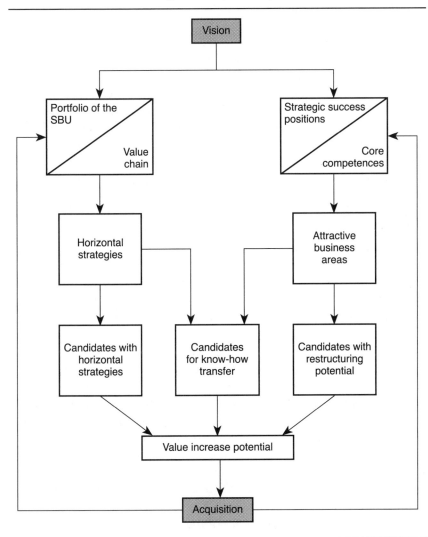

retail outlets selling newspapers and magazines, cigarettes and sweets. These can be found at all locations where there is passing trade, whether it be the smallest stand at the end of a bus route or a 'press centre' usually found at airports with a turnover of millions. The Schmidt-Agence AG (SAG) owned 1100 of these retail outlets and as a wholesaler and outside supplier they supplied a further 3000 retail outlets. Moreover, they also had 35 restaurants and were ranked the number two Swiss book wholesaler. The company had a workforce of 3300 and turned over about sFr720 million a year.

During the 1980s at the level of both business and corporate strategies, SAG consistently and strategically expanded. From about the middle of the 1980s their thoughts turned to acquiring retail companies in order to develop further value potentials. Of course, the first to come up was the second biggest company active in the Swiss CTN business. Yet this could not be realized for many different reasons, the main one being reservations about too large a concentration of market power in the Swiss press distribution business. There were also basic limits on acquiring foreign CTN businesses. In neighbouring countries either the industry structure was non-existent or was firmly in the hands of large publishers. When SAG looked at markets further field, for example in England, they discovered that the CTN business was subject to such completely different legal requirements that the process could hardly be called acquiring a business in a related area.

As it was not possible for SAG to get together with an entire company they started to look at acquiring parts or industries of a company. The starting point for a systematic acquisition process was the value chain of SAG, whose individual links were allocated search fields. This process is set out in Figure 3.44.

The principle of alignment with the value chain lies in identifying sections of the company whose value would increase if they were partnered up. The first area is resources where manufacturers of key products could be taken over. However, possibilities were limited. On the one hand, SAG had already decided – for corporate cultural reasons – not to enter the publishing business and on the other hand, tobacco products are always supplied by the large tobacco companies. That left SAG with manufacturers and wholesalers of confectionery, which only make up a small part of the whole range. Contact was made with a chocolate manufacturer but it did not lead to the desired result as the product did not constitute a large enough share of the CTN range.

The next option to be looked at in detail was the area of stocks, commissioning and IT systems. As essential business logistics are very costly, a cooperation with another company could have a scaling effect. Mail order houses were top of the agenda because they have excellent expertise in this area as well as the corresponding infrastructure. The outcome, however, was that no suitable partner with the desired synergy effects could be found in Switzerland.

The next link of the value chain was their own network of marketing outlets. Ideal partners would have been confectionery chains as well as related businesses such as dry cleaning or even shoe repairs and

FIGURE 3.44   Value chain of a retailer as a starting point for acquisitions

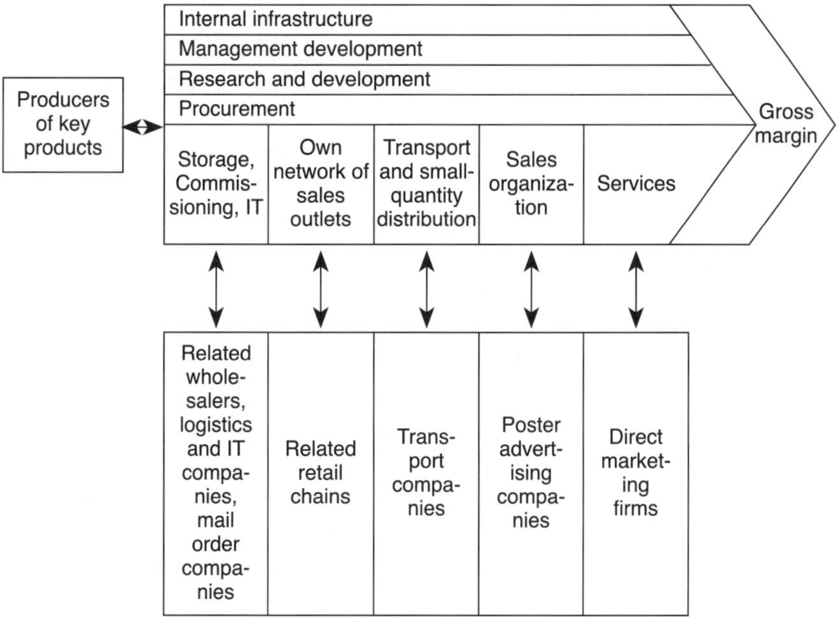

key cutting. Meetings were held with various companies, in Germany too, but these discussions led nowhere. The company appeared to strike gold in the area of low to middle-priced jewellery and watch retailing. Discussions with a company that had 30 retail outlets were progressing well until the very last minute when SAG were gazumped by another purchaser. Acquisition talks within the catering trade followed a similar pattern. Negotiations with a catering company of equivalent size were about to be finalized when the owner opted for a management buyout.

Another key area for CTN companies is transport and small-quantity distribution. Different companies were studied in detail but SAG reached the conclusion that the organization required for such an acquisition went beyond the brief. What was pushed forward however was an alliance in this area with the aforementioned second largest company. This led to important synergy effects and proved to be an excellent solution.

As SAG owned more than 1110 retail outlets the question then arose, could these not be used for advertising? Suddenly a potential candidate was found in a type of company which at first glance had no connection whatsoever with the existing company – a poster advertising company. If one read 'advertising space' for CTN outlet then this was an excellent possibility. So contacts were taken up with potential candidates and finally a poster advertising company was acquired. Of course earnings from CTN advertising was only a small part of the whole but this small part was an assured market.

The final question that needed an answer was whether links could be found to other CTN services? Under consideration was book wholesaling and a subscription business for magazines. In fact a suitable company was found that entered into a joint venture with SAG.

So what do we learn from this company's experiences? One thing is certain: several attempts need to be made before a successful acquisition can take place. The process was roughly the same for all attempts. So as soon as a suitable opportunity arose the company was able to act quickly. Moreover, the company learned more about its own business and how to make use of its strengths and weaknesses. Finally, the company was given a boost by the end result – important acquisitions and alliances.

In 1989 the owner sold SAG to another retail business. This company was in a position to purchase the second largest company in the CTN business as well. Thus they were able to realize those synergies which SAG had felt unable to because of their corporate cultural and social considerations.

The development of horizontal strategies is the most useful way to proceed when it comes to acquisitions in related areas. As Figure 3.43 shows, transfer of know-how and restructuring can also be considered as suitable links. For know-how transfer there is the following:

- marketing know-how;

- cost management;

- employee development;

- strategic know-how;

- asset and cash management;

- financial tools;

- tax construction.

For restructuring, the possibilities are as follows:

- amalgamation of administration;

- business process re-engineering;

- franchising;

- holding structures;

- leverage capital;

- disinvestment.

Buying into related areas does signify a certain distance from the existing business. Despite this, one is still on familiar ground, which is not the case when it comes to diversification. A targeted approach is absolutely essential in order to avoid copying the failures of many companies.

There are different kinds of diversifications: in-house innovations, licensing, alliances, spin-offs or acquisitions. These are often only half-hearted attempts to enter new markets. On the whole it is only by acquiring another company that enough influence can be achieved, thus creating a second or third string to a company's bow. It goes without saying that one has to advance with care. Figure 3.45 shows the steps that need to be taken. To start the diversification process it is essential to examine the core business closely. This means simply that business strategies and integral corporate strategies for the core business have to be in place before a new business can be considered. A strengthened core business provides the framework for establishing a diversification programme. Of course, the intended acquisition does not have much in common with the core business. However, this does not mean that diversifications can happen almost anywhere. It is more important to use corporate cultural standards as a gauge to see which industries and businesses are basically acceptable and which are impossible from the start. And at this point it is still not too early to think about value potentials. The search starts with the company's own capabilities and its aim is to discover value gaps.

The strategic analysis starts with these value gaps and identifies possible synergies and strategic common ground between the company and the acquisition candidate. This step is in fact at the very core of the diversification process and needs to be set out in detail. After this basic analysis comes the risk evaluation. This weighs up possible opportunities and threats of the proposed strategy. If the risk profile is justifiable for the

FIGURE 3.45 Stages of the diversification process (Gomez and Ganz, 1992)

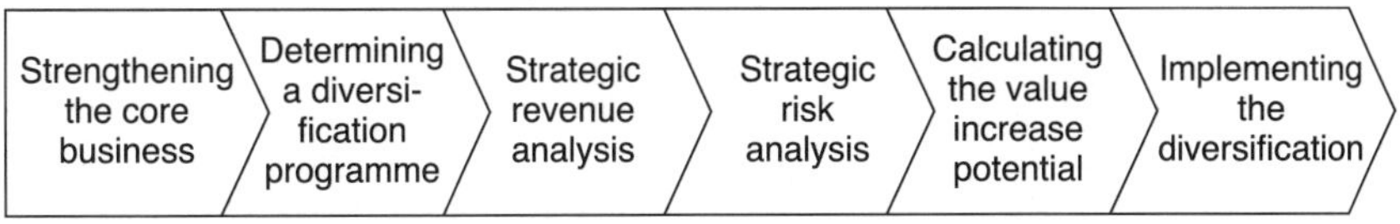

main company then the value increase potentials have to be worked out in detail. If they fulfil the expectations set out in the diversification programme, then steps towards diversification can be taken.

As I said, the success and the failure of the diversification process lies in the quality of the strategic analysis. Figure 3.46 shows the corresponding process for identifying the value increasing steps for diversifications.

In order to assess a candidate for diversification in terms of its value potential, it is important to detect internal improvements after adjusting any possible undervaluation. The next step is to identify operational synergies. There are relatively few synergies if we are talking about a real diversification. However synergies can be found if the administrative boards are combined for example, or if both companies use the same distribution channels or have similar sales or tax constructions.

The next step is to be found in integrating the organization or in re-defining the organizational interfaces. Organizational synergies can bring

FIGURE 3.46   Steps for increasing value through diversification (according to Copeland *et al.*, 1990)

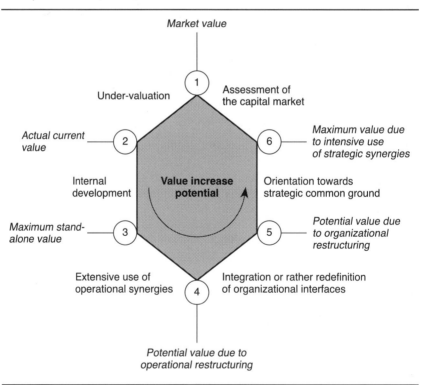

about great leaps forward if the integration is really successful. There are however few value increase potentials to be found if the newly acquired company is viewed simply as another satellite company and allowed its own autonomy.

The best reason for a diversification strategy is common strategic ground between the companies. If one company has excellent marketing prowess and meets a company with activities in a completely different sector whose whole operations are highly efficient but who do not have much marketing experience, then huge synergies can be realized in the area of marketing. Later on I am going to set out in detail the activities of Philip Morris in this field. This example shows how a pronounced value increase was obtained when the tobacco giant passed on its marketing know-how to an operationally efficient yet marketing-naive brewery (Miller beer). Strategic common ground might not be visible at first glance yet contributes considerably to the discovery of value gaps. And in the end it is the only rational reason for entering into the risky business of diversification.

To illustrate the value increase steps of operational synergies, of organizational restructuring and of finding strategic common ground I have set out possible measures in Table 3.12, ordered according to their value generators.

An excellent example of a successful diversification strategy is the tobacco giant Philip Morris. At the end of the 1960s there was a definite shift in the strategic environment and the first stagnation tendencies appeared. At this point many companies began to make unfocused attempts to enter new markets. Not so Philip Morris. It began to strengthen its core business while at the same time developing an organic diversification strategy. In terms of a differentiation strategy within the core business the company pushed the brand image of Marlboro and at the same time steadily increased productivity. The downside of this aggressive differentiation strategy was an extortionate advertising budget. Thus not only did they increase their market share they also greatly increased their marketing expertise, which is an excellent starting point for diversifications.

In the 1960s Philip Morris tried to diversify but they did so with the wrong focus on operational synergies. The company bought the US Safety Razor Company, which manufactured throw-away razors. Philip Morris saw synergies in using similar distribution channels to their own. However the hoped-for mass turnover did not materialize as the competition then introduced new technology for longer-life razors. In 1977 the two companies separated. The diversification was unsuccessful.

A new orientation for diversification strategies was based on identifying and realizing strategic common ground. It soon became clear

TABLE 3.12 Stages of value increase and diversification potentials

Potentials/Value generators	Operational synergies	Organizational restructuring	Strategic common ground
Turnover growth	System solutions Multiple distribution channels	Integration of related businesses Franchising	Marketing know-how Core competences
Profit margin	Purchase pooling Reduction in manufacturing depth	Backward/forward integration	Cost management Control systems
Investments	Central storage operations Combining administration	Divesting property Spin-offs	Asset and cash management
Cost of capital	Leverage capital Optimization of client portfolio	Risk-reducing organizational and legal forms	Equity capital instruments Corporate banking
Income tax rate	Central trading/ purchasing association	International taxation structures	Holding structures

that possible acquisition candidates should come from the consumer goods industry. If the end-products manufactured by this industry were not compatible with the tobacco industry and appeared at first glance to be heterogeneous, the deciding factor was that the necessary managerial capabilities were similar to those of the core business of Philip Morris. Consumer goods have a very long-term growth potential and thus possess great strategic appeal. What is often missing with consumer goods companies is brand cultivation as well as innovation and differentiation. This was precisely what Philip Morris had to offer as this was the essence of their core business.

In 1969 Miller Breweries was acquired. During the first phase Philip Morris placed considerable funds at Miller's disposal so that they could differentiate their product palette from their competitors. At the same time an aggressive marketing strategy was introduced. The only company to have a higher advertising budget than Miller was the market leader. The doubling of capacity required even further investment. Success slowly began to manifest itself and from the middle of the 1980s onwards Miller was in a position to finance the nine figure advertising budget from its own cash flow. At the end of the 1980s Miller had a market share of around 25 per cent and was the second largest supplier in the USA. Synergies were found even in the area of innovations. Experience gained from Marlboro's consumer-friendly flip-top packet and the marketing of lower-nicotine cigarettes helped Miller to introduce a smaller bottle and a low-alcohol beer. Both products were supported by an aggressive marketing policy and proved to be very successful.

Philip Morris discovered Seven-Up during their search for other candidates which shared strategic common ground and certain similarities with their previous diversifications. There were high hopes of functional synergies in the areas of production and marketing. Unfortunately, Philip Morris overlooked the fact that this market requires a quite different kind of advertising strategy. It was dominated by Coca-Cola and Pepsi, both of whom had access to a huge network of contractors with exclusive rights to these products who were therefore unable to sell other soft drinks. The key role that this distribution system played was overlooked and with it the fact that despite their synergies, both sectors possessed other key factors for success. Philip Morris duly disposed of Seven-Up.

Philip Morris now concentrated again on the food and kindred products industry. They were looking for companies which, although relatively ineffective in terms of their operations did possess strategic potential and shared strategic common ground. In 1985 they purchased General Foods, Kraft followed in 1988 and Jacobs Suchard in 1990. Philip Morris is now the second largest global supplier in this area. The importance of this is emphasized by the fact that the new Chief Executive comes from the food processing industry.

The example of Philip Morris shows that it is strategic common ground as opposed to operational synergies which are decisive in determining the success of diversifications. The development between 1979 and 1989 indicates the shareholders also profit from a successful diversification policy. The average growth rate was 30 per cent per year, much higher than with either the tobacco or food processing industry. Even the capital market acknowledged the success of the diversification programme. Since 1985 the relative price-earnings ratio has continually improved.

With the inclusion of a diversification strategy the portfolio of corporate strategies is now complete. As with business strategies, the extensive choice of proven tools available in this area enables companies to position themselves optimally. Until now this positioning had always been seen from the company's managers point of view. There are areas, however, where the competency lies elsewhere. An owner can keep certain strategic decisions to himself. The next step of the strategic methodology considers this perspective.

Creation of an owner strategy

A good understanding of the possibilities and intentions of the owner or owners is essential to the successful development of an owner strategy as part of the value management of a company. I include in this the 'division of labour' between management and the owner. The company is usually only one factor, albeit an important one, in the arena of the owner's interests and objectives. The status of the company can vary according to the owner's orientation. If the owner has a strong connection to the company and wants to leave it to his heirs then he will be thinking of security and maintaining its value. However, if he is interested in more power and a higher profile as a financier then increasing his own assets will be of primary importance. In the latter case the company is only of interest if its value can be increased over time. The duties of the owner towards the stakeholders is also important, by stakeholders I mean the management team, the workforce, customers and society. If he views the company as a quasi-public institution then he will take these stakeholders into consideration when making decisions. On the other hand, if he views the company as his personal property, as something he can do what he likes with, then as an investor he will only keep it in his portfolio for as long as it fulfils his value creation requirements. How the owner sees himself must be clarified before an owner strategy can be formulated as part of integrated value management.

The owner strategy should cover every aspect of increasing the value of a company within his authority as opposed to that which lies in the hands of management. The distinction between a corporate and owner strategy therefore depends on the division of labour between management and the owner. If the owner sees himself as an investor and financier then management has more room for manoeuvre than if he sees himself in the more traditional role as 'patron'. The boundaries between the two are a moveable feast and need to be assessed on a case-by-case basis. For the moment I am going to assume that the owner has allowed management considerable freedom when it comes to operational and strategic matters but has kept for himself any decisions which would fundamentally change the company as a whole. I include in the latter larger disinvestments, reorganization, acquisitions and financial transaction which have to do with the day-to-day running of the business or which give the business quite new dimensions.

This brings us to the sixth strategic principle.

Sixth strategic principle

The sixth strategic principle is: *In view of the owner's overall financial goals and his risk policy, it is essential to exploit his specific value potentials.*

Of course examples of the owner strategy will not be so comprehensive as were examples of business and corporate strategies. This is because many of the corporate strategy methods could just as easily be set out under this heading. Approaches tailor-made for the owner strategy have a rarity value in both practise and theory. Nevertheless, the process will be set out and illustrated with practical examples. The emphasis being on that part of the owner strategy relevant to the company.

As identified in the network set out in Figure 3.28 the different owner potentials are the starting points for strategy development. These were then evaluated as opportunity/threat profiles and set out in Figure 3.29. Broadly speaking, the owner potentials fall into three categories: restructuring potential, acquisition potential and financing potential. If you combine these with the two dominant aims of the owner, namely increasing value and optimizing risk, then the matrix in Table 3.13 suggests possible owner strategies.

Some of these owner strategies were already presented and illustrated with examples in the *Owner strategies for optimization of value and risk* section of Chapter 2. I will now expand on them further. If the restructuring potential is put in motion to increase potential then breaking up the company or parts of the company is the most obvious choice. Breaking up a company means to divide it into two or more independent units. Bühner (1990) used the example of Löwenbräu AG which was divided in 1982. The industries brewing and alcohol-free drinks went into one and real estate went into another independent company. These companies were called Löwenbräu AG (the new one) and Monachia Grundstück AG respectively. Before the announcement of this division the market capitalization of Löwenbräu AG was around DM211 million. After the division the total market value of Löwenbräu (new) and Monachia was around DM640 million. During this time the shareholders assets rose by more than 200 per cent.

A similar case is illustrated in Figure 3.47. The financier Icahn placed an advertisement in the New York Times of 26 April 1990 which was

TABLE 3.13   Company-related owner strategies for value increase and risk optimization

Owner potential/ Owner objective	Restructuring potential	Acquisition potential	Financing potential
Value increase	■ Breaking up the company ■ Disinvestment of parts of the business ■ Divestment/ sale of non-essential business assets ■ Reorganization for tax optimization	■ Takeovers to achieve market dominance ■ Acquisition into non-related businesses with value increase potential	■ Sale of a minority shareholding in the company ■ Application of equity capital instruments ■ Optimization of dividend policy ■ Corporate banking
Risk optimisation	■ Optimization of company portfolio ■ Reorganization for risk optimization ■ Change in legal form ■ Management buyouts	■ Takeover of companies with a low risk profile ■ Purchase and sale of minority shareholdings	■ Going public ■ Entering into joint ventures ■ External financial transactions

aimed at persuading shareholders to agree to splitting the US conglomerate USX (formerly US Steel) into two companies. He pointed out that the USX shares were only showing a fraction of the value increase which Marathon Oil would have shown had it been independent and had it grown at the same rate as other oil companies. Icahn therefore felt that the break-up of USX would bring about a considerable value increase for shareholders. Interestingly enough, the shareholders did not go along with this proposal.

The disinvestment of parts of a company has already been studied in the section on corporate strategies. However, let us take another look at the example of the Swiss-owned Holzstoff AG (today called Holvis AG). At the end of the 1980s this company got rid of its paper production

FIGURE 3.47 'Conglomerate Discount' of USX in comparison to the potential of an independent Marathon Oil (New York Times, 1990)

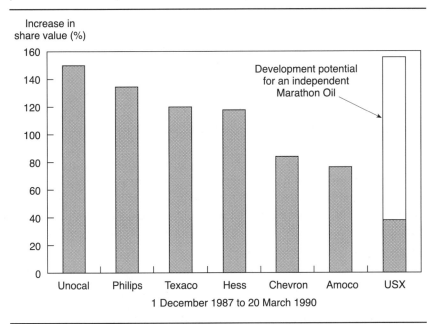

business and with it a turnover of more than half a billion Swiss Francs. It then purchased a US fleece production company which showed a much weaker turnover. As the total turnover was less the revenue picture improved no end, so that the disinvestment policy paid off.

The ability to spin off or sell operative assets lies principally with the owner. As a rule this is usually real estate and property which is either not used for business activities or used too little. When the proprietary family of the Swiss chain of department stores Oscar Weber gave up their business on the best plots and rented out the corresponding real estate to their competitors the value increase was the difference between profits from the department stores and income from the present day rents.

Reorganization for reasons of tax optimization are also a suitable tool for increasing value. It is for this reason that one Swiss retail chain divided their wholesale and retail business into independent units. They were then able to capitalize very cleverly on tax differences between the different Swiss cantons. Reorganizing and creating a holding structure, which enjoys tax privileges in Switzerland is another favourite measure.

The restructuring potential can also be used in other ways to optimize risk. Many companies have recently and actively been clearing out their company portfolios. The Swiss industrialist Stephan Schmidheiny has parted from the Eternit company which had a presence in many different countries. He considered that the risk was too great as it was not possible to replace the asbestos with a safe material in the time allowed and to become profitable in this time-span. It was under consideration of optimizing risk that the whole Anova-Group owned by Stephan Schmidheiny was reorganized and took a new legal form. As figure 3.5 on p. 77 shows, the Anova Group can be seen as a perfect compilation of holding structures. The aim of this construction is to avoid any danger of a domino effect should there be difficulties in one particular group.

Management buyouts also come under the heading of risk optimization and are a natural result of restructuring. As detaching one part of a company follows very controlled guidelines it is possible to keep any kind of future compensation demands to an absolute minimum. Management buyouts are becoming more important, particularly when it comes to less profitable parts of a company.

If the acquisition potential is set in motion within the framework of the owner strategy in order to increase value, there are usually two reasons behind this: one is to achieve market leadership in a particular industry, the other is to take over non-related businesses with considerable value potential. As an example of the former let us look to the Swiss financier Tito Tetamanti. He is in the process of carrying out an acquisition strategy for the express purpose of becoming market leader in the area of weaving machines. Initially he purchased the Swiss company Saurer, which is based in Arbon, then he took over the German weaving machine manufacturers Schlafhorst. The only thing stopping him from achieving his goal is the purchase of the engineering works Rieter in Winterthur. Already initial albeit unsuccessful discussions have taken place.

A good example of entering non-related markets is again Stephan Schmidheiny. When he took over the Eternit-Group from his father in 1974 he had two objectives: replacement of asbestos with a safe material and diversification of the company in order to reduce its one-sided dependence on the building sector. Efforts to diversify were carried out systematically and on a broad front. However, the first acquisition in 1978 still came as a complete surprise to lookers-on. Schmidheiny purchased the leading CTN chain in Switzerland. This was certainly a diversification into a brand new business. Schmidheiny, however, had discovered a considerable value gap, the company had no clear direction for the future in an already saturated market and it needed to introduce modern management and reporting systems. Over ten years he achieved a considerable increase in the value of the company and then he sold it on to the Swiss Merkur-Group for an excellent price. The reason for the sell-on was that Schmidheiny could not see enough possibilities for further value increase. On the other hand, the Merkur-Group could validate their own synergies.

Stephan Schmidheiny is an excellent example of how to work within the framework of a minority shareholding in a company. As Figure 3.5 on p. 77 shows, he has several minority shareholdings in important companies with leading global profiles such as Asea Brown Boveri, the Swiss watch company SMH and the above-mentioned Merkur Group. The minority shareholdings allow him to access the expertise of leading companies without having to risk taking on a majority shareholding. This exchange of know-how has to be seen as a give and take affair, so that the partner company in exchange also profits from Schmidheiny's expertise. This was clearly demonstrated by the merging of Asea and Brown Boveri.

Philip Morris is also an excellent example of how to use the acquisition potential to optimize risk. As the tobacco industry has a high risk factor, one of Philip Morris' main aims was to enter the food processing industry which has a relatively low risk profile. Activities in this sector now account for 50 per cent of the company's turnover. The risk strategy is beginning to show its true value.

Financial potential is number three in the list of owner strategies. Into this category fall the sale of a minority holding of the company and going public for reasons of value increase and risk optimization. Both methods serve to create equity capital and spread the risk load onto extra shoulders. The advantages of such transactions are immediately visible. So it is really quite extraordinary that, for example, Stephan Schmidheiny did not go for this potential. What held him back was the fact that he would have to disclose and justify his company's results. This disclosure could stop him from continuing to manage his company with the long-term in mind, which sometimes means he has to accept possible short-term setbacks. Third parties would hardly accept such oscillations as the capital market likes to see a steady growth. These considerations would not even arise in other companies, as the large number of companies that went public in the 1980s shows. That there has been a certain decline in recent years can be put down to a weakness in the capital markets at present.

I have already talked about the introduction of various equity capital tools. In Switzerland these include bearer shares, registered shares and participating receipts, let us not forget using corporate banking as a value increase tool either. So there is only one further tool in the palette of owner strategies which should be mentioned here and that is the optimal dividend payout policy. It is left to the owner's discretion as to what percentage of the dividends due to him are going to be taken out of the company or what percentage will be left with the company in order to strengthen its self financing power. This putative value increase strategy can also work the other way around as the development of the international oil giants shows. They placed these monies in different diversifications in such a way that did not increase the value of the companies which would have happened to the shareholders in the case of a dividend payout.

Finally, the financing potential can be used to optimize risk. We have already looked at the possibility of a company going public. There is also an advantage from the financing point of view in entering into joint ventures. This is because the high investment required for development and market entry can often be divided between the partners. This lowers the risk – as shown in the *Determining cooperation strategies* section of this chapter. In most cases joint ventures can be filtered through and prepared by management. The owner, however, is required to have the last word.

It is company-external financial transactions which lie completely outside management's area of authority. It is hard to imagine the management of the Swiss company Ems-Chemie buying shares in other chemical companies in order to make a market profit and thus achieve a value increase for their own company. Yet the owner of the company, Christoph Blocher, was able to do this and he did it very successfully. As I mentioned earlier, he realized a value increase of sFr70 million within a few years.

Strategic study DELTA – Creation of the owner strategy

For the owner of DELTA there are four potentials which could contribute to the formation of a strategy: acquisitions, joint ventures, financing and restructuring. The corresponding value creating strategies are set out in Table 3.14.

Once the owner strategy is formulated all the alternatives form a comprehensive future orientation of the company. In the next step these alternatives will be assessed from both a qualitative and a quantitative point of view. Then a definite decision can be taken on the future direction of the company.

Evaluating strategies

By successfully going through the previous strategic development process, a company is then able to make a choice between the different

STRATEGIC METHODOLOGY OF INTEGRATED VALUE MANAGEMENT

TABLE 3.14 Potential owner strategies of DELTA

Owner potential	Value increase through . . .
Acquisition	■ Entry into related industries (paper factories) and non-related industries (packaging machines) ■ Purchase of further European carrier bag manufacturers to extend the European network
Joint ventures	■ Merging with competitors of equal size for market coverage and realization of synergies
Financing	■ Sale of a minority shareholding ■ Going public
Restructuring	■ Sale of non-essential business assets (property) ■ Disinvestment of parts of the business

business strategies, corporate strategies and owner strategies. It is at this point that the question arises: what criteria should this decision be based on? In a very few cases it is quite obvious which strategy should be chosen and so no further systematic process is required. Yet even in these apparently obvious cases it is very easy to make the wrong decision, especially if intuition has been given free rein. In this analysis phase it is not possible to argue simply in cause and effect correlations. Instead the multi-faceted networking of the possible strategic effects have to be considered. And it is precisely at this point that intuition falls on its nose.

Strategies must be assessed from a qualitative as well as a quantitative point of view. A rough estimate of strengths and weaknesses is as ineffective as a purely figure-based assessment. If you look simply at the pounds, shillings and pence you lose many important angles. And although the examples I have listed reflect the importance of increasing the value and thus the shareholder benefits, it is still necessary to include the interests of the various stakeholders. Finally, the question has to be asked: does the strategy fit into its environment, i.e. does it correspond to the legal restrictions and cultural characteristics of the company? These requirements lead us to the seventh strategic principle.

Seventh strategic principle

The seventh strategic principle is: *Strategies have to be assessed from a qualitative as well as a quantitative point of view. It is as important to consider the interests of the various stakeholders as it is to use the company's own dynamics.*

Qualitative assessment of strategy

The qualitative assessment of business strategies, corporate strategies and owner strategies follows similar lines. Three questions need to be asked of every strategy:

- What strengths and what weaknesses distinguish this strategy?

- Does the strategy do justice to the interests of the different stakeholders?

- Is the strategy in accord with the company's own rules and regulations?

The determining of a strategy's strengths and weaknesses can either be purely descriptive or a more systematic approach can be made with the help of a value benefit analysis. The first process will be illustrated by means of the DELTA study, the second appears at the end of this section as Figure 3.48.

Strategic study DELTA – Qualitative assessment of strategies

Business strategies, corporate strategies and owner strategies have been developed for DELTA. The qualitative assessment of these strategies is set out in Table 3.15.

This strength/weakness profile enables initial conclusions about the potential direction for the company to be drawn. However, it is essential to check whether the stakeholders' interests have been considered and whether the company's own rules and regulations have been observed.

So what are the possible interests of the stakeholders? Investors want the strategies to bring about an increase in the value of the company. Employees are interested principally in security, but they also want interesting jobs. Suppliers desire continuity in their relationship to the buyer and competitors wish for fair competition. The terms in which these interests are expressed – 'interested in, desire', etc. – show that the stakeholders cannot actually push through their interests. They are reliant on the goodwill of the company. However, in the long term if these interests are not taken into consideration then the company will in fact be cutting its own throat.

TABLE 3.15   Qualitative assessment of DELTA's strategies

Strategies	Qualitative assessment	
	Strengths	*Weaknesses*
Business		
▪ performance leadership for paper bags	Know-how, protection of territory, quality image	Price of raw materials, paper bag = commodity, strong competition
▪ niche policy for plastic bags	Special bags, services, quality	Slight differences between market segments, strong competition, environmental problems
Corporate		
▪ development of purchasing power	Europe-wide presence	No integration with paper factories
	Purchase large quantities through purchasing with others	Strong competition
	Maintain cheap suppliers	Low price flexibility at top end
Owner		
▪ acquisition of non-related businesses (packaging machines)	Management know-how	Few synergies
	Financial resources	Specialist know-how missing
	Acquisition know-how	Lack of managerial capacity

So how are the strategies compatible with a company's own rules and regulations? Gomez and Probst (1991) came up with some rule guidelines which, if they are followed or neglected, can determine the balance of a strategy. I am going to illustrate some of these guidelines with the example of the magazine publisher, whose strategic alternatives were set out in Figure 3.35 on p. 133.

▪ *'Cut your strategies according to the complexity of the situation.'*
 Strategies should not be confused with recipes. If one wants them to be successful then they have to take into account the wide-ranging interrelations of a situation. If a general interest magazine wants to

keep its level of subscriptions simply by direct-mailing activities this is hardly likely to be crowned with success. Rather a concerted attack is what is needed: employment of representatives, direct-mailing activities, advertising and care of previous subscribers. The secret of success is not to ignore any single part of this mix.

- *'Growth not simply for its own sake.'*
  As in nature growth has to be for a reason. If growth is simply self-serving then it will ail and finally collapse. This is what happened at the end of the 1970s with the large US weekly magazines, *Life*, *Look* and *Saturday Evening Post*. On the sales front and in the advertising market these magazines enjoyed unprecedented success and grew at a two-figure growth rate every year. However, management overlooked the fact that speedy growth would inevitably lead to a jump in costs – new and larger printing works would be required and the distribution channels would need to be expanded. Despite the unprecedented development this led to large losses and in the end the papers folded.

- *'Use the company's own dynamics and the synergies of any situation.'*
  Every situation has its own laws which have to be adhered to in pursuit of goals. Here I am talking about the principle of ju-jitsu: use your opponent's power to reach your own goal. If the magazine publishers wish to keep up or even expand their subscription level then they should start with the cultivation of their long-standing and faithful subscribers. Success looks more likely from reader loyalty though loyalty premiums (discounts cover even travel offers) than the more expensive winning back of subscribers that went astray. What is more, new subscribers have a tendency to take their new reader gift and then leave after one year.

- *'Find a harmonious balance between continuity and change.'*
  All strategies should be examined to see if they are a healthy mix between security and challenge, stability and change, flexibility and specialization. That the print media wants to enter the new media markets is quite obvious as these are the competition of the future. But entry into the new media should only happen in a way that the printed word also profits from it. Advertisement can be in print and on private television companies. If the print media had been completely carried away by the new media euphoria at the beginning of the 1980s then they would not be doing very well now.

- *'Promote the autonomy of the smallest unit.'*
  This principle is generally meant for the organization of companies who are either introducing a holding structure or are working

consistently towards a profit-centre concept. Strategies must be assessed to check whether they are indeed promoting the autonomy of the smallest unit. This is a very important prerequisite to ensuring that the strategy, the organization and the culture of the company all slot in together. The advantage to the magazine publishers is that to outsiders the individual papers appear to be autonomous. It also requires that each individual magazine has the infrastructure of a small company. The strategy of the publishers must take this as a guideline at least.

- *'Draw up strategies in such a way that they develop further in a self-organizing way.'*
  Strategies should not be developed to fit the current situation so snugly that they become irrelevant at the first sign of difficulty. It is more important for strategies to be adaptable in terms of their own evolution. In the USA in the 1980s this magazine publisher built up a bridgehead in the area of pre-printing processes. What started as a small operation with very high quality standards expanded into a large company. Today more than 50 per cent of the company's profits are made in the USA.

So how can we put together the three component parts of a quality strategy assessment into a whole picture? Let us look at an example which will illuminate how the value increase of a strategy can be determined. The company in question is in the clothing industry. It has a jeans division which has been particularly successful over the past few years. However, now it seems to be in the process of stagnating. Competitors were trying to increase their market share with new fashion products and aggressive promotional measures. On top of this the two most important competitors were carrying out rigorous cost-cutting programmes. According to management the business strategy of the jeans division could move in two possible directions:

1 A market penetration strategy:

    - aggressive expansion of the market share by means of a new design, a new positioning of the product line as well as a massive hike in the advertising and promotional budgets;

    - striving for market leadership.

2 A harvesting policy:

    - price increases;

    - gradual reduction of expenditure on marketing.

This would include the phasing out the product line over the next few years with eventual liquidation in the fifth year. Initially, from the qualitative point of view both strategic alternatives were comparable with each other. Figure 3.48 shows this comparison in answer to the three specific questions of strengths/weaknesses, stakeholders interests and the company's own rules and regulations.

Assessment of the strategy passes through three different stages. First, the strategy is evaluated on a stand-alone basis. This is carried out with help of a value benefit analysis which evaluates the individual criteria and then awards marks according to the individual characteristics. At this stage of the assessment the market penetration strategy has 58 points and the skimming off strategy has 50 points. Second, the question is asked: how far do each of these strategies go in fulfilling the legitimate demands of the stakeholders? The market penetration strategy does secure jobs yet the aggressive marketing policy sullies the principle of

FIGURE 3.48 Comprehensive qualitative assessment of a business strategy

Strategic alternatives		Market penetration		Skimming off	
Criteria	Weight	Mark	Mark x W	Mark	Mark x W
• Market share development	5	4	20	–	0
• Investment	4	2	8	5	20
• Profit development	4	3	12	3	12
• Risk	3	2	6	4	12
• Image	3	4	12	2	6
Assessment			58		50

Underlying conditions for stakeholders	Fulfilled	Unfulfilled	Fulfilled	Unfulfilled
• Job security	✓			✓
• 'Clean' advertising and business practices		✓	✓	
• Shareholder benefit		✓	✓	

Compatibility with rule guidelines	Fulfilled	Unfulfilled	Fulfilled	Unfulfilled
• Growth ≠ end in itself		✓	✓	
• Development of synergies	✓			✓
• Autonomy principle	✓			✓
• Development capacity	✓			✓

clean advertising. On the other hand, the harvesting policy, although it represents job losses, does not endanger business practise and provides an important benefit to the shareholders.

Third, and finally, it is time to determine how compatible each strategy is with the above guidelines. The market penetration strategy goes against the principle that growth should not be self-serving. On the other hand, it is totally in accord with the use of synergies, in supporting the autonomy of the smallest unit and promoting development capabilities. The harvesting strategy comes off rather badly when looked at in the light of the last three guidelines. However, as I said earlier a considered decision cannot be made on a qualitative assessment of the strategies alone. It must be complemented by the quantitative assessment, which aims to determine the value creation of each strategy.

Determining value increase

In Chapter 2, I proposed that increasing a company's value was the new yardstick for evaluating strategic success. I showed that profit and profit-related factors are inadequate for this task and that future free cash flows are the only suitable yardstick for measuring the value increase of a company. It was pointed out that not only shareholder benefits but also the interests of the various stakeholders should be taken into this equation. As it is virtually impossible to assess quantitatively the fulfilment of stakeholders' interests we have instead to look for a qualitative assessment of strategies.

To do this I will continue to use the jeans division of a company as an example. The figures came from a comparative study by Alcar (1987). Table 3.16 sets out in figures the expected development of both strategic alternatives: alternative A is market penetration and alternative B is harvesting.

For strategy A, a planning horizon of ten years was proposed. Further development is shown in the terminal harvesting value, which is calculated as a continuing annuity of the profit after taxes achieved in the tenth year. Strategy B's horizon is five years, whereby at the end of the fifth year a liquidation value of 50 million was entered. This was the estimated disposal value for the proprietary brand and machinery. The expansion investment in fixed assets and in net working capital are the same for both strategies. 40 cents have to be found for every extra dollar turned over. A decline in sales means a corresponding release of funds. The final assessment needed is the cost of capital and the discounting rate. As the market penetration strategy was considered risky, the cost of

TABLE 3.16 Turnover and profit forecast as well as expected investments from the penetration strategy (A) and the skimming off strategy (B)

		Development forecast *Current turnover 500 million dollars*									
Year		1	2	3	4	5	6	7	8	9	10
Turnover growth %	A	15	20	20	18	18	15	15	13	11	10
	B	10	5	0	−5	−20					
Profit rate %	A	5	5	7	7	9	10	10	10	10	10
	B	14	14	14	14	14					
Additional investments %											
▪ Fixed assets	A	25	25	25	25	25	25	25	25	25	25
	B	25	25	25	25	25	−	−	−	−	−
▪ Working capital	A	15	15	15	15	15	15	15	15	15	15
	B	15	15	15	15	15	−	−	−	−	−

capital was considered to be 20 per cent, the harvesting strategy on the other hand was considered to have a cost of capital rate of 15 per cent. Table 3.17 shows the value of the jeans division after strategies A and B were carried out.

The harvesting strategy creates considerably more value than the market penetration strategy. There are various reasons for this. Although the market penetration strategy shows a much higher turnover growth, in the early years this has to be set against a much reduced profit ratio and high investment. More favourable conditions do not appear until the fifth year, the effect of which is no longer so important as the cost of capital is so high. The harvesting strategy achieves a consistently high profit ratio over the first five years and there is even the possibility of disinvestment in years four and five. The positive results of this strategy accrue in the first five years during which time consideration of the current market value of the money has not had such a powerful effect. The assessment of the sensitivity of the strategies which was carried out in addition to Table 2.7 on p. 65, shows that a change in the profit margins has the largest value increase effect. Growth in turnover hardly counts at all. The influence of the cost of capital is also important. The simulation shows, however, that the harvesting strategy still wins even if the cost of capital was identical. It is also worth mentioning that both strategies have identical non-operating assets as well as debts and so this neutralizes their influence.

TABLE 3.17 Value of the jeans division when implementing the penetration strategy (A) and the skimming off strategy (B)

Year	Penetration strategy (A)		Skimming off strategy (B)	
	Accumulated discounted free cash flows	Discounted residual value	Accumulated discounted free cash flows	Discounted residual value
1993	(12.06)		19.20	
1994	(31.07)		44.10	
1995	(44.90)		78.55	
1996	(55.84)		107.01	
1997	(61.59)		126.80	24.86
1998	(60.78)			
1999	(60.01)			
2000	(56.81)			
2001	(51.49)			
2002	(45.49)	84.94		
Value increase through strategy		39.55		151.66

If one spread the above case study among executives most of them would intuitively go for the market penetration strategy. I believe there are four reasons for this. First, the influence of turnover growth on the increase in a company's value is usually over-rated. Second, the current value of future earnings is often neglected, i.e. profits that lie far in the future are considered to have the same value as short-term profits. Third, the influence of intense investment is not taken into consideration, particularly when it comes to net working capital. Fourth, broadly speaking it is still considered a managerial failure if part of a company is disinvested. That is why many people plump for forward strategy when in fact all the signs point to a harvesting strategy. By looking at this from a value creating point of view it is possible to show in figures where the strengths and weaknesses of a strategy lie.

After comparing the two different business strategies, I will now explain how to evaluate a corporate strategy and an owner strategy. Let us look at the case of a company in the engineering industry as a possible acquisition candidate. The medium-term figures set out in Table 3.18 are the basis for determining this company's value.

TABLE 3.18 Medium-term planning of a company in the engineering industry in DM (millions)

Year	Turnover	Cash flow	Investments FA/WC	Taxes
1992	573	49	37	23
1993	651	48	62	15
1994	733	60	47	20
1995	820	68	56	24
1996	895	77	45	33
1997	977	81	32	40

Sale price expectations were ten times the pre-tax profits for 1992, namely DM450 million. With profit tax rates at 50 per cent this price expectation corresponds to a price–earnings ratio of 20. Comparable companies at this point were dealing with a price–earnings ratio of 10 to 16.

In order to determine value potentials the following were evaluated: operative measures, strategic improvements and external possibilities. At the forefront were differentiation strategies by extending specialities, second sourcing for bulk purchasers, expansion of the systems business as well as increasing the value creation potential of individual links in the value chain. Other possibilities included backward integration, cooperation in the area of logistics as well as the sale of a small part of the division. All this led to a new interpretation of the value generators:

- Turnover growth rate:

    - The prognosis for turnover in the medium term is considered to be realistic.

- Profit rate:

    - A potential of 3 to 5 percent was identified for materials, for personnel it was 10 per cent of the costs.

- Investments:

    - Investment in fixed assets and net working capital was judged to be too low and should be increased.

- Cost of capital:

    - No significant leverage-potential could be identified. The strong growth in foreign business would bring with it higher risks which could cause the cost of capital to increase too.

- Tax rate:

   - Here an important optimization potential of about DM15 million was found, the future tax rate should not go above 35 per cent.

Different value creating strategies were played through according to the sensitivity model described in Chapter 2. With a cost of capital rate of 8 per cent based on the assumption that all operative, strategic and external improvements are put in place as desired, then the result would be a company value of DM550 million. If the strategy is really to succeed completely and if the company could be purchased at around DM450 million then there was a nice comfortable pillow for the future as well. The company purchasing, however, were of the opinion that these optimistic figures could not be taken as a true measure. They then worked out different and in their eyes more realistic variations, which led to the conclusion that the value lay somewhere between DM300 and DM450 million. In conclusion they made an offer of DM375 million and were promptly outbid by a competitor whose tender was accepted.

So what can we learn from this practical example? The company that discovers decisive value gaps can pay the highest purchase price. In the case above I must mention in defence of our company that this acquisition was in fact a diversification and so very few operative synergies existed. The company whose bid succeeded was already active in the industry and so could identify considerable value potentials immediately. Despite this the magnitude of the prices discussed was quite extraordinary. If a decision had been based on the medium-term planning of the company to be acquired then an offer of DM375 million would go outside the range.

To complete this step of the strategic process I would like to look at the confectionery manufacturer Rowntree, which was taken over at the end of the 1980s by Nestlè. The calculations used were based on estimates from the above-mentioned Alcar. Nestlè paid £2.3 million or £10.75 per share for Rowntree. In order to justify the price over the next few years Rowntree has to achieve the profits set out in Table 3.19. I am going to leave it to the reader to decide whether in fact Rowntree will be able to achieve this high cash-flow increase which would justify their purchase price. Or perhaps one could assume that Nestlè was more interested in using this acquisition to dominate the market rather than exploiting its value potentials.

We have now come full circle in terms of this step of the strategic methodology to define value creation. I am not going to go into value considerations for the DELTA strategic study because at this point there is

TABLE 3.19 Required value increase of Rowntree at a Nestlè sales price of £2.3 billion (Gomez and Weber, 1989)

Year	Free cash flow	Discounted FC F	Cumulated AFCF	Discounted residual value (DRV)	Cumulated AFCF+DRV
1988	71	64	64	1,040	1,103
1989	80	65	129	1,082	1,211
1990	86	63	192	1,126	1,318
1991	124	82	273	1,278	1,551
1992	152	90	364	1,385	1,749
1993	181	97	461	1,464	1,925
1994	207	100	561	1,524	2,084
1995	238	103	664	1,586	2,249
1996	274	107	771	1,650	2,421
1997	316	111	882	1,717	2,599
Total value of the company					2,599
Market value of debts					275
Value of equity capital					2,323

nothing new to learn. The next step is to turn the chosen strategies into reality and to ensure their future development.

Implementation and further development of strategies

There are two things which will ensure the realization and the securing of a long-lasting effect of the chosen strategies, and they are speed and durability. Time management and the examples I have given are enough to prove the importance of speed in realizing a strategy. The success of a product can live or die depending on how fast a company can place the product in the market ahead of the competition. In the same way how fast a strategy is realized can have a direct effect on the exploitation of its potential. If the weakness in strategic management in the 1970s and 1980s was due to the non-realization of strategic measures, the danger in the 1990s is that the strategies worked out by competent management teams will not be realized fast enough.

If we look at examples of successful companies such as Asea Brown Boveri we can see that this was central to their success. After the Swedish Asea merged together with the Swiss Brown Boveri, Percy Barnevik used all his energy to realize the synergies of this merger as quickly as possible and to find a new position for the company on the world's markets. At the risk of making mistakes, he set almost premature deadlines and thus forced his management team to work as fast possible. The method proved to be highly successful for ABB, in a very short time they reached their desired world market position.

How does one achieve this *speed realization*? Perhaps the best prerequisite is a strong leadership that is deeply committed to a consistent long-term direction for the company. Executives must be helped by a suitable range of tools, in this case a sophisticated project management. Experience shows that strategies can only be realized rapidly if they have already been concretized in project form and allocated both managers and deadlines. What was simply a fascinating idea or business potential suddenly becomes a concrete managerial task.

Speed is only one requirement of realizing strategies, the other is *sustainability*. Strategies are often instantly successful at the start but this success becomes impossible to sustain in the long term. The reason is usually that a suitable corporate organization and corporate culture is missing. Strategies are only entirely successful if the necessary structures and management capabilities have been set out. Far too often it is felt that the old organization and the same management team will be able to come to grips with the new demands. Bartlett and Ghoshal (1990) sum this problem up very neatly: 'Companies today design strategies which are impossible to realize due to the simple reason that no-one can effectively introduce third generation strategies using second generation organizations led by first generation managers.' For success to last there has to be optimum concurrence in the area of conflict 'Strategy–Structure–Culture'.

Speed and sustainability are also prerequisites for the healthy future development of strategies. In this case speed means the quickest possible recognition of important changes, whether these be opportunities or threats. The key words here are 'early warning' and the necessary 'alarm system' which is essential to it. Network thinking is ideal for developing a suitable early warning system. Alarm signals can be developed by looking at the time scales between the key corporate factors.

A strategic controller system has to be set up to ensure that the future development of strategies is ongoing. This should test regularly and in an orderly fashion the validity of strategic premises and make suitable adjustments when general conditions change.

Eighth strategic principle

The eighth strategic principle is: *The speed of strategic realization has to be ensured by means of strategic projects and early warning systems. Sustainability has to be ensured by harmonizing strategy, organization and corporate culture as well as by strategic controllership.*

Development of an organization and culture appropriate to the strategies

The first step towards developing an organization appropriate to the strategies is the construction of a project organization, which affects the secondary structure of the company. The adjustment of the primary structure, whether this is organized according to function, line of business or as a matrix, requires more time. For this reason it is not up to the requirement of speed. That is why most companies today have two overlapping structures; the relatively stable organizational structure and an adaptable project organization. How can this be shaped with regard to the realization of strategies?

Figure 3.49 shows the project organization chosen by a retail sales organization to enable them to realize their acquisition strategy. The company has two retail sales chains in the CTN business and now wishes to integrate the two companies.

It is noticeable that only five projects have been agreed on. Experience shows that it is best to keep to a small number of projects otherwise there is the danger of dissipation. Usually it is the line managers who control these projects or are at least responsible for them. There should be someone responsible for each individual project as well as each sub-project. Each project and each sub-project has its own deadline. Those in charge of the projects should report at regular intervals on the development of their project. At set dates they should also present reports and accounts.

Even the planning horizon for realizing the whole project should be defined. A medium-sized Swiss investment bank set a planning horizon of around one and half years for the realization of a strategy. The relatively long deadline was necessary because the development of supporting IT-solutions was time-consuming. Altogether they set up eight strategic projects, each containing five sub-projects. A member of the management team was responsible for the whole project, a manager was allocated to each of the individual projects and an external consultant supported the whole team. At the start individual managers met once a month to report

FIGURE 3.49   Project organization for integrating the acquisitions of a retail company

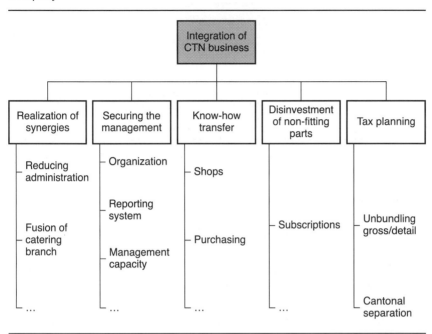

on how matters stood. Towards the end of the project it was considered only necessary to meet once a quarter. The introduction of strategies was carried out according to plan and at the end the project organization was dissolved. This process proved to be successful for the bank and enabled them to steer a clear course through the very unsettled waters of the time.

Strategic study DELTA – realization of the corporate strategy

The qualitative assessment of DELTA's corporate strategy which was illustrated in Table 3.15 proposed a specific new direction, namely building up its buying power. This strategy was turned into a project in Figure 3.50 which offers possible alternative strategies (i.e. purchasing partnerships versus buying into an integrated operation). Here too, each project was allocated a manager and deadlines were set.

   Using an aviation metaphor, if the project organization is there to supply sufficient boost to get the project off the ground, then the adaptability of the organization and the corporate culture allows for a

FIGURE 3.50   Strategic projects of DELTA

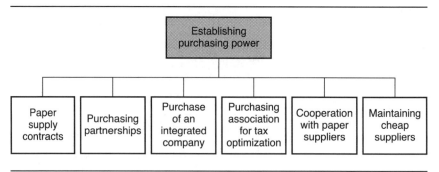

smooth and safe flight. We are talking about the long-lasting effect of following the strategies. There is no one particular shape to a company's organization. Each time the organization should be tailor-made to fit each type of strategy. Of course organizations have tried to achieve the greatest possible fit between the strategic and organizational units. With this in mind Texas Instruments introduced the so-called dual organization in the 1970s, and IBM structured itself into strategic business units. Yet both companies have turned away from this construction because by conforming so much to the business strategies they lost the overview of the company as a whole. Even the holding structure is not actually an expression of turning strategic thinking into organization. Each individual and legally independent unit has in turn to develop its own business and corporate strategies in order to give full rein to their much-vaunted autonomy.

Table 3.20 in support of Gomez and Zimmermann (1992) demonstrates how strategic direction can be turned into a tailor-made organizational form.

First, a basic idea of the strategic direction has to be determined. An example of this is Asea Brown Boveri's mission statement: 'Use closeness to the customer at the same time as international scale effects' which Percy Barnevik turned into 'think global, act local'. The ideal organizational realization of this principle is a multi-dimensional matrix. This cannot be represented graphically according to the chairman of the conglomerate's board, Thomas Gasser. At the centre are relatively autonomous companies anchored to the local markets. They are bound into a network of divisions, countries and functions, sometimes companies and employees are also temporarily locked into global projects. The chosen organization is ABB-specific and could not be applied to other companies. And it has proved itself eminently suited to realizing ABB's strategies quickly and in the long term.

TABLE 3.20 Example for matching strategies with organization

Strategic direction	Guiding principles for implementation	Typical organizational form
Close customer contact *and* general synergies	'Think globally, act locally'	Matrix organization
Development of core competences	Focus on extraordinary capabilities	Core competence organization
Boosting entrepreneurial spirit	'Autonomy of the smallest unit'	Holding and profit-centre organization
Optimization of processes	Responsibility for process and teamwork	Horizontal organization
Going international	Optimizing resources and minimizing risk through mutual operations	Alliances

The other examples in Table 3.20 have been touched on more than once. This only shows that the question of organization should not be left until this late point; it has to be considered in the earlier parts of the process. At this stage we are simply talking about making a definite choice for the way forward.

If the original organization of a company is basically suited to the strategic requirements, it is quite likely to be less suitable for the corporate culture and for the capabilities of both management and employees. Every company has its own 'personality' which is very different from that of other companies. It is almost impossible to determine this personality, rather it has to be grasped intuitively. We have already looked at the culture of Mövenpick, Benetton and Coca-Cola. If a new strategy demands it, how is it possible to change the culture of a company?

The culture of a company is expressed in its perceptions of values and its norms which are at the base of its business dealings. I am not talking about formal rules of an organization but the so-called soft factors, the particular stamp of a certain personality or the emphasis on one particular strength material to the corporate culture. In this way a cost-oriented company differentiates itself from an innovation-oriented company and this will not change simply if the strategies are changed. Sometimes it is unavoidable that an important change in strategic direction is accompanied by a change in the top echelons of management. Only by this symbolic act can old taboos be broken and the path of new strategies be trodden. How should one proceed, however, in a situation when the present manpower wish to realize the new strategies?

We start with the setting out of the present cultural profile as shown in Figure 3.26 on p. 115. This is compared with the cultural profile required to realize the new strategies. The result of this process looks like Figure 3.51.

The present-state cultural profile shows that the company is very employee-oriented and cost-oriented. The new strategies demand that the orientation shifts towards the client and towards innovation. The areas of environment and technology need to be strengthened somewhat as well. Compared to this the cost orientation retreats and employees will have to be prepared for a rough ride. Only in the context of a specific company could I show how this change in culture can be incorporated. It requires a clear and sensitive communication of the company's vision and the strategies that arose from it; it requires that all superiors set an excellent example, the necessary re-forming of the management system and last but not least, re-orientation of the incentive system towards the strategies.

Once the organizational and cultural conditions have been created you have jumped the first hurdle towards strategic realization. That these

FIGURE 3.51 Corporate culture: performance profile and strategy-based target profile

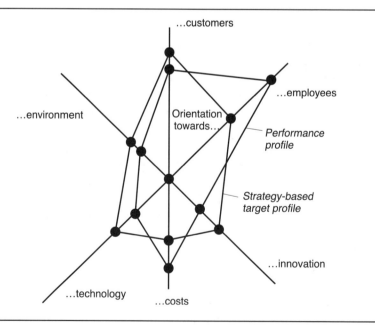

conditions remain viable in the long term requires constant vigilance and the ability to adapt to changing conditions.

Creation of an early warning system and strategic controllership

It is essential to ascertain as quickly as possible whether the practical realization of strategies is going to succeed or not. Then it is possible to take the right measures to support the process or corresponding counter-measures to its failure. Identifying these early warning factors is not easy as they are often the 'soft' factors not normally reflected in data. They are, however, very important if one takes the need for speed seriously.

Gomez (1983) showed the way to developing an early warning system based on network thinking. The disadvantage of conventional methods is that the selection of early warning factors is often intuitive if not downright arbitrary and dependent almost entirely on data. Accounting factors are called upon that can never fulfil the job of early warning. Network thinking ties together all the company's factors into a larger context and places particular emphasis on interrelations and the effects of time. If you start to go backwards from the objectives it is possible to identify early warning factors. Figure 3.52 shows an extract from the early warning system of a computer company. Deiss and Dierolf (1991) have shown how Hewlett-Packard Germany used network thinking while they were realizing their strategies. Hewlett-Packard (HP) identified three factors which were especially suited to early warning: HP's image with its clients, HP's image with its workforce and demand for components and spare parts. Using the latter as an early warning indicator came about in answer to several questions. Hewlett-Packard had already decided that sales and orders on the book were not suitable as early warning indicators as neither allowed enough time for reaction to unfavourable developments. So they asked if there was not perhaps an indicator on the network before the order book. They looked at computer components and the demand from external computer manufacturers. They studied in detail the dates dealing with the demand for components and compared these with the correspondent sales figures for HP computers. These figures revealed a time lag of three quarters of a year between them. So the demand for components came to light as an excellent early warning indicator. In the middle of 1990 sales of components fell. HP felt this was reason enough to stop recruiting personnel. This early measure was one reason why Hewlett-Packard was able to overcome the 1991/1992 crisis in the computer industry better than its competitors.

FIGURE 3.52   Early warning system for a computer company

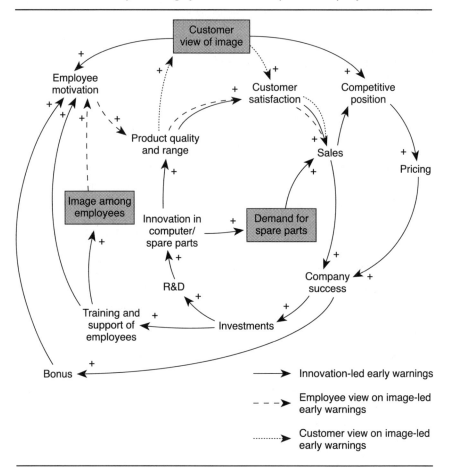

Another important early warning signal for Hewlett-Packard is how employees and clients view them. Both are forerunners for client satisfaction and therefore for sales. If the image deteriorates then it is certain that sales will go down in the medium-term. Hewlett-Packard comes to grips with this factor by carrying out regular internal and external image studies. A change in the image profile gives the company enough time to take counter-measures before sales begin to slide.

The speed or timeliness in terms of early warning is important for the long-term success of a strategy – on its own it is not enough. The durability of a strategy must also be secured and this can be done by means of a systematic strategic controllership. Strategic controllership means checking at regular intervals the premises of the strategy as well as carrying out a running progress control. This process, following Pümpin and Geilinger (1988), is set out in Figure 3.53.

The reasons for deviating from the planned course usually lie in four specific areas:

- changes to the premises and assumptions;

- too high/low strategic targets;

- incorrect or insufficient employment of resources;

- a lack of efficiency and/or execution.

FIGURE 3.53 The practice of strategic controllership (Pümpin and Geilinger, 1988).

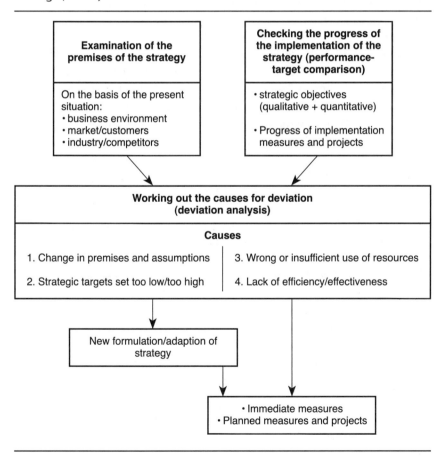

*Strategic study DELTA – maintenance and further development
of the strategy*

DELTA had already taken precautions in the areas of early warning and strategic controllership. The early warning system was installed at different spots in the company. The field workers were supplying information on clients, suppliers, competitors and all kinds of new pretenders with substitute products as quickly as they could so that the company could react in good time. In order to maximize territorial protection interests DELTA provided presidents for the relevant European organizations and thus ensured access to important information. Finally, they had regular discussions with paper manufacturers and integrated paper bag manufacturers to pre-empt and resolve any problems in the purchasing division.

In the sense of strategic controllership, a project group was put together for each new issue that arose. This group researched the effects of any change in the strategic premises. For example, one group looked after the area of territorial protectionism. It not only observed new developments in the EU and related organizations but it also built up close relations with companies in a similar position and if necessary directly intervened, for instance, if there was any sign that this territorial protectionism was dissolving. At the same time the group prepared a package of measures ready for the worst possible scenario.

By creating an early warning system and a strategic controllership we have now come full circle in the strategic process. The characteristic of the strategic controllership shows how much it really is a cycle. Premises change, new strategic sets of circumstances arise, creative ideas lead to a change of direction. The strategic process has to be taken up again, and again and played through. Of course, not every single step of the process has to be carried out in the same detail. Much remains constant and will continue to do so – unless our understanding of strategies goes through a radical change. This is the question I wish to answer in the last chapter of the book.

CHAPTER 4

Integrated value management: back to basics or the rise of a new paradigm?

Why is strategic management always looking for new ways and concepts? The answer looks to be simple: increasing complexity of corporate events, increasing demands from stakeholders, discontent with one-sided competition orientation, failure of feasibility thinking. In other words, there has been a complete turnaround in all corporate matters. Although this explanation is plausible it is not completely satisfactory. One element is still missing, namely the way we manage strategically today. For many companies strategic management equals strategic planning and is often simply an end in itself. In the 1970s strategic concepts sprung up everywhere and were enthusiastically taken up and realized. At the beginning, the results in the marketplace were remarkable and the companies who did not have access to this range of tools suffered considerably. Bolstered up by their initial success, companies began to extend their strategic planning. The largest businesses in particular generously incremented their planning staff. So the responsibility for strategies went from the shoulders of the line managers onto those of the sergeants. The result was the degeneration of strategic planning into an end in itself. The strategies were indeed worked out in the smallest detail, yet they were rarely turned into reality.

This led to a complete re-think in terms of theory and practise in the 1990s. Figure 4.1 shows two rather extreme versions.

One version can be characterized as back to basics. Here it is a matter of re-thinking previous processes and developing methods and concepts onwards. The objective is to re-align the choice of strategic tools to the needs of the line managers. Strategic thinking is a managerial task whereby management is supported by its juniors. Allowance must be made, therefore, for managerial thought-patterns as well as the brief amount of time that executives have available. On the other hand, the new methods and concepts must do justice to the

FIGURE 4.1   Strategic thinking – the road to development (after Pascale, 1992)

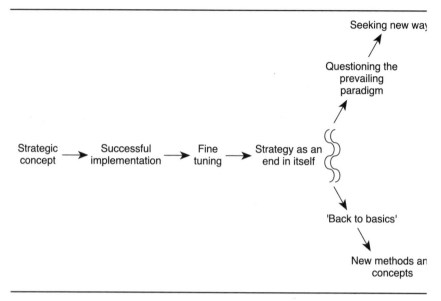

changing environmental conditions as set out at the beginning of the chapter. This leads, of course, to a certain dilemma. On the one hand, strategic concepts and instruments should be simple and easy to handle; on the other hand, they should match an ever-increasing complexity. For present and future strategic approaches it is a difficult task to assimilate these two directions and put them under one roof.

A second way out of the present unsatisfactory situation is to question fundamentally present-day thinking on strategic matters. What is required is a change of paradigm. There needs to be a change in understanding how a company functions. At the beginning of the second half of this century businesses were still considered to be machines whose main task was to manufacture products and services as economically as possible. This changed subtly in the 1970s and 1980s when decision-making took into account social, cultural and political aspects of the company's business. To put it somewhat simply, a social organism and a sense-making system was created out of the machine that was a business (Morgan, 1986; Bolman and Deal, 1991).

More recently, a development has arisen which places this turn-around and a business' learning ability at the centre (Senge, 1990; Moss-Kanter *et al.*, 1992). Of course, the term 'paradigm change' cannot be applied to every change of perspective. Yet the transition from viewing the company as a machine to interpreting it as a learning organization does represent a deep-seated turnaround and as such can be called a paradigm change. This development demands a brand new vision and tools in terms of strategic concepts and methods.

So which of these two paths does this book's integrated value management approach follow? Does it contain sophisticated methods and concepts in the sense of 'back to basics' or is it more an expression of a change in paradigm? The position in Figure 4.2 attempts to provide an answer.

Integrated value management bestrides a middle path between the two extremes. Yes, present concepts are developed further but are then integrated on a higher plane. The first building block is a new company model, which is dedicated to network thinking and finds expression in the St Gallen Management Concept. The second building block is a new strategic model that is characterized by differentiating between business strategies, corporate strategies and owner strategies. And finally, the third building block is a new information model, which determines the yardstick for success for measuring the increase in a company's value as well as a value foundation for stakeholders. Integrated value management does not claim to be a brand new way of viewing a company's business; in

FIGURE 4.2 Major shifts in strategic thinking and the positioning of integrated value management

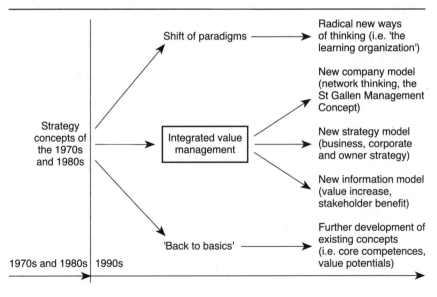

that regard it is not a new paradigm. On the other hand, it goes well beyond the 'back to basics' principle, which places single concepts into a new and changed environment. The prominent characteristic of value management is the integrated way of viewing a company working together with a range of instruments that can be applied practically.

This practical application is the key. It sums up all considerations of integrated value management, a large element of which is the assessment of new strategic approaches and demands on the behaviour of executives and on the infrastructure of a company. Nowadays, one simply assumes that strategic thinking and dealing is the responsibility of line managers and that teamwork plays a vital role. Does strategic methodology fit into this new landscape or does it pass by the needs of executives and the company? This question can be answered in terms of the three building blocks of value management. The new corporate model combines network thinking with the St Gallen Management Concept. The methodology of network thinking and its application to the strategic methodology was developed with management in mind. It should be quite possible to represent and interpret complex and problematic situations and their basic interconnections without requiring the services of an expert. Practical experiences of actual projects has shown that management is quickly able to master the range of tools available.

The St Gallen Management Concept was also developed so that management could categorize corporate problems and identify potential solutions. This tool has also passed its practical test and executives have put it to good use. Both concepts promote thinking as a team and virtually force problem-solving groups to come together in an inter-disciplinary fashion. This is a substantial part of the first step in the methodology of network thinking.

The strategic model of the second building block with its differentiation between business strategies, corporate strategies and owner strategies is also eminently suited to the potential as well as the limits of executives. At each step of the strategic methodology the strategic tools available are described and illustrated with many practical examples. This proffers up a multitude of clues as to which particular approach is suitable for a company's own strategies. Of course, management has the ability to develop and underpin their strategies even further by employing specialists. Initially however there is no need for the interference of a specialist.

The third building block might initially appear difficult for management – how to assess the value increase achieved by a particular strategy? Yet here there are even PC-compatible programmes which will carry out the sensitivity analyses. Of course, if one wants to delve deeper it is a good idea to call in a specialist. However, the programme allows for varying degrees of difficulty and so starting off will not be too arduous for an executive. The only prerequisite is a good understanding of the logic of the value increase approach.

In summing up, I would say that the strategic methodology of integrated value management is tailor-made for today's executives. If they want to face the demands of strategic management then it will not be the range of tools at their disposal which lets them down.

Bibliography

Alcar (1987) *The Value Planner*, Skokie, Illinois.

Ansoff, I. (1998) *Corporate Strategy*, 2nd Edn, London: Penguin.

Barnevik, P., 'The Logic of Global Business', *Harvard Business Review*, March/April (1991) pp. 91 ff.

Bartlett, C., Ghoshal, S., 'Matrix Management: Not a Structure, a Frame of Mind' *Harvard Business Review*, July/August (1990) pp. 144 ff.

Bilanz, 'Schmidheiny', 5 (1992) pp. 193 ff.

Bleicher, K. (1997) *Das Konzept Integriertes Management*, 5th Edn, Frankfurt.

Bleicher, K. (1992) *Leitbilder*, Stuttgart/Zürich.

Bleicher, K. (1992) *Strategische Anreizsysteme*, Stuttgart/Zürich.

Bolman, L., Deal, T. (1991) *Reframing Organizations*, San Francisco: Jossey-Bass Publishers.

Brindisi, L. (1989) 'Creating Shareholder Value', *Corporate Restructuring and Executive Compensation*, Stern J. et al (eds), New York: pp. 323 ff.

Bronder, C. (1992) 'Unternehmensdynamisierung durch Strategische Allianzen', Dissertation, St Gallen.

Brugger, R. (1991) 'Entwicklung eines Frühwarnsystems für die Patria Versicherungen', *Vernetztes Denken*, 2nd Edn, Probst, G., Gomez, P. (eds) Wiesbaden, pp. 227 ff.

Bühner, R. (1990) *Das Management-Wertkonzept*, Stuttgart.

Copeland, T., Koller, T., Murrin, J. (1994) *Valuation – Measuring and Managing the Value of Companies*, 2nd Edn, New York: John Wiley & Sons.

Deiss, G., Dierolf, K. (1991) 'Strategische Planung und Frühwarnung durch Netzwerke bei Hewlett-Packard', *Vernetztes Denken*, 2nd Edn, Probst, G., Gomez, P. (eds) Wiesbaden, pp. 211 ff.

Downes, L., Mui, C. (1998) *Unleashing the Killer App*, Boston: Harvard Business School Press.

Drucker, P. (1994) *Management*, London: Butterworth–Heineman.

Gälwiler, A., 'Strategische Geschäftseinheiten und Aufbauorganisation der Unternehmung', *Zeitschrift für Organisation*, 48 (1979), 5, pp. 252 ff.

Ganz, M. (1992) *Diversifikationsstrategie*, Stuttgart.

Geschka, H., Hammer, R. (1990) 'Die Szenario-Technik in der strategischen Unternehmensplanung' *Strategische Unternehmungsplanung – Strategische Unternehmensführung*, 2nd Edn, Hahn, D., Taylor, B. (eds) Heidelberg, pp. 331 ff.

Geus, A. de, 'Planning as Learning', *Harvard Business Review*, March/April (1988) pp. 70 ff.

Gomez, P., 'Neue Trends in der Konzernorganisation', *Zeitschrift Führung und Organisation*, 3 (1992) pp. 166 ff.

Gomez, P. (1983) *Frühwarnung in der Unternehmung*, Bern.

Gomez, P., Bleicher, K., Brauchlin, E., Haller, M. (1993) 'Multilokales Management: Zur Integration eines vernetzen Systems', *Globalisierung der Wirtschaft – Einwirkungen auf die Betriebswirtschaftslehre*, Haller, M. *et al*, Proceedings of the 54th Wissenschaftliche Jahrestagung des Verbandes der Hochschullehrer für Betriebswirtschaft, St Gallen.

Gomez, P., Ganz, M., 'Diversifikation mit Konzept – den Unternehmenswert steigern', *Harvard Manager*, 1 (1992) pp. 44 ff.

Gomez, P., Probst, G. (1991) 'Vernetztes Denken für die Strategische Führung eines Zeitschriftenverlages' , *Vernetstes Denken – Ganzheitliches Führen in der Praxis*, 2nd Edn, Wiesbaden, pp. 23 ff.

Gomez, P., Probst, G. (1987) *Vernetztes Denken im Management*, Bern.

Gomez, P., Weber, B. (1989*) Akquisitionsstrategie*, Zürich.

Gomez, P., Zimmerman, T. (1992) *Unternehmensorganisation – Profile, Dynamik, Methodik*, 2nd Edn, Frankfurt.

Haerri, H. (1992) 'Generating econmonic value through corporate restructuring: The Alusuisse-Lonza case', *Economic Value and Market Capitlaization in Switzerland*, McKinsey Company, Erlenbach, pp. 10 ff.

Hahn, D. (1990) 'Zweck und Entwicklung der Portfolio-Konzepte in der strategischen Unternehmungsplanung', *Strategische Unternehmungsplanung – Strategische Unternehmungsführung*, 2nd edn, Hahn D., Taylor B. (eds) Heidelberg, pp. 221 ff.

Hammer, M., Champy J. (1995) *Reengineering the Corporation*, 2nd Edn, London: Brealey Publishing.

Henderson, B. (1968) *Perspectives on Experience*, Boston: Boston Consulting Group.

Hinterhuber, H. (1997) *Strategische Unternehmungsführung*, Berlin.

Janisch, M. (1992) 'Das strategische Anspruchsgruppenmanagement', Dissertation Hochschule St Gallen.

Lippuner, H. (1991) 'Zukunftsstrategien eines multinationalen Konzerns', unpublished lecture, Center for Corporate Leadership, Thalwil.

Morgan, G. (1997) *Images of Organization*, 2nd Edition, Thousand Oaks, CA: Sage Publications.

Moss Kanter, R., Stein B., Jick, T. (1992) *The Challenge of Organizational Change*, New York: The Free Press.

Müller-Stewens, G. (1992) 'Der Fall Krupp-Hoesch', unpublished manuscript, St Gallen.

Müller-Stewens, G., Hillig, A. (1992) 'Motive zur Bildung strategischer Allianzen', *Wegweiser für Strategische Allianzen*, Bronder, C., Pritzl, R. (eds) Frankfurt, pp. 65 ff.

New York Times, 'USX stock hasn't stacked up in oil ... or steel', 26th April 1990.

Ostroff, F., Smith, D., 'The horizontal organization', *McKinsey Quarterly*, 1 (1992) pp. 148 ff.

Pascale, R. (1992), 'Reinventing the Future: From Change to Transformation', Plenary presentation at Strategic Management Society Meeting, London.

Porter, M., 'From Competitive Advantage to Corporate Strategy', *Harvard Business Review*, May/June (1987) p. 43.,

Porter, M. (1985) *Competitive Advantage*, New York: The Free Press.

Porter, M. (1998) *Competitive Strategy*, New York, The Free Press.

Prahalad, C., Hamel, G., 'Nur Kernkompetenzen sichern das Überleben, *Harvard Manager*, 2 (1991) pp. 66 ff.

Probst, G., Gomez, P. (1991) *Vernetztes Denken – Ganzheitliches Führen in der Praxis*, 2nd Edn, Wiesbaden.

Pümpin, C. (1992) *Strategische Erfolgspositionen*, Bern.

Pümpin, C. (1989) *Das Dynamik-Prinzip*, Düsseldorf.

Pümpin, C. (1982) *Management strategischer Erfolgspositionen*, Bern.

Pümpin, C., Geilinger, U. (1988) *Strategische Führung*, Bern.

Pümpin, C., Imboden, C. (1991) *Unternchmungs-Dynamik*, Bern.

Pümpin, C., Prange, J. (1991) *Unternehmensentwicklung*, Frankfurt.

Pümpin, C., Pritzl, R., 'Unternehmenseigner brauchen eine ganz besondere Strategie', *Harvard Manager*, 3 (1991) pp. 44 ff.

Rappaport, A. (1997) *Creating Shareholder Value*, New York: The Free Press.

Schoeffler, S., Buzzell, R., Heany, D., 'Impact of Strategic Planning on Profit Perfomance', *Harvard Business Review*, March/April (1974) pp. 137 ff.

Schwaninger, M. (1994) *Managementsysteme*, Frankfurt.

Schwaninger, M. (1989) *Intergrale Unternehmungsplanung*, Frankfurt.

Senge, P. (1994) *The Fifth Discipline*, New York: Doubleday.

Stalk, G., Hout, T. (1990) *Competing Against Time*, New York: The Free Press.

Ulrich, H. (1987) *Unternehmungspolitic*, 2nd Edn, Bern.

Ulrich, H. (1968) *Die Unternehmung als produktives soziales System*, Bern.

Ulrich, H., Krieg, W. (1974) *Das St. Gallen Management-Modell*, 3rd Edn, Bern.

Ulrich, H., Probst, G. (1988*) Anleitung zum ganzheitlicken Denken und Handelm*, Bern.

Weber, B., 'Wertseigerung durch Restrukturierung', *Der Schweizer Treuhänder*, 11 (1990) p. 579.

Wirtshaftswoche, 'Letzter Versuch' 24 (1992) pp. 148 ff.

Index